AF877267

THE DISENFRANCHISED
Stories of Life and Grief When an Ex-Spouse Dies

Edited by
Peggy Sapphire
MS Counselor

Commentary by
Shirley Scott
MS Thanatologist

Death, Value, and Meaning Series
Series Editor: Darcy L. Harris

Routledge
Taylor & Francis Group
LONDON AND NEW YORK

First published 2013 by Baywood Publishing Company, Inc.

Published 2017 by Routledge
2 Park Square, Milton Park, Abingdon, Oxon OX14 4RN
711 Third Avenue, New York, NY 10017, USA

Routledge is an imprint of the Taylor & Francis Group, an informa business

Copyright © 2013 by Taylor & Francis

All rights reserved. No part of this book may be reprinted or reproduced or utilised in any form or by any electronic, mechanical, or other means, now known or hereafter invented, including photocopying and recording, or in any information storage or retrieval system, without permission in writing from the publishers.

Notice:
Product or corporate names may be trademarks or registered trademarks, and are used only for identification and explanation without intent to infringe.

Library of Congress Catalog Number: 2013011960
ISBN 13: 978-0-89503-821-0 (hbk)
ISBN 13: 978-0-89503-822-7 (pbk)

Library of Congress Cataloging-in-Publication Data

The disenfranchised : stories of life and grief when an ex-spouse dies / edited by Peggy Sapphire, MS Counselor.
pages cm. -- (Death, value, and meaning series)
Includes bibliographical references and index.
ISBN 978-0-89503-821-0 (cloth : alk. paper) -- ISBN 978-0-89503-822-7 (pbk. : alk. paper) --
ISBN 978-0-89503-823-4 (e-pub) -- ISBN 978-0-89503-824-1 (e-pdf) 1. Grief. 2. Bereavement--Psychological aspects. 3. Loss (Psychology) I. Sapphire, Peggy.
BF575.G7.D5497 2013
155.9'37--dc23

2013011960

Cover Photo by Peggy Sapphire

Table of Contents

Contributors' Acknowledgments and Dedications vi

Peggy Sapphire and Shirley Scott

Foreword ix

Darcy L. Harris, Ph.D. FT

Editor's Preface xi

Peggy Sapphire, MS Counselor

Preface to Commentaries xvii

Shirley Scott, RN, MS, CT, Grief Counselor

Introduction 1

Dr. Kenneth Doka, Ph.D. Gerontologist

SECTION 1
Moving Toward Forgiveness 3

CHAPTER 1
Harold 5

Rosemary Wyman

CHAPTER 2
Rubber Man 13

Anne Bower

CHAPTER 3
Selected Slides 27

Elizabeth Kerlikowske

CHAPTER 4
Never Given a Name 37

James McGrath

SECTION 2

"He's Dead and I'm Not" 45

CHAPTER 5
When Pawpaw's Spearmint Went to Heaven 47
Linde Grace White

CHAPTER 6
The Absence of 57
Barbara Traynor

CHAPTER 7
He's Dead and I'm Not 65
Anonymous

CHAPTER 8
Missing You 73
Jean Gant

CHAPTER 9
The Ride 77
Kristina Grey

SECTION 3

". . . A Change of Worlds . . ." 87

CHAPTER 10
Barking at the Knocks 89
J. Bradley Brandts

CHAPTER 11
Un-grieving a Death 103
MM

CHAPTER 12
Chronic and Acute 109
Marion Cohen

CHAPTER 13
The World Cracking Open—or Living Atop a Cultural, Emotional
San Andreas Fault 123
Deborah Dashow Ruth

CHAPTER 14
Then, a Deep Silence 137
Korkut Onaran

SECTION 4
As the Dust Settles 143

CHAPTER 15
Geography of a Marriage 145
Barbara Hoffman

CHAPTER 16
Jake 155
Denise Handlon

CHAPTER 17
How I Survived 169
Penelope Scambly Schott

CHAPTER 18
Postmortem 179
Joyce Lombard

CHAPTER 19
Ex-humation: Digging Up the Past 187
Mary Kolada Scott

Afterword 195
Peggy Sapphire

APPENDIX
Grief Reactions to the Death of a Divorced Spouse 199

Further Readings 205

Contributors 211

Biographies 215
Sapphire, Doka, Scott

Index 217

Contributors' Dedications and Acknowledgments

Dedication—Peggy Sapphire

To the Contributors, whose courage has made this book possible.
To my daughters Lori and Jill, with my love, always.
To Bobby who knows "I wouldn't be here if I hadn't been there."

Dedication—Shirley Scott

To Hal and Chuck

And to my children,

Tom, Sherry, Linda, and Bob.

Thank you for your love and your support.

Contributors' Acknowledgments

"How Do The Guilty Survive?" *The Perfect Mother*, Penelope Scambly Schott, Snake Nation Press, Valdosta Georgia, 1994, winner of the Violet Reed Hass Prize for Poetry

"Gemini Under Glass," "First Marriage: Going For Broke," Elizabeth Kerlikowske, Big Scream, Nada Press, 2003

"Discovery Bookstore, San Francisco, 1965," Deborah Dashow Ruth, *CQ* (California Quarterly), Vol. 25 #3, 1999

Acknowledgments—Peggy Sapphire

In March 2008, long before there was a complete manuscript to present, I mustered my resolve and contacted Dr. Kenneth Doka, Professor of Gerontology, whom I'd never met. Ken Doka's seminal work and writings on disenfranchised grief were well-known to me. Ken (from the beginning he signed each message, "Warmly, Ken") responded immediately with word of his support and encouragement. He then generously agreed to my request that he write the Introduction for this book. Ken's Introduction is a validation of singular value, without which this project may well not have succeeded.

Ken directed me to Shirley Scott, whose commentaries accompany each narrative, and provide an essential dimension. Shirley, again someone I'd never met, has very graciously worked with me on this project during these last 3 years of its development. As a well-published Certified Thanatologist, practitioner and educator, she has unfailingly given untold hours and outstanding expertise to this endeavor. In the process, I feel I have gained a treasured friend, as our conversations deepened far beyond the bounds of this project. Often, at the end of our countless conversations, I have sat in pure contemplation of my extraordinary good fortune. Shirley's long-standing commitment of service to all those who have and do experience disenfranchised grief, has taught me profoundly. I am confident it will do the same to the readers of this work.

Dr. Dale Lund, the editor at Baywood Publishing Co. with whom I made contact in 2009, offered affirmation of the concept of this anthology, and his suggestions for its further development have proven vital. His sustained encouragement was invaluable. Dale Lund shepherded this work to Dr. Darcy L. Harris, the current editor of the *Death, Value, and Meaning Series* for Baywood Publishing Co., who responded with immediate support and continued assurance of the value of this project. In her extraordinary hands this breadth of this work has gained immeasurable dimensions, and moved from possible to definite. I couldn't have asked for a more collaborative experience. Great thanks to Ramona Fernandez, research assistant, who has enthusiastically lent her expertise and resourcefulness.

My thanks to Dr. Ben Lapkin, my graduate school professor, my first and only mentor in my academic life. More than 30 years have passed since I was his student. When I wrote him about this project, in hopes he'd remember me, his response was all I could have hoped for. I have always remembered a particular class when he expressed (paraphrasing), "You know, when I see a student on campus, I will sometimes just pass him/her by. We've become so used to 'Hi, how are you?' that we don't take it literally. If I pass you by, please understand that I won't ask unless I can and want to give you the time to listen." Such a simple act of caring, so rarely given.

Always in hopes of emulating that ethic, I composed my Call for Submissions to potential contributors to summon their trust. I asked for "fiercely, honest, first-person narratives" about intensely personal aspects of their lives. Essentially, I wrote, "Hello, will you share your intimate story, for publication, of grief and disenfranchisement?"—a stranger asking strangers a great deal more than "How are you?" Thank you, Ben, for teaching me how.

I am grateful to the Vermont Studio Center in Johnson, Vermont, for the month-long fellowship—the gift of time, a private writing studio, fantastic food, accommodations, grand companions and 24-hour access to their meditation room, all of which nourished me in every sense.

And Bobby, without whom . . .

Peggy Sapphire, July 2012

Acknowledgments—Shirley Scott

My thanks to Dr. Kenneth Doka for suggesting Peggy Sapphire call me to work with her on this anthology. It has been an amazing journey to walk with her through the creation of this book. Her sincere kindness, patience, and understanding during times I was not able to work on the project are much appreciated. It was Peggy's vision, persistence and hard work that brought this work to fruition.

A book like this could never be written without the participation of the generous people who contributed much time and effort to share their very private lives so that others can understand what it means to be grieving for an ex-spouse.

I want to thank the anonymous women and men who graciously completed the extensive questionnaire for my original research project, *Grief Reactions to the Death of a Divorced Spouse* (1984–85). Many of them took the time to write notes and letters that explained in more depth their reactions, their problems, their dilemmas.

I also want to thank all the contributors to this anthology for their courage in unveiling their very private stories in poignant, beautifully written prose and poetry so readers, whether lay or professional, can learn from their experiences.

My special thanks to my good friend, Judy Peterson, who spent many hours reading and commenting on the manuscript as it developed. Her counsel was invaluable.

Two early readers, Dr. Kathleen Moore Brotherton and Lydia Vorhees, also provided suggestions and encouragement that are much appreciated.

Last, but certainly not least, I want to thank all my longtime friends in the Association for Death Education and Counseling (ADEC) and in Women in Thanatology (WIT). They are pioneers in the field of thanatology and have taught me so much over the years. I could not have written the commentaries without their numerous publications in which they share their accumulated knowledge and wisdom so the rest of us can continue to learn.

Shirley Scott, July 2012

Foreword

In this book, Peggy Sapphire provides us a glimpse into the experiences of individuals who have already faced the death of a marriage...and who now are faced with the death of the person to whom they had once been married. In divorce, the marriage is what has died, and the two individuals who shared that bond continue to live their lives apart. But the attachment and relational bonds often transcend the legal papers.

We know that the divorce rates in North America indicate that approximately half of all marriages will end in divorce. It is also apparent that the baby boomer generation is aging; this was the generation where the meaning of what marriage is supposed to be and the acknowledgment of the realities of divorce as an outcome to marriage began. The baby boomers whose marriages ended in divorce are now growing older and are more likely to develop life-threatening illnesses. In many of their backgrounds exists a relationship that was once primary, and even though it endured divorce, may still have tendrils of meaning that exist long after the divorce decree was granted by a judge.

Peggy Sapphire acknowledges the grief of those left behind, whether these individuals initiated the ending of the marriage or not. Sharing one's life, family, children, and everyday world with another individual is no small thing, and in reading these accounts, it becomes apparent that the breaking of an attachment bond with all of its meaning is not confined to a legal document. These relationships are profound in their ability to shape us and contribute to how we became the people we are today, even if they did not continue as expected when they were first initiated. For many, the death of a former spouse reverberates with poignancy and reflection, which is often misunderstood by others. In this book, we have powerful narratives written by individuals who reflect upon the death of a former spouse in ways that are profound and relevant.

As human beings, we are programmed at a deep place to form attachments and to be in relationship with others. Definitions and terminology may seem irrelevant upon the realization that the person with whom you shared a portion of your life, who was special above all others at some point in your life, and who left or whom you left for whatever the reason is no longer living in this world with you. The grief may feel complex and layered; it may be as simple as a pause to remember the good moments along with the reality of the times that led to the demise of the relationship. Most often, it is dismissed and not recognized—or not shared with others out of fear of being misunderstood or dismissed. The death of a former spouse is a form of disenfranchised grief, fraught with social stigma and expectations (or lack thereof). In this book, Peggy Sapphire captures these moments through the stories that were shared with her, providing us with insight about the complexity of the human experience—reminding us all of the need for compassion and understanding for the times in life that are not tidy, and which may defy conventional expression.

Darcy L. Harris
Series Editor, *Death, Value, and Meaning Series*

Editor's Preface

Peggy Sapphire

First, I am not a "surviving ex-spouse" in the literal sense, but as one of the courageous and intuitive contributors to this anthology generously wrote to me, I am "surviving," and chances are I will be disenfranchised with my own story of life after the death of my ex-spouse.

I have remarried since my divorce from the father of my two daughters. For more than 20 years I have lived within a deeply loving and peaceful union we call "beshert" . . . meant to be.

As of this writing, it has been over 5 years since our daughters told me their father had been diagnosed with a terminal illness and since then, though in remission, he has been diagnosed with a second terminal illness. Our daughters, throughout this ordeal, have been lovingly attentive to their father. As a daughter whose father died decades ago after a long and historically significant life, and whom I miss daily, I wish for my own daughters to draw deeply for comfort on their having given and received love and compassion with their father, in whatever time remains to them.

My ex-spouse has been happily remarried for over 20 years. He and I have maintained an amicable though distant relationship, making contact when either of our daughters' health concerns has drawn us together as their parents. This is what we promised them when we divorced over 3 decades ago, ". . . We'll always be your parents."

With their father's death will come the death of my only companion and witness to the intimacies and circumstances of our 17 years of marriage, begun when I was 20 and he was 23 . . . the first marriage for each of us, two pregnancies, first birthings, first parenting anxieties, early poverty, first professional positions, first home and mortgage, first credit card debts, first and continuous arguments about money, first and fatal disenchantments. These are the thoughts that led to my decision to seek the stories you'll find here.

Their father and I committed ourselves to amicability, so much so that as we walked out of the final divorce settlement meeting with our lawyers, one of the secretaries remarked that she'd never seen such fairness as she'd found in our proceedings, even wondering aloud why we were getting divorced.

I later struggled about whether I'd been naïve to be so eager for peace. Should I have been, as some friends advised, adversarial, more aggressive about the terms? They were talking about money, of course.

There may be unease for my daughters with the publication of this book, though to date, each has been entirely encouraging, for which I'm profoundly grateful and relieved.

I raise this issue here because I think it's a major aspect of the courage of the contributors to this anthology. There are grievances our children carry or surely did in their work of finding resolution.

Our daughters' grief at the death of their father will not be mine, nor can or should it be. It may well be they that my grief will remain beyond their comprehension and I suspect that is how it must be for any child of a parent suffering disenfranchised grief. My daughters' grief will not be disenfranchised.

It's one thing to give some "explanation," but as with anyone beyond the couple, I think the dissolution of any marriage is unknowable to any but the two whose marriage dies. The grief awaiting me, my "life after the death" of my ex-spouse, will find me joining a community of "the disenfranchised."

as other wife
in other life
she was dust
underfoot.
Peggy Sapphire

Perhaps one day there will be another volume, written by children of divorce who have experienced the physical death of one of their parents. Their personal histories will add yet another perspective. I hope to read that volume someday.

I suggest personal history carries the concept that 'truth' is how we remember, and what we bring to memory. As the sole survivor of a marriage, each contributor's perspective is therefore purely individual and not meant to imply that the contributor's truth is *the* truth. Personal history is not legal testimony. I believe it is more powerful than that.

Neimeyer (2001) and Neimeyer, Botella, Herrero, Pecheco, Figuera and Werner-Wilder (2002) deepen the process of one's search for the meaning of their loss, as each contributor in this anthology has. Neimeyer's work reveals, and in my writer's mind, re-confirms, that the act of each contributor's "master narrative" offers what has so far been elusive: the author's definitive expression, told in the only voice in which it can be told, of their life's essence. These writers have become *the* standard-bearers of their histories.

In announcing this project, each writer whose work appears in this anthology recognized the phrase "surviving ex-spouse," the term I'd used in my search for stories: former wives, husbands, life-partners surviving the death of their ex-spouse.

Many contributors have written of their dread as they sat to write their stories. Yet the invitation to write their stories was compelling. Some spoke of many failed past attempts to commit their stories to paper, and all expressed their sense of long-awaited resolution when their stories were finally written. Silence, until now, has been accomplice to their disenfranchisement.

As recipient of these deeply personal stories, and editor of this collection, I have felt a personal responsibility to affirm each contribtor's trust in having offered their story and to respect the integrity of each. Any editing I have done has been for length, clarity or proofreading purposes. Above all, I honor and have committed to preserve each writer's voice.

The publication of this anthology will finally bring the long-overdue affirmation, laced with hope, that these beautifully written personal histories and the powerful poems within many of the narratives will reach other disenfranchised ex-spouses in our midst, their families and friends and all who know and have known grief, disenfranchised and otherwise. I believe their need for comfort and compassion will be found here in unparalleled consonance.

These personal histories are offered to a general readership and, very importantly, to new generations of undergraduate and graduate students and scholars. Readers drawn to this anthology will, I hope, be mindful of the privilege they have been given by each contributor.

Another person's grief, disenfranchised or not, so often feels beyond our reach as we try to provide solace. As friends or family we wish to be delicate in our approach, not wanting to cause more pain, against which we feel helpless. We search for the "right" words, perhaps a classic turn of phrase.

We know we can find generic cards for socially accepted grief in the "Sympathy" section of Hallmark and American Greetings cards. None exist that speak the particular language of disenfranchised grief to those whose loss exists within a social context, which denies them recognition and validation.

The writers whose work you are about to read were largely left to their own devices as they sought solace or needed compassion as they stood apart—the "ex." A few tell of compassionate friends and family, and in one case, an exquisitely sensitive clergyman. But for most, no such condolence was forthcoming. Characteristically, disenfranchised grief marginalizes all upon whom it descends.

The writers in this anthology are, I believe, deserving of recognition for their courage in offering their stories. Each has given us collective guidance, inspiration and wisdom. Readers will 'hear' authentic first-person voices within intimate, unsparing disclosures. This anthology is the first to provide such narratives.

Given the recently reported statistics (AARP, 2012) that the divorce rate for people 50 years and older is doubling, the certainty exists that there will be a new generation of ex-spouses. Hopefully, their grief will not be disenfranchised.

When I placed my Call for Submissions for this project, I invited writers to include their poetry, published or unpublished, within their narratives. I believed their narratives would provide an essential context within which poetry could potentially express long-withheld distillations of memory, feelings and countless moments which often defy prose (Cameron, 2009).

In precisely that context, Dana Gioia, writer, poet, essayist and former Chairman for the National Endowment for the Arts, in his best-selling *Can Poetry Matter?* (1992), brings readers a glimpse of T. S. Eliot's reflection on silent periods when nothing is written, ". . . the unconscious is working all the time."

Most of the poetry within this anthology has resided in the personal papers of its authors—unpublished, likely never submitted for publication due to its intensely intimate and disenfranchised expressions of grief. One of the contributors, Joyce Lombard, speaks for many in this anthology and those anonymous undiscovered others, when she says of herself, "I've gone to the venue which historically sanctions the unacceptable, disenfranchised, shadow side of life: the arts."

Beloved poet, the late Ruth Stone, was a young mother to three when her husband committed suicide. Thus began Ruth Stone's sorrowing struggle with disenfranchised grief, though it was never identified as such.

Therese Rando (1993) clinical psychologist, founder of the Institute for the Study and Treatment of Loss, writes in *Treatment of Complicated Mourning* of disenfranchised grief when one suffers the suicide of a spouse who has chosen death rather than life with his spouse, "Lowered self-esteem, shattered self-worth; and feelings of inadequacy, deficiency, and failure are typical."

Ruth Stone's heroic resurrection of her Self, through her eight volumes of poetry, speaks to the power of art to heal, to rescue any of us from a fate of personal perdition. With the publication of two volumes of poetry, which, in part, refer to my personal and family history, I am often asked, "Did this really happen?" or, "Is this true?" My response is to remind readers that poetry is not photography. Poetry does not seek to recreate circumstances of an event, but rather, as a writer or poet, to release one's self in the full swing of emotional freedom; to heal, forgive, remember or give metaphor to the otherwise indescribable. Of particular value to me, both prior to and while attempting to produce a book of poetry, were the writing exercises I found in Julie Cameron's *The Artist's Way* (1992, 2009). With her guidance, I exercised the freedom-giving skill of daily dislodging boulder-like obstacles, which would have blocked my progress toward writing in a pure state of release. This free-write practice allowed me to push past what would otherwise have been lost to me. With that awareness came the practice of revision, and more revision. I view revision as the ultimate introspective process, the single most essential writing tool.

T. S. Eliot (1933) wrote in *The Uses of Poetry and the Use of Criticism* that, "At these moments, which are characterized by the sudden lifting of the burden of anxiety and fear which presses upon our daily life so steadily that we are unaware of it, what happens is something *negative:* that is to say, not 'inspiration' as we commonly think of it, but the breaking down of strong habitual barriers—which tend to re-form very quickly. . . . The accompanying feeling is less like what we know as positive pleasure, than a sudden relief from an intolerable burden."

Consider the concept of *disenfranchised*: Until 2005, *Roget's Thesaurus* (Kipfer, 2005) proceeded from *disenchanted* to *disengaged.* The word *disenfranchised* did not appear.

Interestingly, *enfranchise* did appear: *citizenize, emancipate, empower, free, grant citizenship to, give rights to, liberate, manumit, naturalize, release.*

In other words, disenfranchisement as applied to grief has only recently achieved clinical legitimacy, as offered in *Disenfranchised Grief* (Doka, 2002), whose researched-based text serves to confirm the narratives presented here.

As contributors to this anthology expressed to me, they had not previously attempted to write about this part of their lives, did not know they could endure the revisiting of that part of their lives, and often were not confident they could see it through. Others consciously avoided approaching any sort of expression of their grief. Many shared with me that having finally given themselves their "voice," (and I say, deeply deserved) long muted, elusive, and inaccessible. I regard each contributor with absolute admiration and gratitude for having accepted this challenge.

Years ago I discovered Ira Progoff's *Intensive Journal Workshop* (1992). Then as now, particular passages reaffirm that "[The] quality of sensitivity and openness to the inner unfoldment of our lives becomes a major source of life-confidence enabling us to overcome the anxieties and trials of our existence."

In that vein, you will find strong revelatory poetry here, often woven into these intrepid narratives.

Let the poetry here, the unparalleled prose, both created as if by an inexorable push not unlike breathing. Let it move you to unchartered places of healing.

The finest writing takes the greatest risks, dares to be intimate, urges readers to consider the unconsidered.

REFERENCES

Abrahms, S. (2012, June). Life after divorce. *AARP Bulletin*, pp. 26–28.

Cameron, J. (2009). *The artist's way.* New York, NY: Penguin Books.

Doka, K. J. (Ed.). (2002). *Disenfranchised grief: New directions, challenges and strategies for practice.* Champaign, IL: Research Press.

Eliot, T. S. (1933). *The use of poetry and the use of criticism.* Cambridge, MA: Harvard University Press.

Gioia, D. (1992). *Can poetry matter?* (p. 137). St. Paul, MN: Graywolf Press.

Kipfer, B. A. (Ed.). (2005). *Roget's 21st century thesaurus* (3rd ed.). The Princeton Language Institute. New York, NY: Bantam Dell.

Neimeyer, R. A. (2000). Searching for the meaning of meaning: Grief therapy and the process of reconstruction. *Death Studies, 24,* 541–558.

Neimeyer, R. A. (2001). The language of loss: Grief therapy as a process of meaning reconstruction. In R. A. Neimeyer, (Ed.), *Meaning reconstruction & the experience of loss* (pp. 261–292). Washington, DC: APA.

Neimeyer, R. A., Botella, L., Herrero, O., Pecheco, M., Guigueras, S., & Werner-Wilder, L. A. (2002). The meaning of your absence. In J. Kauffman (Ed.), *Loss of the assumptive world: A theory of traumatic loss* (pp. 31–47). New York, NY: Brunner-Routledge.

Progoff, I. (1992). *At a journal workshop* (p. 101). New York, NY: Penguin Books.

Rando, T. (1993). *Treatment of complicated mourning* (p. 524). Champain, IL: Research Press.

Stone, R. (2002). *In The Next Galaxy* (p. 86). Port Townsend, WA: Copper Canyon Press.

Preface to Commentaries

Shirley Scott

A telephone call from a stranger, who had heard I was a grief counselor, was my first introduction to the topic of grief reactions to the death of an ex-spouse.

She told me she was afraid her mother, Sally (not her real name), was going crazy because she had been crying most of the time for the past 2 weeks, ever since she learned her ex-husband had died suddenly of a heart attack. "But they have been divorced for over 10 years!" the daughter exclaimed. "And they seldom talked to each other in all that time. If they did, it always ended in an argument, screaming at each other. Why would she be so sad now?"

After asking a few more questions I suggested that it sounded like Sally was having a normal grief reaction to the unexpected death of a person she still cared about. I told her I would be glad to have Sally make an appointment to see me.

Sally's consultation confirmed she was indeed having a very normal grief reaction to a loss situation, albeit one society, family members and friends do not usually recognize, support nor mourn. Dr. Kenneth Doka calls this "disenfranchised grief" (Doka, 2002).

The above took place in 1983. Even after all these years there are three things Sally told me that stand out in my memory. First, she still had some affection for her ex-spouse and always hoped that someday they would sit down and calmly resolve some of the issues that caused the divorce in the first place. Now, that could never happen and it made her cry every time she thought about him.

Second, she recounted how much she appreciated a sympathy note she received from a friend who understood Sally's pain because she had gone through a similar experience.

Third (and perhaps most important), Sally was very relieved to know that what she was experiencing was a normal grief reaction; she was not going crazy.

Shortly after Sally's visit I decided to check the professional literature for any information on the topic of grief reactions to the death of an ex-spouse. I found none specific to the subject so I embarked on a research project that ultimately involved 79 self-selected participants from 15 states.

Results of my research were first reported at the 1985 annual conference of the Association for Death Education and Counseling (ADEC) in the same breakout session as Dr. Doka's first report on his research of the subject. This was a surprise for both of us since neither had any idea the other was investigating the topic. Our results were remarkably similar, which gave validity to our findings.

In 1998 I revisited the subject because I could find no additional information in the literature. I felt it was an important subject that needed to be brought before the ADEC members and the public again.

The same questionnaire was used. Although I had a smaller number of respondents the results were remarkably similar. I then combined the results of the two studies to reveal that almost 79% of the respondents said they had experienced some degree of grief ranging from slight to overwhelming. This shows that in our society a grief reaction to the death of an ex-spouse is a common occurrence. However, the grief experienced by the surviving ex-spouse is often not recognized, acknowledged, accepted or mourned. Their grief is disenfranchised. (To read the results of my research see the Appendix.)

Another telephone call from a stranger (now a friend) in 2009 was my first introduction to this anthology of stories written by people who had experienced the death of an ex-spouse. Peggy Sapphire had talked to Dr. Doka about this project and he suggested she contact me to write the professional commentaries in order to help readers better understand the grief reactions the authors were experiencing.

As I first read the stories I was amazed at the courage of the authors in their willingness to revisit extremely painful times in their lives. Also, I was reminded of similar stories people had sent to me with their completed questionnaires. The commonalities were legion; stories of physically and emotionally abusive relationships, addictions, betrayals, mental illness, angry family and/or ex-family members, concern for the children's welfare, loss of dreams of what might have been, unresolved conflicts from the marriage and/or divorce, problems centered on caring for a dying ex-spouse, disagreements concerning funeral arrangements and/or financial problems.

In the past 50 years the divorce rate in this country has been around 50%. Our population is aging and that means we will have an increasing number of people who will experience the death of an ex-spouse.

My goal in writing the commentaries for this book is to enable readers to recognize some of the reasons people might grieve after the death of an ex-spouse, and to understand it is a normal human reaction to the loss of a significant relationship. Society in general needs to understand the necessity for supporting the survivors in the same way they would support them if the death involved more socially acceptable circumstances.

This book is an opportunity for readers to gain some insight into why a grief reaction is common for the survivor after the death of an ex-spouse, and how people can help themselves and others through the healing process. How long that will take varies widely; it is different with every person. Some people say, "It takes as long as it takes."

Grief affects every aspect of our being; emotionally, physically, spiritually, cognitively, financially. Knowing what grief is and how it affects us is a powerful tool to help us survive and heal over time.

REFERENCE

Doka, K. J. (Ed.). (2002). *Disenfranchised grief: New directions, challenges and strategies for practice.* Champaign, IL: Research Press.

Shirley A. Scott, RN, BSN, MS, CT
Nurse Thanatologist

METHODOLOGY FOR WRITING COMMENTARIES

1. Read Preface, Story and Epilogue, make notes on individual situations and pertinent grief-related topics.
2. Place topics in logical order within boundaries of the story.
3. Write paragraph(s) on each topic.
4. Select references from the literature for specific topics that will lead professional and non-professional readers to gain additional insight into what grief is all about.
5. Use online resources to give readers more in depth knowledge of topics like memorial tattoos and living wakes/living funerals that are not covered extensively in the literature.
6. Revision process of editing/rewriting to improve clarity and impact, keeping in mind the sensibilities of the contributors.

Shirley Scott, RN, BSN, MS, CT

Introduction

Kenneth J. Doka

Almost half of all marriages in America end in divorce. That divorce ends a marriage—not necessarily a relationship. In many cases, especially if there are children, the relationship is likely to continue. That relationship may be fraught with ambivalence, torn by continuing conflict, wearyingly peaceful or, in some cases, truly friendly. But it does continue, connected through all the transitions of the life cycle, even possibly coming together periodically perhaps to celebrate events in the lives of shared children and even grandchildren.

It was my interest in ex-spouses that began my foray into a concept that I later defined as *disenfranchised grief* (1989, 2002). I was teaching a graduate level course in family life. As we were discussing the grief of widows, one of my older students commented, "If you think the widow has it tough, you should see the ex-spouse."

To be honest, even though grief had been my area of study, I had not really thought much, or at all, of the grief of ex-spouses. The student continued. She had been married for close to twenty-five years when she caught her husband in bed with another woman—a neighbor whom she'd considered a friend. She threw him out of the house, beginning a long and acrimonious divorce proceeding. He soon remarried and within a year after the marriage, less than two years after the divorce, her ex developed a cancer that rapidly consumed him.

She was surprised both at the depth of her own grief and the little support she received from her friends and family. *Why be so upset? He was only an "ex"—and an unfaithful one to boot.* Yet she still grieved him—her old high school boyfriend, her first husband, and the father of her children. In fact, the very ambivalence, wrought in the betrayal itself, complicated her grief. Who was she mourning—the spouse she had once loved with all her heart or the unfaithful man whose duplicity cast doubt on all she held dear in her marriage?

The student's story inspired me to do research on the grief of ex-spouses, beginning an intellectual journey that would lead to research on the grief when an intimate but unmarried partner dies, and eventually leading me to coin the term *disenfranchised grief* to address losses where the bereaved survivor has no right to grieve. That is, where persons experience a loss, but where their grief is not socially validated and their loss cannot be publicly mourned or socially supported.

Bereaved readers then taught me one of the great values of that concept. As one reader wrote, "It gave my grief a name." The fact that someone addressed these types of losses eased the isolation and the stigma.

THE DISENFRANCHISED: Stories of Life and Grief When An Ex-Spouse Dies does that in a very powerful and personal way. The narratives and poetry reaffirm the many types of relationships that exist after a death, and myriad ways that ex-spouses mourn the demise of an erstwhile and failed partner. This alone is validating—reminding surviving ex-spouses that others have experienced this grief as well.

These stories offer more, though, than simple validation. They offer tools, strategies to cope with the loss. In doing so, they offer even another gift: hope. These stories reaffirm not only the complexity of human relationships but also the resiliency of the human spirit to surmount even the most complex and difficult losses.

REFERENCES

Doka, K. J. (Ed.). (1989). *Disenfranchised grief: Recognizing hidden sorrow.* Lexington, MA: Lexington Press.

Doka, K. J. (Ed.). (2002). *Disenfranchised grief: New directions, challenges and strategies for practice.* Champaign, IL: Research Press.

Kenneth J. Doka, PhD
Professor of Gerontology, The Graduate School
The College of New Rochelle
Senior Consultant, The Hospice Foundation of America

SECTION 1

Moving Toward Forgiveness

CHAPTER 1

Harold

Rosemary Wyman

Preface: I had been with our adult children for two days as they trooped in and out of the Asheville ICU where their father, my ex-husband Harold, was unconscious and on life support.

During the next couple of days I was not there. I requested an emergency appointment with my L. Ac. (licensed acupuncturist) for some acupuncture. At the beginning of the session I was asked just a few questions about what was going on with me. Then I was told, in effect, "You need to look around your psychic house and see what needs to be returned to Harold. It is important for his journey that he has everything that is his."

During my treatment, I realized I had been keeping Harold's shadow hidden; all the wayward things about him I had not revealed. The poem "Peter Pan Ending" resulted from my meditation during the hour of acupuncture. It portrays the psychic ceremony of intention by which I returned the shadow to Harold respectfully, and with love.

I was back in Asheville when his kids requested staff turn off Harold's life support. He didn't stop breathing right away, and we transferred him to a little hospice residence.

I rested in a recliner alone beside him for about an hour while his sons did the paperwork and orientation involved. Blessedly, he no longer had any tubes or tape on him. Nothing was blinking or beeping, and he looked a lot like his old self, fast asleep.

When he was alone at last, he lifted off for Neverland. A few weeks later, a member of my writer's circle handed me a copy Peggy's call for writing on the subject.

❧ ❧ ❧

In July of 2007 the man with whom I began an illicit affair in 1971, whom I married in 1975 and divorced in 1983, died.

The last week of his life was spent in ICU on life support, and then in a palliative care center in Asheville, North Carolina, surrounded by his three children and me.

When I'd first met this man, 6 years my senior, he was my boss. I was not yet out of high school.

To me, his incredible intellect, outspokenness, physical allure, and daring were like drugs I was unable to resist. I'd just turned 18 and the full court press was on.

Our affair and subsequent marriage was full of passion, anger, drama, and heartbreak. I escaped with my self-esteem in tatters and our two beautiful children. At the time of our parting I cursed him.

I have moved on to a new life as part of a blended family and managed, with the unconditional love of my new mate, to grow and change and become a better person.

My ex was not so fortunate. He struggled with mental illness, homelessness, diabetes, and heart disease. For the most part, depression kept him isolated from his children. Sometimes there were months at a time when no one heard from him or knew where he was. He was stuck in a universe of his own making, where he could not grow up, could not father appropriately, could not partner with anyone.

In the last 10 years or so I've been able to see how my negativity toward him was hurting me, keeping me from growing. I started to work on softening my heart without smudging my boundaries. At first I worked hard to find forgiveness.

Eventually forgiveness for him came with ease, and I believed it was genuine. From that point on I made an effort to stay connected through infrequent letters that he never answered. I heard he enjoyed them.

In the winter of 2005–2006, as a result of being unable to afford to keep up his numerous, expensive prescription medications, he had fallen in his little apartment and gone undiscovered for a few days.

From that point on he never really walked again. His mind still worked, but was not as sharp, and his depression was like a tangible wall most of the time.

The last 18 months of his life were spent either hospitalized or in a nursing home not far from his son (from his first marriage), who lived and worked nearby as a physician's assistant.

In early July 2007 he contracted a severe infection. My stepson took him to the emergency room and left only after it was determined that they would admit him some time during the night.

He "coded" within the hour. Staff worked to revive him for 17 minutes before getting a pulse. From that point on he was neurologically unresponsive except for one freak moment, when our son audibly expressed his love and forgiveness.

At that moment, there was distinct movement in his hand.

His three grown children and I worked as a loving team, supported by hospital and hospice personnel, to gradually and gently release him.

I wrote the following poem after a vivid visualization, while trying to process my role in that energetic release.

Peter Pan Ending

Wendy must
Open the drawer in her chest
The Neverland Compartment
Of her heart

She scans its musty interior
For the folded secret hidden
His silent shadow
That must now be returned
Peter lies unresponsive in a hospital bed
But a certain *Pan*-ness prowls
The frigid ICU room
Hunting what is his

Time here is kept
Not by the tick-tock of the Clock
But by the whoo-SHHH
Whoo-SHHH of the ventilator

Twenty-first century Tinker Bells live
Trapped inside IV drip machines
Blinking mechanically dispassionately
Uncharacteristically resigned to their fate
Wendy must
Carefully consciously
Sew Peter's shadow back on
Wendys are bound by nature to do so

Her precise stitches
Bind his slippery shadow
To left foot to left side to left arm
That is hot with clot

At his head she pauses for
Dramatically dark lashes
Hair she once kept neatly cut

Hers has grayed but his will not
His lips are no longer visible
Tape is stretched like a long loud scar

Across his jowls and mouth
To hold the ventilator tube

Beneath which his broad chest
Rises repeatedly falls predictably
Hypnosis hook dragging her
Into a fog of her memories

Wendy must
Resume shadow needlework
Push herself now
Round the crown of his skull

Now past his right ear
Lobe adorned with red
Flashing pulse ox-clip
Now trace the sleeve

Of that awful green gown
Not Peter Pan green
All down that bruised arm
Past the IV lines

His right hand lies engorged
Rests swollen discolored
On a pillow all its own
A surreal hand sculpture

Wendy hums an unknown song
Tinder for her rhythmic chore
Her stitched descent to marble toes
Her ending where she'd first begun

Peter Pan will want to do

What boys who won't grow up will ever do
Fly off to Neverland
Bringing Wendy to mother *all* the lost boys

Wendy must
Open the hospital window

She crosses the room loving the layers
Of blue mountain vista beyond

A sudden temptation plays her
To stand at the risky rim again

Beside a crowing Peter Pan
But she'll not fly with him this time

Wendy must
Strip off all her artificial skin
Protective gloves protective gown

Slip out into the hall alone and leave him to it.

EPILOGUE

Harold died on July 13, 2007, his eldest son's 37th birthday, and one day before his daughter's 30th birthday. She was just 2 weeks away from taking the Bar Exam and slightly less than 1 month away from her wedding.

I felt fiercely angry about the timing of his death. I'd witnessed him slowly self-destruct for almost 30 years and he had to climax on his children's birthdays? Right when his daughter was trying to finish studying for the Bar? Just before she married? Jeez! That anger hovered just above my hurt.

But, for me, relief was there as well. Finally there would be no more havoc wreaked by this man. There would be aftermath, yes, but nothing freshly complicating coming at us. As children and young adults, his kids had been through every kind of emotional turmoil at his hand: promises and abandonment, mania and depression, times when he projected responsibility for his well-being onto them, blatant favoritism, cutting put-downs, unpredictable, scary, sometimes violent behavior.

After his death, I just kept telling myself, "Thank God it's over." My dear friends and family could sense both of these powerful emotions and offered me the chance to speak about both. No one seemed to think I should feel any way except how I was feeling at any given moment.

There is a persistent sadness in me that Harold's life was so difficult. A lot of it wasn't his fault. I knew the patterns of self-destruction were seeded in his post-WWII Jewish childhood. His family circle included many Holocaust survivors whose mission was to reunite other such families and support them in healing.

But I think his parents and grandparents were severely traumatized by what had occurred in their world, by their undeniable vulnerability, their personal and cultural loss.

His parents taught him that he had a superior brain, which would make the world a safe place for him and ensure him a life of success.

I think he knew from the outset that their premise was not necessarily true. Sadly, his great intelligence and subsequent mental illness isolated him. He knew who he was supposed to be, but simply could not achieve his parents' expectations.

All the way home from Asheville, where I'd left him at the hospice, mere hours from death, I played Dave Matthews' song, "You Never Know." It resonated with me in a deep place; it's a song about the fleeting nature of life, the perils of not tuning in to what's really happening, and the ultimate spiritual twist of leaving our bodies. Those lyrics howled my frustrations, soothed my sadness and helped me connect with the departing soul of someone I had loved imperfectly. I played and sang that song a lot in the next month and it helped me release him as well as remember him.

For our daughter's wedding I decorated a special candle, which she placed on the altar to represent his spirit presence at the ceremony. I came very close to a real sobbing fit just moments before her stepfather and I were to walk her down the aisle together.

I felt (not unexpectedly) a tidal wave of regret for all that he, and the kids, had missed, *would* miss. I got through it by focusing on shockingly blue eyes in a portrait of someone I'd never met, which hung in the narthex where we were queuing up for our entrance. That man's eyes seemed to say to me, "Stop that right now!" And I did.

Recently, my ex came to me in two powerful dreams. In the first he was healthy and happy. He wanted me to tell him the story of how he died. A friend pointed out that my ex-husband might actually need such closure, since he had been in a coma.

In the second dream, he let it be known that he was working to ensure our financial support in a way that he had never done in life. The job he was working was one he'd had when our kids were young. I saw him carrying big stacks of money, putting it away for us.

I interpreted the dreams in two ways: one as signs of his ongoing healing in some spirit realm, the second as an indication that aspects of our soul contact still continue, previously irreconcilable but now within reach of resolution.

Harold's children each seem to grieve and find support in different ways. The three siblings agreed on a good time and place to scatter Harold's ashes the winter after he died. They stay in loving contact with each other. Perhaps they converse with one another about how grief and healing manifest in their lives, but if so, they are not telling me.

I suspect that they will have some ongoing, unfulfilled longings not unlike the ones I have carried because my father was an emotionally damaged person who was ultimately not available to me. If our children are fortunate enough to have children of their own, they will find surprising avenues of healing by parenting differently.

COMMENTARY

Forgiving yourself or others is an opportunity to free yourself of pain and anger that has built up over time. It may not be easy, but the alternative is choosing to live with the pain of bitterness and resentment toward yourself and/or others (Murphy, 2012).

Forgiveness is the tool that made it possible for Rosemary to eliminate the anger and negativity that was holding her back, hurting her ability to grow as a person, to become someone better. She had lived through a tumultuous affair and subsequent very difficult marriage for 12 years that involved "passion, anger, drama and heartbreak." After the divorce her self-esteem was shattered. She was full of anger and cursed her ex-husband when they parted.

Some time later, she was able to form a new, supportive relationship with a man who loved her unconditionally. Her self-esteem improved. However, in the past 10 years or so, Rosemary finally realized it was necessary to address the unresolved negative emotions she had held on to for so long.

To forgive means to "give up resentment [and] the desire to punish" (*Webster's New World Dictionary,* M. Agnes, Editor in Chief, 2003), a daunting task after many years of misery and a bitter divorce. Some people may be able to accomplish this on their own. Others need the help of a therapist, an understanding friend or family member, and/or their religious or spiritual advisor.

Rosemary states that at first she "had to work very hard to soften [her] heart without smudging [her] boundaries." She had to learn that when we forgive someone, even when they may not deserve forgiveness, it will unchain us from the person we hate. "Forgiveness accepts the past as it was, embraces the present, and faces the future. . . . It frees us from our emotional baggage" (Byock, 2004).

Eventually Rosemary was genuinely able to forgive Harold, who, over the years following the divorce, experienced many physical, mental, and social problems. Rosemary made an effort to stay connected with him by writing infrequent letters that he never personally acknowledged. She heard he had enjoyed them.

Because she had forgiven him, she was able to work with her children and stepson as a loving team to provide support for Harold during the final chapter of his life. Had she not forgiven him completely for all he had put her and the children through she would have missed the opportunity to accompany him through his final hours.

The stress of sitting by Harold's bedside day after day, expecting him to die any time, led her to visit her acupuncturist to foster relaxation and relief from the tension. In response to what Rosemary told her about what was going on, that Harold could not seem to "let go," the practitioner suggested Rosemary "look around her psychic house and see what needed to be returned to Harold" to ease his transition into death. During her meditation Rosemary realized what she had kept hidden: "all the wayward things about him that she had never revealed—the shadow of his being."

Sometime later, as she was again at his bedside, she experienced "a vivid visualization." In the resulting symbolic poem, "Peter Pan Ending," she very sympathetically and lovingly portrayed Wendy sewing Peter Pan's shadow in place, allowing Peter Pan, the boy who could never grow up (Harold) to once again fly away. She was able to say goodbye to the imperfect man who had been her husband. Through the act of writing, Rosemary was able to free both Harold and herself.

In her epilogue, Rosemary states that after Harold died she again experienced anger. This time it was in response to the unfortunate timing of his death. But there was also great relief that he could no longer create havoc in the lives of their children. That she expressed her hurt indicates there was still some love or affection for this man who had been a significant, albeit disruptive, part of her life.

Rosemary was fortunate to have the support of friends and family who understood her conflicting reactions after Harold's death. They were willing to let her talk about how she was feeling, understood and/or accepted whatever she said. Many people in a similar situation do not have that support. Their grief is disenfranchised; it is neither recognized nor socially acknowledged (Doka, 2002). They are left to their own devices to get through the pain.

As parents usually are, Rosemary was concerned about how her adult children would be affected by their father's death and the unresolved emotions from their traumatic interactions with him over the years (Scott, 2000). She understood they were processing their grief in different ways and was encouraged by the knowledge they stayed in "loving contact" with each other. She hoped they would find some peace and consolation by learning how to forgive him for the trauma he had created over many years. Experts say the most effective way for children to learn forgiveness is to see their parents modeling forgiveness in their daily life (Enright, 2001). Hopefully, the children learned the rewards of forgiveness from Rosemary.

REFERENCES

Byock, I. (2004). *The four things that matter most: A book about living* (pp. 38, 70). New York, NY: Free Press.

Doka, K. J. (Ed.). (2002). *Disenfranchised grief: New directions, challenges and strategies for practice* (pp. 10-13). Champaign, IL: Research Press.

Enright, R. D. (2001.) *Forgiveness is a choice: A step by step process for resolving anger and restoring hope.* Washington, DC: American Psychological Association.

Murphy, P. (2012). Retrieved May 24, 2012, from www.thepowerofforgiveness.com/pdf/Forgiving_oneself.pdf

Scott, S. (2000). Grief reactions to the death of a divorced spouse revisited. *Omega: Journal of Death and Dying, 41*(3), 216.

Webster's new world dictionary. (2003). Paperback edition. New York, NY: Simon & Schuster.

CHAPTER 2

Rubber Man

Anne Bower

Preface: The central incident described in this narrative happened a lifetime ago it seems, but when I read Peggy's call for essays, time dropped away and once again I was in our little farmhouse kitchen facing an irrational, tempestuous husband. Writing about that episode and the years that followed has eased some of the anger I carried, but it still amazes me how little my husband and I understood ourselves and each other.

❧ ❧ ❧

Spring 1973

"Rubber Man wraps his left arm around Amanda and Thomas. 'Hold on tight,' he whispers."

It's a quiet Sunday afternoon in our crowded farmhouse. Lee has our three kids entranced with another episode of "Rubber Man." He's leaning forward across the kitchen table, sandwich remnants and empty milk glasses no obstacle, cigarette smoke drifting up from the ashtray. The kids wait, silent. Lee's left arm is folded against his chest, but now his right hand reaches forward.

"Rubber Man holds the kids snugly; his legs twist around the chimney. He s-t-r-e-t-c-h-e-s his strong right arm up, up to where Mr. Snargly's magic knife is lodged deep in the pine tree's bark. . . ."

As I put the Mason jar of goat's milk back in the fridge, I'm again amazed at my husband's imagination and voice, and how well he uses it for these stories.

When Rubber Man pulls at some distant object, Lee's tone extends out and out. When the hero grabs a bullet, Lee can ping or whang his voice so you feel that damned bullet graze your skin. He barks for the wild dog, howls, snarls, roars, and trumpets various animals across our kids' minds.

Peter, Becca, and Nettie watch his hands and arms, his face, and I know they're inside the story, seeing Rubber Man's black shiny suit and fearless actions. Upstairs, I can hear my foster daughter, Judy, practicing her cello. My own destination is the barn where piles of bedding must be removed from the goats' stalls. The weather is mild and gray, a perfect early spring day for shoveling shit.

My husband's inventive capacity shocks me. He can make up these stories whenever the kids need them—when they're fussing in the car, restless before bedtime, or just at loose ends. He remembers exactly where he's left off an episode, so that when shouts of "Rubber Man, Daddy, tell us another Rubber Man story," fill the air, he knows exactly where to start the next installment. He lights another smoke, inhales, looks up at the ceiling to think for a moment, exhales, and when his head comes back down, and the cigarette is resting in the ashtray, it's story time.

He strokes his beard slowly to indicate a villain in thought, opens his blue eyes wide when some innocent child is needing Rubber Man's aid, flaps his long arms when a vulture is about to swoop down on the blind man's Seeing Eye dog.

When it's my turn to tell a story, I pull a book from the shelf and make sure the kids see the illustrations. Yes, Lee is the creative one in our couple. The English professor—the poet, the storyteller.

I cook, clean, do the bulk of farm work on our marginal little spread, keep track of bills, though I'm also the one who paints and draws, with or without the children.

Shoveling soiled straw out of the goat stalls, I anticipate the rest of this day. Lee has papers to grade, Judy has homework, the kids will get up to some game—another exploration of our neighbor's cornfield or a long session of Monopoly. Maybe we'll make some cookies. At ages 5, 7, and 9, they're almost always eager for cookies.

Our friend Mike is coming over later. He likes cookies too. He's been talking to Lee about whether or not he should flee to Canada rather than serve in Vietnam. Mike hates the idea of leaving all his friends and family behind, but he can't accept fighting for something he doesn't believe in. Lee served in Korea. He hated it. Mike trusts him.

My barn work goes well, and after an hour there's a good-sized pile of manure-y straw beside the garden. My hands are calloused, and though my 32-year-old back aches, I'm pleased with my body's efficiency—its warm, sweaty, earthy smell. Pleased too with the order of the yard and garden.

Walking from barn to house, I scan the fenced pasture where the three goats graze, catch a glimpse of our aggressive rooster chasing his hens, note that the gander isn't in sight though his mate is over near the blackberries. The yellow cat is sitting on a saddle we've hung on our small porch and I stop to scratch behind her ears, her instant purr gratifying, and a non-verbal "thank you."

Lee is the only one still in the kitchen, sitting at the table reading a magazine.

"Hey, Babe," he murmurs, glancing up, "How's it goin'?"

"Good. Got the stalls all manured out, clean bedding down."

His eyes are back on the magazine page. "Get me some cereal, will you?"

Right. He didn't have dessert at lunch and wants his usual Rice Krispies and fruit now. I want to say, "Hey, buster, get it yourself," but I know better.

"Sure. Let me wash up first."

A hum of comprehension . . . he reads on. I can hear the kids upstairs. The cello has stopped so maybe they're with Judy.

We've been married a dozen years and the habits are set. Once in a while Lee will wash dishes. If I'm truly sick, he'll cook. But the kitchen is basically my zone.

This often strikes me as totally nuts. We've been through the 60s, we all know about women's liberation. And yet among the couples we know, few of the men do any major childcare or domestic labor.

Now my hands smell of Ivory soap, even though the warm scent of manure still clings to my clothes. I place a washed peach, the jar of goat's milk, a bowl, a knife and spoon, and the box of Rice Krispies near my husband. The sugar bowl is on the table. I'll take care of the lunch remnants later—the bottle of ketchup, bread crusts, rumpled paper napkins, plates and glasses, a bowl of homemade bread and butter pickles.

What kind of cookies should we make? I cross the room and pull *The Joy of Cooking* from the shelf beside the stove, while Lee mindlessly pours cereal into his bowl, adds milk, and picks up the peach to slice.

Maybe the kids would like hermits; my grandmother's favorite—easy and a little bit nutritious.

"Jeesuz, Anne." His tone is sharp. I turn to see him holding part of a peach in his hand.

He spits out a bite right onto the table. "This goddamn peach is mushy."

"Maybe it's just one section that's over-ripe?"

He turns the peach and pokes it with a finger. "The whole damn thing's mush, and . . ." he points at the bowl where I see fragments of peach among the cereal and milk, "now the whole thing is ruined." His brows are drawn together, his nose crinkled in disdain at the offending peach. "Why'd you buy fuckin' bad peaches?"

"Oh good grief, Lee—I didn't knowingly buy *bad* peaches."

I start to explain how expensive they were, how I took time to pick out the four that looked best, but before more than five words are out of my mouth he picks up the offending bowl of cereal and heaves it across the table toward me, milk splattering the table and wall, cereal and peaches jumping out of the bowl among the lunch detritus.

"Take this fuckin' mess out of my sight," he yells, "Can't even buy a decent peach," and smashes the remaining unsliced peach down onto a plate, cracking it in half.

My stomach tightens and my tongue feels heavy in my mouth. Everything seemed fine when I left the house, but here we go again. Even after this many years, Lee's "moods" still terrify me, and what's almost worse, they close me down. I just don't know what to do.

Lee is tall and thin, wiry and surprisingly strong. He has never hit me or the children, but when he's in one of his moods he flails out at any piece of the world that's around him—a wall, a chair, a dish, a plant, and the same voice that can tell a story with such fluid variation or tell a joke so well, becomes a harsh, cutting knife or a blunt weapon.

His blue eyes go a shade darker, his beard seems to shine, and his body expands like a threatened male baboon in the jungle somewhere demonstrating he is the strongest and toughest critter around.

And don't try to argue with him. He's always right. He'll always find a way to top your logic, your fact, your idea. The easiest thing to do is placate him. Later he may apologize. May. . . .

I should keep calm, make nice, and just bring him a clean bowl, another piece of fruit—a banana. But not this time.

I sit down across the table from him. "It's not my fault the peach isn't perfect. *It's your* fault for being an asshole."

His brows pull together and his jaw tightens. Oh yes, any second and he'll spew vile words to shut me up. I look down at the bowl of bread and butter pickles. What the fuck, maybe I can get satisfaction out of fighting back? He sure seems to get something out of this kind of display. So deliberately I reach forward, pick up the pickle bowl, and slam it back down on the table. Slices of green pickle leap from the bowl and flop onto the table, pickle juice and little mustard seeds spread out. I almost laugh at one seed that lands neatly on a butter knife blade.

"Don't start with me," he warns in a low voice.

"I'm not starting anything. You're the one who started it."

He throws a lunch plate across the room. It hits the far wall and cracks into pieces, shards, crumbs, and a bit of mustard spattering the floor where it lands.

"I told you, don't start with me," his voice loud now.

Please don't let the kids come downstairs, I think. I can't stand to see their faces when Lee gets like this.

I should stop. He's warned me, after all. Yet my right arm reaches forward and I grab a glass, aim for the same spot the plate hit, watch his eyes widen, watch the glass arc across the room, and blink at the sound of glass shattering. Danger. I worry the kids will come downstairs barefoot.

Lee sweeps an arm across the table and two plates, another glass, butt-laden ashtray, and the open bottle of ketchup hit the floor, spilling out across the linoleum like thick blood.

"You think you're the only one who doesn't get what he wants?" I ask. "You ever stop to think maybe I'd like someone else to cook once in a while, someone else to weed the garden or clean out the barn?"

"Shut up, shut up with that crap," he snarls. "I'm the one earning a living here. I deserve to have at least a decent bowl of cereal."

He throws the jar of milk off the table. Perfectly good milk, fresh this morning. At least the Mason jar didn't break, I think, and lean forward, grabbing the Rice Krispies box.

"You want a fucking bowl of cereal?" I ask, standing and emptying the box onto the floor, shaking it to make sure every tiny Krispie drops from the wax paper liner. "Then you get it yourself."

I walk out of the house, my heart beating fast but my pace deliberate. I grab the car keys off the peg by the door and head straight for the car. Rice Krispies and milk and pickle juice cling to my jeans. I don't care. The car starts promptly and I drive away, determined that whatever happens I will not clean up that mess. Lee can clean it up. I don't care if broken glass and cereal crumbs and cigarette butts stay on that kitchen floor forever. These hands aren't cleaning up that crap.

The worst thing is that throwing out words like that, acting angry, heaving things around didn't make me feel one whit better. Not at all. Worse if anything. Ashamed. Stupid.

Half an hour later I pull the car off the road and wonder where the hell I am. It takes me a while to recognize the field. Lee, the kids, and I gleaned potatoes here last autumn. A family outing, the kids running up to show Mommy and Daddy oddly shaped spuds or super big ones that had somehow escaped the mechanical picker. We filled two bushel baskets. Anyone driving by would have smiled to see the five of us laughing together despite poverty, sharing the work.

Those passing strangers would have thought us a perfect family.

I sat in the car another 20 minutes or so, unsure what to do, worrying about what Lee might say to the kids to explain the shouting and the mess. It's horrible to hear your parents swearing at each other. Scary enough to know Daddy had another temper tantrum, but now Mommy's doing it too?

I'd always been the calm one, the one who didn't panic when someone cut a knee or spiked a fever. The one who paid the bills, showed the plumber what leak needed to be fixed. I had to go home and make sure they were all okay. But I was damned if I was going to clean up the broken dishes and food we'd splattered around the kitchen.

I turned the car around and drove home, repeating to myself, "I will not clean up the mess, I will not clean up the mess, I will not clean up the mess."

No problem. When I walked into the kitchen, the table was clear except for the salt and pepper shakers neatly placed in the center. The floor had been swept and washed. No traces of food on the walls. As I later learned, Judy cleaned it up.

In the living room, Becca and Nettie were making paper dolls. Peter was drawing with Judy. Lee had retreated to his study. No one mentioned the fight.

January 1981

Lee had a cancerous growth on his back. It looked like a golf ball was buried under the flesh below his left shoulder blade. His mother arranged for a specialist in New York to do the surgery, and he stayed with her a few days after the surgery. When he came home, he joked magnificently about the gouged out area of flesh and muscle. "The shark bite," he called it, *Jaws* having entered everyone's cultural vocabulary.

He warned the kids he wouldn't be able to roughhouse or lift anything for a while, and when he winced in pain they winced with him. The wound was so large it couldn't be closed with stitches, and most of the skin graft the doctor attempted didn't take. So healing went slowly as the raw flesh grew back from the wound's edges. Lee needed me to clean and treat the hole in his back every evening.

Each night, he knelt on the bathroom floor, leaning on the edge of the tub, and I carefully untaped the large gauze pad that covered the whole area. I had to wash the healthy skin around the incision, pat the area dry to carefully inspect the raw flesh, and make sure healing was progressing.

Where the skin graft hadn't taken, muscle, I guessed it was muscle, it gleamed a deep pink, mottled, moist, and shiny. The first time I saw it I almost puked, but I kept my hands steady and my voice calm.

"Whoa . . . that's . . . that's amazing looking. It's really clean, Lee." The excised section measured about 3 by 4 inches. At the center, it went a good half-inch below the surface of his back. After I washed and sterilized the existing skin, the tricky part of the nightly routine involved rolling a thin stick coated with silver nitrate evenly across the vulnerable unprotected area—leaving a film of the chemical behind. My first attempt was awkward, of course. My hands trembled for fear I'd poke the wound and cause Lee more pain.

I twirled the end of the stick lightly across the bare flesh and saw how the silver nitrate adhered to the skin. It took me about four rolls down the wound to coat the pink horror with a film of gray chemical. Then I covered the treated area with loose clean gauze and taped it in place. Lee told me he couldn't feel anything on the open wound, although the nerves all around it were hypersensitive.

That was a relief in a way, although startling. Not a nerve in this large a section? But knowing he couldn't feel the treatment stick on that sickly looking flesh reduced my nervousness.

By the time we'd gone through this routine for four or five nights, I'd become quick and skillful. And after a week or so I actually derived satisfaction from the even rolling of the stick across the wound, watching the silver nitrate smoothly flow across the nastiness, seeing that the skin did gradually creep forward and grow to cover up the raw flesh.

The kids and I waited on Lee, and he maintained a surprisingly good attitude. Later, months later, he'd bitch about the way the missing muscle in his back affected his golf swing. When twinges of pain stabbed him, he'd bark at whoever was closest or blame the pain on something one of us had or hadn't done. He'd have swamping moods of depression, hours and days in front of the TV. Panic attacks too, horrid debilitating seizures of fear and confusion.

He consulted with a psychologist, a colleague at the college where he taught, a fool who didn't see the depth of pain and misery this man suffered. I knew it was more than the cancer, knew from all the years of ups and downs, of alternating silences, tempers, and hilarity, but had no idea what to do. His needs were just too much for me.

Yet we slogged on. Just as we'd managed the treatments for his back, we managed his legally blind mother moving in with us, we managed our teenage children's sports events, band concerts, plays, applications for college. In 1982, when the kids were 13, 15, and 17, I began graduate school, and went to a therapist in nearby Morgantown, West Virginia, for 6 months.

"When you're ready for a divorce," he said, "come back."

I wasn't ready in 1984 when his mother moved in, or in 1985 when I earned my Master's degree in English, which, if I remember correctly, was the same year Lee converted to Catholicism. (We'd both come from Jewish backgrounds.)

November 1987

I waited. One of the things that kept me married long after I should have left was my confusion over how my children would maintain relationships with their father if we divorced.

His temper was so fierce, and I knew he'd be so angry with me, that I couldn't picture either of us being decent to the other. I imagined we'd take our nastiness out on our kids.

By 1987, Peter was 18, Nettie 20, and Becca 22. That same year, I discovered that, quite early in our marriage, Lee had had a string of affairs, all of them with girls. I mean girls. High school-age girls.

I hadn't realized. I should have known. I'd been stupid, fooled, blind, trusting, unperceptive.

The actual divorce, in 1987, just formalized the emotional separateness in which we'd operated for years. Although he was angry and begged me to give us another chance, I think he too was relieved.

I told him, "You'll be married again within a year or two." And he was. To a woman he'd met at church. She moved in just a few months after my departure and they were married by the time I earned my PhD and moved to Ohio to become an English professor.

When we divorced, our circle of acquaintances was shocked.

"You seemed the perfect couple." (*Seemed* would be the operative word there. Yeah, we put on a good show.)

"But you've been married almost 25 years; you have all that history together." (Hmm . . . but so much of that history hurts . . . my own blindness and fear as well as his angers and cheating.)

"We didn't realize you guys were unhappy." (Maybe we didn't let ourselves realize it either. He hid from his discontent by cavorting with young girls. I buried myself in the busy domestic scene, volunteerism, whatever jobs came my way.)

I don't know what Lee told people about why we divorced. He maintained friendships locally and people accepted his new wife, I presume. He went on teaching at the same college, playing golf, was active in the Catholic church, writing poems—now with a religious flavor, and smoking, despite his doctor's warning.

A Warm Day in 1991

Here I am, back in the driveway of Lee's house to pick up his mother, Rose, so she can come again to stay with me in Ohio for a 3-week visit. I had told her when the divorce occurred that I wasn't divorcing her. After all, we'd become friends and she was the grandmother of my kids.

Since Lee couldn't be civil to me, usually Rose and I arranged these pick-ups for times when Lee was teaching or playing golf or at church.

I notice the new patio furniture Rose had bought Phyllis and Lee. I notice the yellow cat, Butterball, hiding under a pine tree. Beyond the trees, the land rises gradually, a sloping hayfield, then acres of woods.

During the last few years of my marriage, I'd escape Lee's tantrums and the constant fights between Lee and his mother by taking long walks up that hill. Walking through our neighbor's land, I would catch glimpses of deer and rabbits, once a Pileated Woodpecker. I'd inhale the smell of pine, let my mind go blank and find peace.

Today I knock on the door, but nothing happens, even though Lee and Phyllis's new puppies yip boisterously and scrabble around in the hallway.

When I cautiously open the door, the two miniature dachshunds dash out, bumping into my ankles, circling me, completely cute. I stoop down to touch their silky fur. They're all wagging tails and twisting bodies, long ears flapping, little paws scrabbling on the patio stones as they work figure eights around my legs.

Their fur is shiny, a chestnut brown, and they've got those lovely soft bellies puppies always have. I squat down and tickle behind their ears.

He's standing above me and the voice is like a stone. "Don't touch my dogs."

I straighten up and step back, almost tripping. Lee stands in the doorway in a navy terrycloth bathrobe, thin legs pale. I haven't seen him for over a year. His receding hairline has crept further back, but his beard is neatly trimmed and his posture is still good. At 58, he remains a handsome man, but his face is distorted by anger. It shows in his rigid body, in the way his long-fingered hand grasps the belt of his robe, in the line of his eyebrows drawn together.

I step back further, hands raised to show him my empty palms. Bastard, I think, you believe I'm gonna hurt your damn dogs?

"Don't worry. I'll never touch your precious dogs again. Tell Rose I'm here."

I turn and march back to my car.

Why can't he act like an adult? Would it be so hard to just show a little courtesy? After all, it's *his* mother I'm here for; after all, it's always me who makes the drive to get her and to bring her back.

You'd think he'd appreciate the way I've maintained a relationship with Rose and the time free of responsibility for her that he and his wife have each time she's away with me. Damn the man.

I want to throw stones at his house, kick his dogs, race out of the driveway without his mother. But no. I sit there squeezing the steering wheel and wait.

When Rose emerges, hand on her new daughter-in-law's arm, walking cautiously across the uneven patio stones, I make no effort to help. I let Phyllis make a second trip with the suitcases, get out of the car to open the trunk, and don't utter a word.

Autumn 1993

Each time Rose came to visit, her stay would last a little longer. She found Phyllis cold, Lee's ongoing angers confusing, and enjoyed the more social life in my household—little dinner parties, an occasional lecture or concert, a monthly trip to the mall where, even though she couldn't see the clothes with her blind eyes, she'd use her scrap of peripheral vision and tactile abilities to enjoy buying a new blouse or skirt.

In 1993, during one of Rose's visits, Lee called to tell me he'd been diagnosed with a virulent, incurable chest cancer and was undergoing chemo.

Rose spoke to Lee, listening carefully, trying to offer notions of hope, as much for her as for him, I thought.

"It's not right," she said, after she hung up the phone. "Why can't it be me instead?" At 88, she showed no signs of failing. She railed at a God in whom she'd always said she didn't believe.

"Take me," she demanded, tears running down her face.

A week later, Lee called again and spoke to her, then to me. The voice at the other end of the line contained Lee's familiar firmness and resonance, but he spoke calmly and slowly. He knew he was dying, he told me, and hoped I could help his mother through this. I believe he said something about keeping her with me rather than having her at the house during his last weeks. When I hung up, I wrapped my arms around Rose. How dreadful to survive your own child, your only child. He was 60.

She kept saying it wasn't fair, "how could this be." She had to go back and help Lee.

I drove her back to visit with him. He chose to die at home and refused further chemo. From my son and younger daughter, I learned that he accepted death and was gentle to them in his last days.

I'd always thought of him as someone dreadfully afraid of death, someone who wanted to control the world around him and would see death as wresting that control away. Perhaps his religious beliefs helped him, and certainly a loving wife made a huge difference.

Rose was back in Ohio with me when my son called to tell us Lee had died. Rose burst into body-shaking sobs, inconsolable. I stood there, blank, empty, waiting to feel some shred of sympathy for my ex-husband and all he'd been through.

Then I felt my body relax and let the relief flow through me like a gentle, meandering stream. Never again would I have to hear that angry or icy voice. Never again could those unpredictable moods descend upon me.

When friends and colleagues learned of my ex-husband's death they reached out with concern. They knew we'd been married almost 25 years, knew the divorce wasn't amicable.

"Even though you were divorced, there's a lot of history there," my friend Mandy said, her hand atop my own. "I know his passing must still cause you pain."

Another friend poured wine for us and said, "After all those years, no matter how much shit you guys went through, you can't help but be sad about his death."

They meant well. They thought better of me than I deserved.

Of course, I was sad for my three children—especially my son, who was close to his father and who helped care for him during that painful, rapid death. I was sad for Rose, who'd lost her son.

In an abstract way, I was sad for his wife. They'd only had 5 years together. But my own heart didn't shrink or throb with sorrow or pain. No, I have to admit I felt lighter, more at ease, free.

When we'd first met, back in college, I'd lusted after that man and during the early years of our marriage, I must have loved him. He had a huge presence, immense often manipulative smarts, great charm, and a brutal temper.

For years after his death, he still showed up in my dreams, furious and demanding, telling me what to do, or yelling about some mistake I'd made.

After his mother died, I dreamed the two of them were together, enjoying themselves. It pleased me to imagine him peaceful, though I don't believe in any kind of afterlife.

But that sneaky guy lives on. Even now, when we've been divorced 2 decades and he's been dead 14 years, he occasionally stretches out to the land of the living and smashes my dreams in anger.

EPILOGUE

If I were a truly mature person, perhaps my long-dead husband could vanish from my dreams or at least assume only minor roles. But no. Loud-voiced and scowling or full of desperate worries, he still barges in. I wake and wonder why I harbor his discord after all this time. Do I, in some perverse way, require his form of nasty passion? But at least there's this: Each year he makes fewer appearances. And each year I can more easily shake my head and even smile when I recall our mutual stupidity and ignorance, the unfortunate way our psychological needs dovetailed and locked us into a cycle of attacks and withdrawals.

Then too, it's easier now to remember some of the good things. Family trips in the car with all of us taking part in a fake opera, belting out arias about "I see seven COWS in the field," and "Peter's sweater has stripes and its colors are red, red . . . and blue, blue . . . and greeeeeeen," and "Grandma's going to meet us, she'll meet us at the museum, the museum full of din-o-saurs." Or a wonderful afternoon by the shore in Spain—olive oil fried potatoes, fresh sardines, the kids playing in the sand, the two of us enjoying a local white wine in the ocean-scented air. Or the amazing "light shows" Lee invented using slides in the projector, his waggling fingers in front of the projector's light distorting the images cast upon a sheet hung on a wall while The Doors or Country Joe and the Fish blasted on the stereo.

Part of what helps me smile is that our three children—now all in their 40s—are such healthy, creative people. Their quirky senses of humor, their sharp intelligence, and their ability to have fun all owe much to Lee's influence. We seldom speak about their father, but from a few things each one has said it's clear they have some good memories to counterbalance the recollections of the man's frightening mood swings, temper tantrums, and the tensions between me and Lee they couldn't miss.

But part of my smile has a sardonic twist. Despite much healthier relationships and some insights and good memories, Lee still bugs me. I guess this is the way the human psyche works, but damn it, if he must show up, couldn't he leave the temper behind? Bring dream flowers, tell a joke, put on a phantom light show, make me a cup of cocoa?

Or, maybe, just maybe, one night he'll finally wave goodbye and fade out of my dreams forever.

COMMENTARY

The first thing Anne mentions in her epilogue is her wish that her long-dead ex-husband would disappear from her dreams. They had been divorced for 20 years and he had been dead for 14 of those years. She adds that at least "each year he makes fewer appearances" to disrupt her sleep with his loud-voiced and scowling demeanor.

Just as she did during the marriage, Anne wishes that in his dream visits Lee would leave his temper behind and be nice to her, tell a joke, or bring her dream flowers. This may be an indication she is subconsciously still looking for acceptance and/or affection from him.

While grief is the normal response to a significant tangible or symbolic loss, mourning is the process of adapting to that loss by detaching from the person or object (Balk, 2007). Sometimes when a person denies grief and feels only relief concerning the death, as Anne does, there are still unresolved problems lingering in the subconscious that must be attended.

There are two aspects to working through these situations that need to be considered. The first is an internal, private, intrapersonal process. It is the inward struggle to cope with reactions to the loss and/or the problems. The second is the outward, public or interpersonal process that includes the social aspects, the religious or other rituals, and the support of family and friends (Corr, Nabe, & Corr, 2006). According to Worden (2009), dreams offer an intrapersonal parallel mourning process that reflects the perplexing circumstances with which the person is struggling.

Dream research shows that dreams can help integrate the troubling effects of trauma in a way that sometimes cannot be done in a waking state (Scott, 2000). This allows submerged feelings of anger, frustration, guilt, and/or anxiety to be processed over time. After so many years of violence, anger, uncertainty, betrayal, and verbal abuse, the fact that Anne's dreams are happening less often may signify that her intrapersonal process is working well for her. It is gradually allowing her to detach from the nightmare that was her life with Lee.

Anne states she is now able to remember some of the good things in their years together, has much healthier relationships and some insights into what the problems were. But she adds, "Lee still bugs me." This may be another indication there is lingering ambivalence about her feelings for him. This is a common occurrence when one has a long, albeit troubled, relationship (Scott, 2000). Anne said she had no grief, only a great feeling of relief, when she got the news that her ex-spouse had died. However, memories of the trauma and loss of her marriage, plus the anger and bitterness from the divorce, have apparently persisted for years.

Many people who have experienced the death of an ex-spouse do not receive sympathy and support from family, friends, and co-workers (Scott, 1992). In Anne's case, the opposite was true. Family and friends were unable to understand why Anne and Lee divorced in the first place for they appeared to be such a "perfect couple" for so many years. After his death their perception was that despite all the problems and their long history together, Lee's death must still cause Anne pain. She received condolences from so many people she felt guilty and not worthy; she felt only relief that Lee was gone. This is just one of the dilemmas confronting survivors of the death of an ex-spouse.

Concern for her children has been dominant in Anne's mind for years. She now takes comfort in the fact that her children survived their tempestuous early years, "even have some good memories [of their father] to counterbalance [those of] frightening mood swings, temper tantrums, and tensions" between their parents. She is pleased they exhibit some of their father's good traits such as his quirky sense of humor, sharp intelligence, and ability to have fun. She is comforted that now, in their 40s, they are "healthy, creative people."

REFERENCES

Balk D. (Ed. in Chief.). Wogrin, C., Thornton, G., & Meagher, D. (Assoc. Ed.). (2007). *Handbook of thanatology* (p. 132). Northbrook, IL: Association for Death Education and Counseling.

Corr, C. A., Nabe, C. M., & Corr, D. M. (2006). *Death and dying, life and living* (5th ed., p. 220). Belmont, CA: Thompson Wadsworth.

Scott, S. (1992). Death of a divorced spouse: The survivor's dilemma. In A. Tiemann, B. Danto, & S. Gullo (Eds.), *Divorce shock: Perspectives on counseling and therapy* (pp. 64-65). Philadelphia, PA: The Charles Press.

Scott, S. (2000). Grief reactions to the death of a divorced spouse revisited. *Omega: Journal of Death and Dying, 41*(3), 212, 215.

Worden, J. W. (2009). *Grief counseling and grief therapy* (4th ed., pp. 171-173). New York, NY: Springer.

CHAPTER 3

Selected Slides

Elizabeth Kerlikowske

Preface: I wrote these poems as my life unfolded. My ex-husband died unexpectedly at a moment when I was already furious with him. He was in the process of having our marriage of 30 years ago annulled. All the loss I felt for him and our history was tainted by this fury, this attempt at erasure, which our daughter's existence belied.

Since resolution with him was no longer an option, I turned to writing as I always do. The poems helped me to draw a circle around the parts of our life I could still love.

❧ ❧ ❧

For the wrong reasons, my husband and I were happily married in 1973.

He wanted to be a radical, and I wanted to be a hippie.

I saw him as a way to get revenge on my conservative grandparents; he viewed my trust fund with desire.

We played a lot of Scrabble, smoked a lot of dope, and went to college.

Reality set in when our daughter was born in 1975. It was time to grow up and get jobs, which I did.

He remained a dreamer who felt a certain sense of entitlement, and his dream included inheriting some of my father's money. I worked; he watched our daughter. On the Fourth of July, 1977, I asked him to grant me my independence.

Our daughter lived with me until I moved across the country to attend graduate school. Then he became her custodian.

Because he can no longer represent himself, I must speak on his behalf. He was a wonderful father who loved his daughter utterly. Having to peel her away from his casket was one of the most difficult things I have done in my life.

At the time he died, I found out he was in the process of having our marriage annulled. He wanted to become a better Catholic.

I was infuriated by this, by his secrecy, and most importantly, by the effect it would have on our daughter.

He was not in my good graces when I received the terrible midnight phone call. I thought I would be happy that he was dead. God had granted him a certain annulment. I guess I thought he was asking for it.

As the news sunk in, and my daughter flew home, I became a participant in a ceremony of honoring.

My ex's wife and I have always gotten along, and because of our mutual parenting, I've been included in everything. I spoke at his memorial service. Our old counter-culture friends came by, cleaned up, middle-aged, and successful.

The more I let myself feel, the more I realized the loss. There was no one else who remembered when I worked for The Galloping Gourmet. No one else was searched repeatedly at the Canadian border. He was the one who helped me with the first awkwardness of motherhood. An entire clump of my life had just disappeared.

I still had it in my head. I could speak of it, but no one on Earth had shared it with me but him.

It wasn't until he was gone that I understood how important he'd been to me. The lasting legacy is the use of my name. I had always had a nickname, but when I met him, he began calling me Elizabeth, my grown up name.

I have been her ever since.

First Marriage: Going for Broke

Unplayed in a decade
the clarinet ditched in
its plush velvet coffin
reeds snug in sleeves

pads peeling from keys
like antique band-aids.
*"You don't need this,
do you?"* he said.

She tasted AJ "Bill"
Johnson's music store,
her licorice stick real
wood, not Belwin plastic
but only plastic tones
clotted in its bell.
$200 used
and good for asthma.

He closed the lid, left
and an hour later returned
with pizza.

Swing poured
from the radio. He ate,
but her mouth was lined
with velvet.

Lunch After Twenty Years

It took that long to see what you once saw in each other
and now you note his easy etiquette:
he ordered for you, picked up the tab
finally comfortable in a suit and tie.
And there you are both gray as ghosts.
He's bald but bearded and your hair's long.

"Great witch hair" your third child compliments,
eleven years younger than the one you had together.

That daughter's the main topic of conversation
but the words ramble and veer carefully
on terrain disquietingly familiar.
You both look so nice.
It would be a shame to be disheveled by a spat.
he points out his boss across the room

in this restaurant you've never been to.
You are still statuesque.
The two of you make a handsome couple
if people aren't intimidated by size.

He sits straight and throws his chest out.
"That's all he ever had to do," your father had said.
"Ah," you think, *"but if it works . . ."*

However, you came today because you had
one thing you wanted to say,
but before you get to that,
you grind some gentle axes. So does he,
which leaves the room freshened with cleansing
and look, you're both whole!
Your clothes aren't shredded, cheeks remain unscathed by claws.

He's pushing his chair back
which is your fault because you looked at your watch,
so now you have to say your piece.

Remember you invited him.
From the archives you erase all fighting and enmity.
Let it all evaporate, like his hair, your waist.

Swallow any fury and thank him.

Thank him for your real first name,
which he recovered and sent with you on the
road to yourself.
He was the stile through the glass fence.
He was the first father.
For these gifts and time served,
let everything else be forgiven.

Gemini Under Glass, 2003

The next slide is my dead husband
squeezed between window panes.
Squished dreams squirt from his ears:

the doctorate, entrée to aristocracy.
See how his pillow exudes a stream
that pools into our daughter. A hookah

twists overhead or is it an IV?
His chest hair matted fleur de lies, rope
descending to his navel, gesture
of rescue too late. He can't climb away
from his heart-wrenching legacy.
Ceremonial gear litters the thought

balloons popping from his occipital
lobes: I am the asp around the pen,
his wife an owl's feather, the child

we didn't have a Celtic warrior, the one
we did, Quetzalcoatl. Silver and jade
circle his former neck. A habit of braces
keeps teeth together, marbles laughing
behind coke-bottle lenses. The deceased
knows he does not look fifty-three or
human or 3-D, ash impression, lip
print on the drained mug. Orange and
red smoke bombs from the Days of

Rage, fill in the blank color outside
his shifty outline, all he left behind,
an R-crumb dreamer counting off

something I can't yet know
on the fingers of his free hand:
one down, three to go.

Annulled

Our daughter calls from the West Coast with news:
you're having our marriage annulled. The action will be
complete by June, thirty years exactly since we threw
crepe paper from the windows of the old hall, needed
pots and bedding but accepted joints and candles. Erase
the Scrabble games, re-runs of Dragnet and Star Trek.

Return your Cribbage victories during labor. Murder memory.
Replace the tainted years of failure with faith once spurned.
A surgeon's already re-routed your bad, bad heart.

Say your rosary: blue green algae, Feng Shui, New Age,
Beatnik, Celtic, crystals. All failed. Your best part
is not in Heaven, but in Oregon. Still you are on a rampage
of excision. You can twist a Bishop's pen to say we weren't, but a
repaired heart should know it's Kate, not me, who's hurt.

Epitaph

Preposition: anywhere
a life could go-down the tubes,
in the toilet, out the window,
up the Gorgon, around
the whale, over the Cuckoo's
Nest, under the nose picker,
on the cleat, and above the toast

Images slapped on paper
snow shovels of paint
loose and running
him racing to convert drips
to sense before they dried

Or with precision
calculation of a just-flipped
egg over easy sliding onto
a Butter Wagon platter

Rote, his epitaph
rewritten a hundred times
to have it read the same

(the writing of worms
universally cursive
whereas moles undermine
the stability of exclamation
marks and onions)

His pen supported
on the staff of a minor key
transcribed a crescent moon

Abecedary bodies in motion
before the paper scrim
gels rotating NO
A fellow spot
they fought over

Grits bubbled and broke
hot onto his page.
He played with his food
until no one was looking,
but by then it wasn't food.
What was it?

A gift once
lost in an x-ray

A rubber band strangling a wrist

A clam is not a girl except
on the end of the boy's stick
or in the fisherman's hand or
at the end of my fingertip
When is the door ajar?

Legal pads filled
with illicit thought swung
on monkey bars of verbs
until everyone saw
underpants and the rapture
of cubing lust in words

(a wall of heliotrope suggests

action only when unobserved
at intervals by the cigarette
of twilight)

Hate After Twenty Years
for my ex

Your shields flew up whenever we were on the phone
as if you didn't want to speak for fear I'd steal

a thimble of your voice and cast it into spell.
What power I assumed in your imagination,

mossy glamour of money. You nailed me
the week you were Freud: I *was* looking for a father.

Email lectures I deleted without reading;
acquiesced to your gift request for Kate
at holidays. Your move to my town caught me
by surprise; soon friendships intertwined,

but it was known you wouldn't tolerate my name.
O passionate loathing I did not comprehend

the depth of your regard, although your wife knew,
on guard against possible reconciliation. Old man,

I mourn the years we missed two miles apart,
littered with bitterness and skewed attempts at

communication. Your absence traces the streets
each school day and when I lean into the benign

universe, you're not pushing back from the other side
keeping me in my place. How could you die?

EPILOGUE

When I answered the phone and heard my daughter say, "Dad's dead." I actually said, "You're kidding." But I could tell from her tears that she was not.

My ex's death was incomprehensible. Unexpected. He was only 52. I felt the loss immediately. A swath of memory disappeared; there was no one now who shared my early 20s when he and I had moved to Canada.

Although we were married only 4 years, he had a profound influence on who I became and what I've done with my life. The irony was that our divorce was required to do that.

Although it had been over 20 years since our split, his fury was just as intense when he died as it was at the final hearing. He was happily remarried and the hub of a wheel of friendships. He loved his life, but for me, he felt only smoldering and often outright fury. I did not feel the same. I had hoped for some reconciliation after all these years.

When he died, I knew that reconciliation could not happen, and I grieved that wasted time and fury, part of the hypertension that killed him. He came from a family of haters, and when a relationship became difficult, they lopped it off like an animal with its foot caught in a trap.

I thought when he and his wife moved to my town, that meant things would improve. We shared friends. I thought that would help. I hoped beyond hope, and then he died.

I spoke at his funeral, which was reminiscent of *The Big Chill.* He lay in his coffin with a half-smile on his face as if he would sit up at any moment. Friends had prepared him for his journey with scotch and joints, books, CDs.

I tucked a poem into his vest pocket. Later there was a huge party with only one person absent. My current husband did not participate in any of this. He did not care for my ex. He only knew the angry, "entitled" part of the man. He understood that I'd lost part of my past, but for him, I was well rid of it.

The depth of my grief surprised me.

No friends seemed to understand how the death of someone I'd never even mentioned could hurt so much. Mercifully, one of my colleagues, who'd divorced her husband, who also later died, was the one person who understood the kaleidoscope of feelings. She helped me believe I was not emotionally unstable.

Witnessing my daughter's grief was the most unbearable experience. We finally had to escort her from the coffin so it could be closed. A couple months later she decided to move back to Michigan from Oregon. I drove there to help her.

As we packed up the final load, she picked up her phone to replay the last message her father left her. It was full of hope and encouragement and bespoke his pride. That was what I would miss too: his best self.

COMMENTARY

There are many factors that affect the intensity of the grief response to the death of an important person in our lives. For example, the stronger the attachment in the relationship the greater the intensity of the grief reaction will be (Wolfelt, 2011). However, sometimes grief is more intense when there have been strong negative feelings between the parties. This may be the result of knowing it is no longer possible to confront the deceased, to vent the anger, or perhaps to resolve some of the problems.

Elizabeth's relationship with her ex-husband was very difficult before the divorce, which she instigated, and anything but cordial in the following years because of his smoldering fury at her.

She did not feel the same. Elizabeth had long held the hope they could somehow stop being adversaries; they could at least be on speaking terms. This is a common theme among survivors of the death of an ex-spouse, especially when the death is unexpected. One researcher found that 92% of the people reporting a severe grief reaction said the death of their ex-spouse was sudden (Scott, 2000).

In her poem "Lunch After Twenty Years," Elizabeth expresses her attempt at some reconciliation. At the end of their time together she decides to "erase all fighting and enmity [...] swallow any fury and thank him for resurrecting her real first name." For the things he had done for her, she decided to "let everything else be forgiven."

All of that was forgotten when Elizabeth's daughter informed her of her father's goal to have the marriage of 30 years ago annulled. She felt betrayed and infuriated at his attempt to deny their marriage, erase the history they had shared and the legitimacy of the daughter they had conceived. She turned to writing to find solace in the parts of their life she could still live with.

Many people experience great relief in writing their thoughts and feelings, no matter how jumbled or crazy they seem. It helps to vent emotions, to break the circular thinking that so easily keeps us awake at night when we are grieving. Writing can allow us to gain insight that can help change painful feelings in some ways.

A good example of disenfranchised grief is Elizabeth's report that none of her friends could understand the depth of her grief for someone none of them had heard of. However, one colleague knew from personal experience what she was going through. She helped Elizabeth believe she was not going crazy.

Feeling that we are losing our sanity is another manifestation of grief. The lack of concentration, feelings of unreality, anxiety, panic, helplessness, confusion and depression are just some of the symptoms that combine to create doubt that we are still sane. There can also be physical, behavioral, cognitive (thought processes) and spiritual manifestations during the grieving process (Worden, 2009). As we work through the grief process, these symptoms diminish and we begin to feel more control over what is happening to us.

Elizabeth was fortunate that she and her ex's wife were on good terms because that made it possible for her to participate in the funeral. This is not always the case. Some people are forbidden to view the body, attend visitation or participate in the rituals in any way even though the children are present. Often this causes additional grief, especially when the surviving parent of the deceased's children is not even acknowledged at the services.

Dealing with the grief of our children is a main concern for parents. After all, the first responsibility of a parent is to protect his or her child. In this case, however, the parent cannot protect the child from the pain of grief. But he or she can be lovingly supportive, listen when needed, comfort when possible, seek grief counseling when necessary. On top of that, parents have to deal with their own grief—not an easy task.

REFERENCES

Scott, S. (2000). Grief reactions to the death of a divorced spouse revisited. *Omega: Journal of Death and Dying, 41*(3), 212.

Wolfelt, A. D. (2011). *Exploring the "whys" of grief* (p. 2). Ft. Collins, CO: Center for Life and Loss.

Worden, J. W. (2009). *Grief counseling and grief therapy* (4th ed., pp. 17-31). New York, NY: Springer.

CHAPTER 4

Never Given a Name

James McGrath

Preface: Good, bad, indifferent, angry and joyful memories are the roots of my writing. It was the opportunity given in *The Disenfranchised: Stories of Life and Grief When An Ex-Spouse Dies* that brought together those solid and fleeting memories nourished in my poems.

The complex narrative—the story—the voice of it is only partially here. Memory has a life of its own to be lived each day, piece by piece. How fortunate for me (and others) that the life of memory can be expressed and shared. Thank you.

❧ ❧ ❧

I think of how Jean and I met in an art class at the University of Oregon. We were art majors. I wrote the following poem as I see her face in my memory today. I feel her standing near the photograph she took of the Northwest landscape, for our first Christmas together in 1951.

The Color of Ice Melting

I envisage all the words, colors, faces,
hands at the tip-of-my-tongue.

If I gather the words together
to shape a phrase, a description
a picture blazes
of where we danced among noon-hot sage,
stirred up dust.

I would have few words.
The sounds would be spring and rain.

If you would press your hand to the small of my back
  I would recoil in bliss,
  melt my shoulders into your breasts,
  sweat sweet dreams on your pillow.
  I would have few words.
  The colors would be bougainvilleas and guitars.

If I could mold your profile into clay,
  turning you to face the mountain one day,
  then to face the West
  where the sun melts the desert
  into lakes of lava
  you would see why I stare at you
  in the night where the colors are stars.

What lies at the tip-of-my-tongue
  is what I love most,
  what bites my lips,
  what I feed on.

It is the years I have been nourished
  by you touching me in the silence.

What words are left are indecipherable as the voices of the
  tides going out over small stones
  turning them on their backs.

The sound and color would be ice melting.

Jean and I married the same week we graduated, each of us with degrees in art. She with a major in weaving and ceramics, I with a major in art education.

We spent the last 3 years of our 9-year marriage in Europe. I taught art to American students in Germany. Jean was a dedicated housewife, a generous mother to our two girls, and a devoted companion.

After our divorce, Jean and our daughters, Jeni and Jain, returned to Jean's home city in Oregon. I stayed in Europe 4 more years.

Jean died on Christmas day, 2004.

Our daughters did not tell me of her death until after they'd scattered her ashes on Monterey Bay, several days after their mother died.

I wrote the following poem 3 years after her death.

Feeding The Fire

There is a fire in my kitchen
  that will eat years of birdsong,
  leaving only a pile of silent gray ashes.

There is a fire in my heart that flickers and flames
at the whim of a photograph
or a handwritten name on an envelope.

I will shovel my winter fireplace,
drop the ashes into a glass bucket,
layer the vanished trees
into my garden on a windless day.

I will smear the ashes from the burning
of my heart across a sheet of white paper
to remember where they came from.

The burning will say it's over.
The wound is healed

What ashes remain, I shall spread into my garden
with the others where the seeds of memory
bloom and ripen with spring plantings
and the conversations of mourning doves.

In the summer, when I pick the first zucchini
and open a leaf of lettuce,

I will taste the name of the beloved
in the greenness of what I have left behind.

Now Jeni and Jain have children of their own. When we speak on the telephone at odd times or when we exchange letters and cards that acknowledge birthdays and holidays, a fleeting, pressing remembrance of family comes into our conversations. The following poem was written to acknowledge the phantom that comes and goes with the memory.

Searching For a Reflection

This morning I see your figure in the phantoms
left by a night bird that dreamed you.

You come and go
unexpected, uninvited.
I don't invite ghosts
when morning glories open their eyes.

When you arrive in a fog,
I welcome your invisibility,
even ask you to stay a while.

In all those years we dribbled time away,
we never questioned the shape that time
would leave behind.

For now, I only see you when your image
floods the day in drought driven light.

By noon, you will have vanished again,
melted, turned into a hollow bird-bone flute.

If you come to me in a dream
hidden in a pile of night leaves,
I will twist and tumble about
vomiting those leaves into the air,
calling them ravens.

I will speak to these ravens,
telling them winter is coming,
they must fly South to circle you
with a crown of hibiscus.

I will tell them to watch for you
searching a bottomless pool
of sunset water, searching
for your reflection for the last time.

At 79, I write poetry. Two books have been published in the past 3 years. My third collection is ready for the publisher. When I write my poems with the sense of loss for Jean, the sense of the incompleteness, our movements together continue in the mysterious present that is only felt, never completely unwrapped, never given a name.

EPILOGUE

As I write this, it will be 5 years this 2009 Christmas-time, that Jean died. My daughters told me of her death a few days after she had died. Jeni and Jain were still in their shock and grief.

They said, "We just didn't tell you right away; that's what Mom wanted."

I can only believe Jean had more anger at me than either of us knew. Anger and grief was the order of those days.

Anger and Confusion After Death

There is anger after death.
The kind of anger that has no one thing
or person to be angry at.
The kind of anger that is pure,

dark, a room full of blinking lights
and shadows without names.
There is confusion after death.
The kind of confusion that rattles
the ribs, stirs up the well of tears
behind the eyes. I could list the words
that describes this confusion: fluster,
muddle, disturbance, displacement,
unsettling, tangle: words that have
one meaning: the red blinding WHY
without an answer.
There is anger and confusion after death
that is expressed only by inviting memory
and grief to walk with me hand-in-hand
searching for peace on the long road home.

COMMENTARY

Through his gift of poetry, James gives us a moving glimpse of the myriad feelings of grief he still feels after the death of his ex-wife some years before.

Since he did not know of her death until after all the mourning rituals were past, he did not have an opportunity to share with family and friends the memories, stories of her life and the support for each other in their mutual loss—all significant parts of the rituals (Worden, 2009).

James does not mention a second wife, significant other or family and friends with whom he could share his grief. Even if they were nearby, who would understand his grief reaction more than 40 years after being divorced? He apparently was left alone to work out his conflicting feelings in the best way he knew how—through heartfelt poetry. His is a significant, often unexplored example of how disenfranchised grief makes it more difficult to process the complexity of emotions that can come in a flood or in waves as we try to make sense of the death of someone we still care about (Doka, 2002).

Throughout his poetry James seems to feel his loss as if Jean died only yesterday. No one can judge the normality of another's response to a death, or of how long another will grieve. Both depend on numerous variables including the individual's own coping style.

Many people have a very difficult time processing their grief for reasons related to the quality of the relationship, the circumstances of the death (expected, or unexpected and/or traumatic), how long they were married, how long since the divorce, how they processed the loss of that relationship, ongoing involvement with the ex-spouse because of issues with children or business, to name just a few (Scott, 2000).

When asked how long grief lasts, some people would answer, "Until I die." For others it may be a few weeks, months or years. For some it may be decades. For the latter, their inability to address the "Tasks of Mourning" may complicate their lives with emotional pain and longing that keeps them from getting on with their lives. Those tasks are to accept the reality of the loss, process the pain of grief, adjust to the world without the deceased, and find an enduring connection with the deceased in the midst of embarking on a new life (Worden, 2009).

James tells us very little about his marriage, but he seems to remember Jean fondly as illustrated in his words, "She was a dedicated housewife, generous mother, and devoted companion."

Neither does he tell any details about the divorce, but given the intensity of his grief after Jean died it may be that he never was able to grieve for the great loss of his wife, children, and sense of family. Only when Jean died did the finality of loss of the relationship trigger the unattended grief from long ago (Despelder, 2009).

In James's poem, "Anger and Confusion After Death," he expresses two very common reactions people have when first hearing of the death of a loved one. His later description of "inviting memory and grief to walk with me hand-in-hand searching for peace on the long road home" shows his increasing ability to accept the reality of Jean's death, express his negative feelings, and begin the painful journey of adjusting to his loss.

As James reaches out to his adult children with phone calls, occasional letters and cards he experiences a "fleeting, pressing remembrance of family." We can only speculate that through increasing interactions with his daughters he may be working toward gaining their forgiveness. As very young children they may have felt deserted by their father when he stayed in Europe for 4 years after the divorce.

Reconciliation sometimes happens after a death when people realize the importance of family connections, that now all they have is each other. It is also possible that, as he ages, James will choose to nurture his relationship with his grandchildren.

In his poem, "Feeding The Fire," James indicates that even though Jean is gone she still lives in his memory. Over time, when the grief process has been allowed to progress, it is possible to remember the loved one without the severe pain of the initial loss. James can now hold Jean in loving memory, maintaining a continuing bond (Klass, 1996) with her that may allow him to proceed more comfortably with his productive life as a poet.

REFERENCES

Despelder, L. A., & Strickland, A. L. (2009). *The last dance: Encountering death and dying* (8th ed., p. 327). Boston, MA: McGraw-Hill.

Doka, K. J. (Ed.). (2002). *Disenfranchised grief: New directions, challenges and strategies for practice* (p. 11). Champaign, IL: Research Press.

Klass, D., Silverman, P. R., & Nickman, S. L. (Eds.). (1996). *Continuing bonds: New understandings of grief* (pp. 349-351). Philadelphia, PA: Taylor & Francis.

Scott, S. (2000). Grief reactions to the death of a divorced spouse revisited. *Omega: Journal of Death and Dying, 41*(3), 210-213.

Worden, J. W. (2009). *Grief counseling and grief therapy* (4th ed., pp. 39-53, 118-119). New York, NY: Springer.

SECTION 2

"He's Dead and I'm Not"

CHAPTER 5

When Papaw's Spearmint Went to Heaven

Linde Grace White

Preface: Stereotyping is rampant in our society while relationships become more and more complicated. The emotional bond between spouses changes throughout that relationship, and although people need to come and go from each other from time to time, the basic bond remains, particularly if there are children and grandchildren. I wrote my story to highlight the kind of change that happens when the change is permanent; the way a person can rise to the occasion and put aside negative feelings to help a person in transition and those who love that person. Besides, my grandson is hilariously funny.

❧ ❧ ❧

"Nuts! This can't be good. Maybe it's a wrong number."

When the phone rings at 1:30 a.m. on December 29th in Ohio, somebody's either drunk or dead. Good options do not abound. I struggled awake and grabbed the phone.

"Mom!" my daughter's strained and tearful voice quavered. "My daddy's dead."

The denial is instantaneous. "No! What happened? Does Karen know?"

I am assailed by questions that need answers and my main thought is about my children . . . well, our children.

Laura is my oldest child, happily married, the mother of two sons. Right now, she sounds about 6 years old.

"He died. Mary Kay (stepmother) called. I don't know if she's going to call Karen.

I ask if my son-in-law, Pete, is awake too. Of course, he is. Her children are asleep. She has just gotten off the phone with her stepmother, has not called her sister across town, and is in shock.

She starts recounting what she knows so far. Her father, Herb, and his wife were at a restaurant in California where they were visiting her family. He parked the car, ran up a hill, and collapsed inside the door. They moved him to an empty room. He didn't recover well, so a stepson called an ambulance. He "coded" in the ambulance, was revived, and died in the emergency room. That's the short version, the factual version.

I call a good friend of mine and tell her about it.

I can't believe I have any real feeling about the situation, but I give her the quick run-down, and still have to get in touch with my younger daughter, Karen.

I dress, phone Karen, don't reach her, wonder what to do, try again, and finally get her. She has just come home from a night out with friends.

If she wasn't sober when she picked up the phone, she is now—in a matter of seconds when I tell her that her dad has died. I tell her to stay dressed and I will pick her up in a few minutes. I head out. Ten years ago, none of us had cell phones.

With some difficulty, I get Karen in the car. She is in shock, quite distraught, and when she's reluctant about anything, it's a job to get her to move in the direction she needs to move.

We drive across town to Laura's, where we sit, dumbstruck, the rest of the night.

Mary Kay has agreed to call my son, Jeff, who lives about a hundred miles from her in San Francisco. The girls want to talk to their brother too, so we call him.

There is no plan for what to do, but Herb's body will be coming back to Ohio no matter what plan develops.

I find I am more involved in this death than I ever thought I would be. The suddenness of Herb's passing is a major factor. When he was at my house on Christmas Eve for a small celebration with our daughters, Pete, and grandsons, he had not been feeling well.

Since our divorce and his remarriage, he had put on weight, too much weight. Not only was his food intake unhealthy, he did not exercise in any way, nor was he under a doctor's care. His wife, very much into vegetarianism, naturopathic medicine, yoga, and so on, had virtually no influence on his health practices.

On December 23rd, with his wife in California, he suffered the classic symptoms of heart attack for men. He took some ibuprofen or aspirin or something, thinking he had pulled a muscle (he was actually very intelligent) and had called the doctor the next day. The doctor told him to come in and get checked out, but Herb had a wedding that day and three worship services (he was a Presbyterian minister). He didn't see the doctor. He called me, he called Laura, and he called Mary Kay. We all told him to see the doctor. He was afraid he'd be hospitalized on Christmas Eve. Instead, he came to my house, looking gray, feeling bad, and leaving early. It was the last time I saw him alive.

Our daughters were worried. I was worried. I had no idea I could be so frustrated with him after a full 16 years of divorce. Yet, I could say and do nothing to influence the situation. I didn't want my children to lose their father. That was my bottom line.

I ended up helping my daughters choose his burial plot although my recollection was that he had preferred cremation. When Mary Kay called with the information that his body could not be moved out of California until he had a permanent address, as it were, it fell to me to write down her wishes for his ultimate disposal.

Mary Kay dealt with the funeral home and made all the other arrangements, most of which Herb wouldn't have liked. Apparently they didn't talk much about final plans. He was only 55, so I guess it seemed premature.

Since most of the family had to travel from out of town, Herb's house was teeming with extra folks. Everybody pitched in to manage shopping, meals, supplies, and beds for about 15 people. The girls and I stayed, of course, at our own homes, but spent hours at Herb's. It was actually fun to visit with relatives and friends who came by or were staying there. Herb would have had a ball!

The funeral had to be scheduled for shortly after New Year's Day. Fortunately, the ground at Spring Grove Cemetery was not too frozen for burial.

The service was to be the held at the church Herb was serving, and the ladies of the church put on a spectacular luncheon after the burial.

Explaining this funeral "stuff" to Andy, our 3-year-old grandson, became the task of his mother and father. Andy had been told that "Papaw" had gone to heaven. Since his great-grandmother, Herb's mother, had died earlier that year, Andy was somewhat familiar with the concept.

Andy told me that he was wearing his "funeral suit," a little gray number in size 3, with a white dress shirt and tie. It was sad to think of such a little child owning a "funeral suit."

When he saw Papaw laid out in the funeral home, he made everybody cry by saying, "Mommy, Papaw's not in heaven. He's right here in the treasure box!"

Next day at the funeral, Andy got quite restless. The service went on for over an hour. We let him move around in the pew, and his daddy spoke to him a number of times.

Finally, the soloist launched into a beautiful rendition of Albert Hay Malotte's "Lord's Prayer." Karen, seated next to me, started to cry. As I put my arm around her, Andy appeared between us, gazing up into Karen's tear-stained face and said, "Don't cry, Aunt Karen. It's the last song."

At the cemetery, after his first limousine ride, Andy fairly danced around the grave, which gaped, shadowy, in the bright sunshine. The pallbearers placed the casket on the bars across the concrete vault.

"Papaw's spearmint has gone to heaven!" he exclaimed to the amusement of the mourners. Herb would have loved it.

As ex-husbands go, Herb had been totally responsible in caring for our children. Child support payments appeared every month in the right amount. He provided extras when he could. When Karen had mononucleosis and couldn't go to school for weeks, she stayed every day at his house where he or Mary Kay could look after her.

I would pick her up after my school day ended (I was a teacher).

He took the children on vacations, bought clothes and other items that they needed. On a few occasions, when the children wanted to do something that cost some money (camp session, school trip, etc.) we split the cost between each of us, letting the children share the costs, depending on their ability to come up with their third of the cost.

Herb and I worked out college expenses, cars, and insurance. When social or emotional crises occurred, we were able to cooperate to solve the problems. The children preferred to live with me, but Herb was usually available to help out with transportation, discipline, or party-hosting.

When Karen graduated from high school, we jointly hosted a luncheon for her girlfriends. We sat in the kitchen and chatted while the girls partied in the dining room. His house was the bigger one.

Karen's friends commented, "I can't believe your parents are in there talking. My parents can't even be in the same room!"

The children were never a point of disagreement between Herb and me, and I never refused to let him see them or to let them go to see him. The fact that we lived in the same neighborhood simplified matters.

At the time of our divorce, I promised myself and Herb that I would be cordial and do whatever was necessary to limit damage to our children. I initiated the divorce because I objected to his dating other women during our marriage.

He'd said there was something wrong with me.

I don't know what would have happened if, after he died, his widow had stayed here. Fortunately, Mary Kay returned to California where she still lives.

When Jeff married 3 years ago, she traveled to Pennsylvania to be part of the celebration. It worked out all right.

I am not completely comfortable with her. Mary Kay seems to regard me as a co-wife, but none of us is Muslim or Mormon. One wife per husband is the Protestant-Christian norm around here.

The children have, it appears, mixed feelings about her. They occasionally contact her. She calls on their birthdays and on holidays. She says that her estate will be distributed six ways when she dies. She has three children of her own.

I resent the fact that I wasn't consulted more in his funeral service. I know that it wasn't my place to do it, but I knew more about what Herb wanted than his widow did. I resent that when that minister wanted to present one of Herb's grandchildren to the congregation, he chose one of Mary Kay's grandchildren, not Herb's actual flesh and blood 6-month old grandson, Tyler.

I resent that my children received virtually nothing from their father's estate. I have come to a better understanding of my own personality and psyche through therapy, writing, and living.

I still resent that I did not have a silver wedding anniversary to celebrate with him, and I resent that Herb didn't recognize good advice when he heard it. I think he regretted not trying harder in our marriage. I feel I did as much as I could to save our marriage.

It would have helped had I known much earlier about my own childhood experience of sexual abuse. Some of our problems would have been put into perspective. I think he might have been willing to work harder if he'd known that about me, but I didn't know it about myself.

Marriage to Herb continues to inform and influence my life these past 26 years (16 of divorce, and the 10 years since he died). This is mostly because of our children. It is also because of where I live and the many people I've come to know because of that marriage.

I have in-laws with whom I am still friendly. My life is inextricably entwined with his, and elements of that life have never, and will never, cease to affect me. The alternative is to give up family, home, work, and friends to move far away and start over. It isn't worth it.

EPILOGUE

My immediate response was shock. No phone call at 1:30 a.m. is likely to be good news, and this was particularly shocking. I am no stranger to shocking events, but this morning's news of Herb's death was a stunner.

Once my finger-in-the-light-socket phase was over, I became somewhat annoyed.

First of all, I was the only person available to help my daughters with the news. My older daughter had her husband for support, which was great, but he had little experience of death of close family members at that time. My younger daughter was single. I lost a night's sleep, but that was nothing compared to what else occurred.

It turned out that state law complicated everything. We live in Ohio. Herb died in California. You can't ship a body from California to Ohio unless you have, as it were, a permanent address for that body. This has to be a gravesite of some kind. Of course, no such arrangements had been considered because people are not supposed to die suddenly at age 55.

Since Herb's wife was in California, she couldn't buy a gravesite in Ohio. Therefore my daughters were asked to do this, but they were very upset and asked me to help them. In fact, I took the phone call from Herb's wife explaining what had to be done.

Although I knew that Herb did not want a traditional funeral and burial, that is the plan we undertook to follow. (Years later, his widow remarked to one of my daughters that she thought maybe Herb wouldn't have wanted. . . .)

We climbed in the car, drove out to a wintery, freezing cemetery, and shopped for a gravesite. The people at the cemetery were very nice, but rather confused as they had been dealing by phone with the widow. Now the ex-wife showed up to help the daughters. Once we settled on a plot, the body could be shipped.

On the day of the funeral, I became resentful. Our children were not seated in the first pew. The widow and her children (from a different marriage) were on the front row.

My children and I were on the second row.

This would have been fairly palatable had the preacher not gone "folksy" on us. He didn't know us well. He decided to parade an infant grandchild around the room, presumably to illustrate that life (and DNA) goes on. Instead of picking up our 6-month-old grandson (an actual recipient of Herb's DNA), the minister took one of the widow's grandchildren. Of course, not many in the congregation realized this slip. After all, it was only symbolic, right?

The wrangling over property started early, and I was mainly an interested bystander. I had collected my own belongings years before, when Herb and I divorced. It could have been much worse, I agree, but it's ugly to see your children needing something of their father to hold on to, while someone else with another agenda is making all the decisions.

Nobody was distressed when the widow pulled up stakes and moved to her home state of California.

Over the 12 years or so that have elapsed since the death, I have mellowed considerably. I can only imagine how horrible it would have been had our children not been mature adults. I have stayed out of their relationship with their stepmother. I am cordial to her and can get along with her on occasions such as my son's wedding. She sent a very helpful gift of money for my younger daughter's wedding reception last year. She remembers the grandchildren's birthdays and Christmas. She is not on my "usual e-mail suspects" mailing list. I send her a Christmas card although she has not considered herself a Christian for years.

I have learned that there is no way to predict what your reaction will be to the death of an ex-spouse. There is also no way for others to know what to do or say to you. It is a limbo, vast and vague. No social structure exists, either real or imaginary, into which the ex-spouse fits. It is the stuff of which TV movies are made.

I expect that, to some extent, I will continue to resent many aspects of my divorce and Herb's death. In this age of changing partners, instant communication, and totally unconventional family structures, we need to consider our whole grieving process and our commemorations of the lives of the ones we love or have loved.

We seem to be just beginning to grasp that every person is different and that every situation is unique. We can't make assumptions about what people feel or what they want to do. We need more openness and more cooperation among us.

COMMENTARY

In her epilogue Linde very clearly expresses some of the dilemmas (Scott, 1992) that plague those who experience the death of an ex-spouse. There are the external problems where we don't quite know what is expected of us, whether we should speak out against decisions that we feel are not what the deceased would want, and how others often don't understand and/or judge whatever our feelings are. Then there are the internal struggles of resentment, concerns for children, and of not "fitting in." In this anthology we can see we are not alone in our uncertainty, and that these problems are common to all who have walked this path.

In addition, there are two significant issues Linde has raised in this account of her experiences that need to be addressed.

The first is the importance of letting our family members know, before the need arises, what our wishes are for both end-of-life care and for funeral and burial rituals to be followed after the death occurs.

It would have been much easier for everyone if Linde's ex-husband, Herb, had made his wishes known before his sudden death. Linde knew he wanted cremation rather than burial and would have objected to many of the other plans made by Mary Kay, Herb's wife. But Linde was not in a position to interfere. This is one basis for some of the resentment she still carries.

One of the most important things we can do to help our families at the time of our death is to prepare an Advance Directive (also called a Living Will or Health Care Directive) letting them know what our wishes are beforehand.

An Advance Directive is a legal document that is recognized in every state as being the decisions of the person who signs it. It can be a very simple document (Legacy Writers, 2011) or much more detailed such as the Five Wishes document (Five Wishes, 2011). They are both state-specific and spell out details for end-of-life care and the choice of a health care agent (surrogate) to make decisions when we are unable to do so. Five Wishes also includes plans for the funeral or memorial service, burial or cremation instructions, what we want our loved ones to know, how to give and ask for forgiveness, how we wish to be remembered, and much more. Copies of the documents should be given to anyone who might be involved; i.e., family members, health care agent (surrogate), doctors, the hospital, caregivers, clergy, lawyer, friend, and so on.

Many people avoid thinking about preparing a Living Will because they are still fairly young, healthy, and "too busy" to do it. Others are superstitious and feel that if they do it they will die soon. Some people talk to family or friends about their wishes, but never put them in writing. Oral information may be acknowledged by the doctors and/or other family members, but it is better to have our decisions in writing in order to avoid confusion and possible disagreements. The greatest gift we can give our loved ones and healthcare providers is to let them know what our wishes are. Then there will be no second-guessing. They will know they did the right thing by following our wishes. There will be fewer regrets and less guilt.

The second issue involves how we talk to children about death. Linde states that it was Andy's parents who helped the 3-year-old understand what was going on with the funeral "stuff." He had already experienced the death of his great-grandmother and his parents had obviously talked to him about the current situation. But still his ideas of Papaw being in the "treasure box" and that his "spearmint" had gone to Heaven illustrate how words and ideas are easily confused in a young mind. Children of this age often put bits and pieces of previous knowledge and overheard conversations together in their own way to come up with some unusual, sometimes disturbing and often amusing combinations (DeSpelder, 2009).

A hundred years ago people lived in rural areas and had to be very self-sufficient. Theirs were multi-generational families under the same roof. When someone was sick and died it was usually at home surrounded by family members. They all took care of the details of caring for the body, making the casket, digging the grave, conducting the service and burying the body. Children stayed with the adults, were included in all activities, sometimes even slept in the same room with the corpse (DeSpelder, 2009). Children were aware of the never ending cycle of life and death.

In modern times, in our urban communities, all of the above are most often taken care of by strangers. Children are frequently excluded leaving them to wonder why the adults are so upset, and what is happening. They can be confused and fearful of what will happen to them. No one is talking to them.

Children grieve at all ages in different ways according to their level of understanding of the event. They fear what they don't know. They need support and opportunities to be with adults who can communicate with them about this difficult subject.

Some guidelines for adults when talking about serious illness, death, and/or grief with children are: begin on the child's developmental level; let the child's questions guide the conversation; provide opportunities for the child to express feelings; share faith and how it can help one cope; encourage feedback to clarify the child's perceptions; encourage children to express their feelings through stories, games, play, art, or music (Doka, 1995). Utilize other resources such as age-appropriate books (DeSpelder, 2009).

There are support groups that offer a safe, supportive space that children and families can attend. One such group is The Dougy Center: The National Center for Grieving Children and Families (Dougy Center, 2011). Over many years they have trained others to open similar centers all over the country.

Andy's mother and father apparently have done a good job of helping him cope with the deaths of two people he knew. No doubt there will be more questions and concerns as Andy moves through the developmental stages, but his family can be there to give him loving support, answers to his questions, encouragement and understanding.

REFERENCES

Despelder, L. A., & Strickland, A. L. (2009). *The last dance: Encountering death and dying*. (Eighth Ed.) (pp. 34, 353-354, 377-383). Boston, MA: McGraw-Hill.

Doka, K. J. (1995). Talking to children about illness. In K. J. Doka (Ed.), *Children mourning, mourning children* (pp. 35-39). Washington, DC: Hospice Foundation of America.

Five Wishes. (2011). *Aging with dignity*. Retrieved September 22, 2011 from agingwith dignity.org

Legacy Writers. (2011). *Living will*. Retrieved September 22, 2011, from www.legacy writers.com

Scott, S. (1992). Death of a divorced spouse: The survivor's dilemma. In A. Tiemann, S. Gullo, & B. Danto (Eds.), *Divorce shock: Perspectives on counseling and therapy* (pp. 59-67). Philadelphia, PA: The Charles Press.

The Dougy Center. (2011). *Support in a safe place*. [Video file]. Retrieved from dougy.org

CHAPTER 6

The Absence of . . .

Barbara Traynor

Preface: I have long believed that placing words on paper dilutes anger and frustration from most issues. Before, during and after the divorce, my anger/frustration was not directed at my ex-husband per se, but at his total disregard of the opportunity to participate in the lives of our children. The ramifications of his indifference, regardless of reasons, scarred those involved much more deeply than he could have imagined. Not that it would have mattered to him. This is why I wrote. This is why I continue to write.

❧ ❧ ❧

During our divorce, when my ex-spouse once again decided that the grass was greener elsewhere, my children and I breathed a sigh of relief.

Remember Yogi Berra, "It ain't over 'till it's over?" He was right.

We were to endure more months of drunken violent tirades, until he finally departed on Valentine's Day. Ironic. Anyway, after a few months of relative peace, we could stop looking over our shoulders and really breathe.

From that point forward, about a week before his birthday, my ex-spouse would call the house, as a reminder to say "Happy Birthday."

I suppose it was nasty, but my oldest son would play the game of not responding to his hints, although he knew he was setting us up with a series of disruptive phone calls which would leave everyone exhausted and frustrated.

For a while, my eldest played the game, and became an expert at distracting his father. And some parents wonder how children become vindictive?

I am sorry to say I did prolong our troubles by arguing and accusing, but eventually realized it was futile. I did learn.

A number of years were to pass with his sporadic calls, which served only to distance any relationship that might have been.

One day my middle son received a call from an uncle who lived in the same state as their father. His uncle explained that their father was dying, and that he wanted to see his children.

Now, past history had not been good—no holiday or birthday cards (never mind presents), no acknowledgment of accomplishments such as graduation, marriage, grandchildren. And of course, no child support. This was back when the courts did not track absentee fathers. When he'd left, the children were 10, 13, and 16.

Before and during these years, my children and I developed a survival relationship. You know the kind—loving, sequestered, and defensive thoughts of the traumatic past slowly dissipating. We allowed ourselves to anticipate happiness, keeping details to ourselves.

It's not that my family did not know what was going on. I did share to some degree. Most relatives were sympathetic, some not. This was back when good Catholic women with young children did not divorce. They were supposed to persevere.

I was never good at persevering. Times were lean; single parents an oddity. We literally survived until gradually finances improved.

So, my son took his uncle's call and, after speaking with his siblings, they all called me. Given their father's track record and given that this particular uncle had painted a picture of me as the Wicked Witch of the West within the paternal side of the family, I thought they'd have told him where to go.

Wrong.

Their question to me was: "He's dying. We want to allow him to visit. What do you think?" What did I think? Truthfully, I thought they were crazy, but I was never so proud of them. After all they had been through, all they had done without, due to the circumstances their father had constructed, they chose to honor his request.

As much as I thought I'd ruined their childhood, I began to think maybe I'd done something right.

It seems my daughter wanted to see who this person was, this person she was supposed to call Dad.

My sons had more ulterior motives. They figured he would realize he was setting himself up for a fall and cancel at the last moment (he'd previously threatened to visit), or show up and hope his children had not done well without him. Either way, they wanted to see his reaction to them as adults.

They requested their uncle send a recent snapshot since it had been 15 years and they had no idea what he looked like or how his cancer had altered his appearance. Later, they described the scene at the airport:

> Mom, we figured he might have lost weight (their father had been 5′9″, 250 pounds), and would look older, so when we heard his plane had landed we

> went to baggage and waited. We waited and waited until all the passengers had picked up their luggage. We looked around, speculating on maybe "that guy over there," getting a little silly in the process—or perhaps nervous. Anyway, over to the side was a white-haired, short, stocky old man, too old for Dad. Could it be? We walked over—there's safety in numbers—and introduced ourselves. Mom, he was old beyond illness.

Prior to the visit, they had discussed the schedule and parameters with their uncle; where their father would stay, that he would visit with another uncle (with whom he'd remained on good terms) in an adjacent state. They discussed the fact that they would not tolerate drinking of any kind.

My middle son who had two young children said, "I'll throw him out if he gets drunk."

At best, the interaction was awkward.

They had planned his time: so many days here, so many there, but could not have planned on his fragile physical condition. Adjustments were made, and things progressed accordingly within a pleasant atmosphere.

My children were incredible. I do not know if I would have been as tolerant.

During one family activity, he needed to rest and came to my condo. While the children took a respite from care-giving, he and I talked a bit. He did acknowledge that I'd done "a good job," but continued to brag and embellish his current circumstances. Some things never change. I should mention that through his drunken mis-statements, we knew exactly what his circumstances were (i.e., a series of low paying jobs while living with his mother).

The past was not discussed or debated. We stayed in the present and, to their credit, my children got through the week. This had taken a great deal of scheduling, shuffling of cars, and hours on the road. One lived 2 hours away, the other was finishing college. The only one in the immediate area was my middle son, so he provided room and board.

When their father had arrived, they'd telephoned their uncle to say they would be attentive to his medical needs.

When the week was up, they escorted him back to the airport, waiting until his plane was called before they left—fully aware of the abundance of bars in airports, and made certain he boarded sober.

They told me later, "We couldn't get out of there fast enough."

Why had they chosen to do this? They each had their own private reasons, but the public one was that he was their father. They felt if they granted this request, he could see that they were responsible members of society.

They also would be able to say goodbye.

Yes, perhaps there was spite involved, but it takes a great deal of fortitude, forgiveness, and perseverance to carry off a week of visitation with someone you hardly know nor have much feeling for. All three said, "We did what we thought was right. We saw him, recognized that he just never grew up, and said our goodbyes."

After 2 days, my oldest son called his uncle to ask if their father had arrived safely. To his surprise, the uncle berated him. Their father had chosen to drink on the plane and, upon arrival, had to be taken to the hospital.

My son was dismayed, defended their actions, and hung up. Three months later, the same uncle called to say their father had died, asking when someone would arrive for the funeral. After discussion, all three declined, stating they had already said their goodbyes.

Their uncle was furious. He had to confess his reason for calling. Their father had listed my oldest son as next-of-kin, and in that particular state, that person must sign for the body to be released to the funeral home. He had called out of necessity.

A bit of clever Internet research and telephone deception traversed this issue. No one went anywhere. They had done their duty, above and beyond.

Their father was dead. My ex-husband was dead. According to my children, they felt pity, not love. There had been no father to love, therefore no father to grieve over.

It is an emptiness no child should have to suffer, but each has reconciled that issue. Therefore, they will be a different kind of parent to their children.

As for me, I wish I could have felt sad, but there was nothing, no feeling. My ex had become someone I might have glimpsed at occasionally but who no longer affected my life one way or the other, despite procreation.

Our divorce was not like most. It was brutal, with threats that could have been avoided.

During the divorce, my daughter was in the process of making her Confirmation, discussing the rules of the church, divorce and all. Apparently she had observed more than I knew, because when informed of the restrictions on remarriage, she was naïve enough to ask the priest, "What happens if a divorce isn't someone's fault? Can one still get married in the church?"

Well, the priest answered, "Rules are not always black and white, there are many grey areas."

She was not pleased with his answer, staunchly defensive of her mother.

Her father had been blatant in his disregard of marital obligations, financial responsibility, and parental involvement. She, in effect, along with her brothers, did not have the benefit of a father's love or presence. That is the sad part. The absent father. The absent husband.

We learned, but are jaded by the experience.

Life goes on. We have done more than survive—we have succeeded.

My children did what they felt was right, and I did congratulate myself for instilling in them a sense of compassion beyond my expectations.

My ex-husband refused to acknowledge his responsibilities, and in doing so, missed the opportunity to be a father.

Meanwhile, I had the joy of watching three wonderful children become mature, responsible adults, ready and willing to accept a role of their choice in the future.

By being absent, his negative example turned positive. Perhaps that is the kindest way to view his death.

EPILOGUE

In retrospect, there are insidious repercussions scattered in the wake (no pun intended) of an absent—yet existing elsewhere—father and husband, much like when a truck whizzes by you on the highway, the backdraft is not felt immediately.

Many years later, there remains the hesitancy to trust, the compulsion to be financially responsible, and a necessity to raise children without the pain and violence experienced in childhood. Some adjustments are physical, obviously, like a stable financial lifestyle with the material goods and services commensurate with higher education. Other after-effects are more subtle, like a sarcastic tone used for an inside joke, a defensive maneuver . . . the best offense is a good defense . . . or avoiding alcohol.

In the course of my everyday activity, I notice my deliberate patience and kindness directed toward children who I know have enjoyed such relationships with their father. I sense my desire for calm and a demonic aversion to moving trucks.

Ironic. I am describing my own childhood, a time I vowed would not be repeated.

Grief is not exclusively defined by death. There are those who grieve a leg lost in war, a home in a fire, a child taken, sentencing everyone involved to exist in limbo. Therefore it stands to reason that grief, when extended over time, can become internalized, a secret deep inside, demeanor composed until disrupted. That disruption can be as simple as a color or melody, or as complex as reaction to violence.

For myself and my children, our grief process occurred prior to their father's death. Their father existed in his separate world, we in ours. Unlike most families, we had a 20-year period to ponder the why and wherefore, diluted by adolescence and adulthood, attention to daily pressures, school, work, family. When death came, it was more an, "Oh, OK—it's over."

But it wasn't.

The pain of being ignored never left my soul. It's the type of pain that simmers until placated or dismissed.

It would have been easier if he had been a constant rather than intermittent thorn, someone to grieve and put aside. Instead he was a silent needle, ever remembered, never forgotten.

Grief after a loving relationship fades into pleasant memories; grief after terror and longing becomes resentment, if allowed. When the children were young I would placate, saying, "Do not hate. He doesn't know you hate him, much less care. Hate hurts you, not him." It seemed to help, but internally the needle was always there.

I did not grieve for my ex-husband when I heard the news of his death. I grieved for my children—for their loss of paternal memories, camaraderie, and laughter.

The children had said their goodbyes by accepting his visit. Did those outside our nucleus realize or sympathize? How could they, when most was not shared. It wasn't as if we lived next door. Distance precludes details.

If I have learned anything, it is if I do not include (or am unable to) share intimacies, I automatically exclude negating sympathy. If his death was mentioned, there was the awkward, "I'm sorry," or simply, "Oh." My children and I discussed—and dismissed—attempting to forget, for the past rarely goes away, you simply speak about it less. Each passing day dilutes.

When my aunt died, I cried. I loved her. At the funeral I spoke a eulogy laced with kindness and laughter, a celebration of life, memories that all had shared during her lifetime. No such release when he died. Simply . . . nothing.

It is better to have loved with passion and bear the sorrow of grief than to experience a void. Nothing is relentless. It leaves a continual "what if?"

A cruel legacy.

COMMENTARY

In her narrative, Barbara speaks mostly about her children and their responses to the turmoil of their lives. However, her writing reveals her inner strength and resolve to get through the challenging times with intelligence and grace. She is aware of what grief is, what it has done to her, and how their absent father affected her children. She tried not to let her memories of the terror, and the longing for a peaceful, loving existence that could not be, turn into resentment. She knew that would negatively affect her children who already had enough to deal with.

Boss (1999) describes the loss the children experienced as "ambiguous loss." It is a non-death loss occurring when the person is perceived as physically absent but psychologically present. The children "lost him" a long time ago—long before he died, but psychologically he was still a presence in the family system. Such is the case when a divorce has occurred and one parent is physically absent but is still in the minds of the children.

Barbara and her children have experienced many emotional challenges from before the divorce and in the many years since. Perhaps the theme of Barbara's account could be, "That which does not kill us makes us stronger" (Nietzche).

This may not always be true, but in this case, with the love and guidance of their mother, Barbara's children managed to mature in positive ways and carry out the difficult week-long visit of their estranged, terminally ill father with grace and dignity.

Did they forgive him for the past? Barbara does not know. They each had their own ways of dealing with their traumatic early years. Their father's total indifference after the divorce inflicted pain that could not be easily resolved. George Bernard Shaw (1901) wrote, "The worst sin toward our fellow creatures is not to hate them, but to be indifferent to them; that's the essence of inhumanity."

Despite their pain they were able to do what they felt was right, honor their father's request for a final visit, recognize that their father had never grown up, and say goodbye.

As well she should, Barbara congratulated herself for having instilled a "sense of compassion beyond my expectations" in her children over the years.

Barbara states she did not grieve for her husband at the time of his death, that she and the children had experienced their grief over the many years following the divorce. Her grief was for the children's loss of paternal memories and how their father's behavior affected them.

When death came they felt "it was finally over." However, they discovered that all the pain of the past still simmers until it is addressed. Barbara's pain was based in a complicated grief that is difficult to resolve. Worden (2002) states, "It is a kind of grief for what we wished for or never had or never will have."

During the weeks and months following the death, Barbara found she did not have much support or understanding from people around her for she and the children had shared little about their situation with family and friends. Some of them felt she had done the wrong thing when she divorced. Others just didn't know what had occurred over the years. Barbara experienced disenfranchised grief when her need for understanding and support were not expressed or acknowledged by others.

When the children were young, Barbara instructed them not to hate their father. She explained that hate would hurt them more than it would hurt him. He wouldn't even know about it. Instinctively she recognized that when we hate someone, that person is still in control.

Hers was very good advice for it takes a lot of energy to sustain feelings of hate for someone. It may also be indicative of avoiding dealing with the pain the situation or person produces in us. Playwright, essayist James Baldwin (1963) states it well: "I imagine one of the reasons people cling to their hate so stubbornly is because they sense, once the hate is gone . . . they will be forced to deal with the pain."

Love and hate can be two sides of the same coin. According to the dictionary, hate is an intense hostility and aversion usually deriving from fear, anger, or sense of injury. Certainly Barbara's children experienced all of these reactions to the behavior of their father both before and after the divorce. Had they kept the hate going through the years it could have permeated their state of mind and negatively affected their lives in many ways. Martin Luther King, Jr. (1967) stated, "I have decided to stick with love. Hate is too great a burden to bear." Life is too short to waste time and energy hating anyone.

REFERENCES

Baldwin, J. A. (1963). *In the Fire Next Time*. New York, NY: Dial Press.
Boss, P. (1999). Ambiguous loss. Cambridge, MA: Harvard University Press.
King, M. L. (1967). *Where do we go from here?* Annual report delivered at the convention of the Southern Leadership Conference, August 16, Atlanta, GA.
Nietzsche, F. (n.d.). http://www.brainyquote.com/quotes/quotes/f/friedrichn101616.htm
Shaw, G. B. (1901). *The devil's disciple.* Whitefish, MT: Kissinger Publishing.
Worden, J. W. (2002). *Grief counseling and grief therapy* (3rd ed., p. 84). New York, NY: Springer.

CHAPTER 7

He's Dead and I'm Not

Anonymous

Preface: How curious I was when sitting down to write a brief essay for this anthology: Curious to know what I'd say if I let myself go freely. After all, it would be anonymous, and I could be as candid as I wished, if I wished.

As a teacher of poetry and writer of both fiction and poetry, I know the virtue of understatement, how an ordinary voice can be more effective than a flourish. With all the drama of Jane Eyre, Charlotte Brontë knew this too. After the orphanage, the cruel stepmother, the mad woman in the attic, the fire, Jane simply says, "Dear reader, I married him."

So, I'd leave out his mood swings, his paranoia, his temper. I'd not write of his spraying Round-Up on my beloved rose bed or the terrible lies he told our son in his attempt to alienate him from me.

I'd attempt to limit the damage. Who wants a list of grievances? What was that like?

It was like emptying the trash, cleaning a closet, sweeping up after a heavy rain—it was cleansing to be rid of all that. I would have to admit, "Dear Reader, I married him," a serious error in judgment for which, after all this time, I forgive myself.

❧ ❧ ❧

In retrospect, the biggest favor he ever did for me in close to 30 years of marriage was to say, "I could shoot you when you come home from the airport. I could say I thought you were an intruder. It will still be dark then."

It was mid-November, he was still in bed, and I was dressing in semi-darkness to take his 80-year-old mother to the airport for her 6:30 a.m. flight clear across the country. I was probably pulling a sweater over my head, I really can't recall. I do remember asking, in as steady a voice as I could summon, "Are you threatening me?"

He pulled himself up a little, propping himself on an elbow to glare at me as he hissed: "I'm just expressing my fantasy."

My own fantasy was that he'd drop dead, done in by his own horrible temper and bile.

Another fantasy was that since he didn't have to be at his office until 9:00 a.m., he might have seen his way to driving his own mother to the airport at such an early hour. The airport was less than half an hour away. God knows at such an early hour there wasn't much of a commute, and he would have been home with 2 hours to read the paper, eat his breakfast, then drive the 7 minutes it took him to get to his office.

Nothing was to be gained by voicing either of these thoughts, but when I left the room, I found his worried mother down the hall, where clearly she'd heard raised voices. "He's just being himself," I said.

"Disagreeable," she muttered. We left, and as we drove, she reminded me of something she'd told me upon our engagement: "I'll always be on your side."

Naïve, I thought it a terrible thing for her to say.

That was then.

When I dropped my mother-in-law off at the airport, I considered what I'd learned about him in all those years: he collected guns, had a horrible temper, all of which was probably a view into the dark window of what passed for his soul.

This was before cell phones. As soon as I drove into our driveway, I went into the kitchen and shut the door to the hall. I picked up the phone and called my sister to report his earlier threat.

"If he makes good on it, nail the son of a bitch," I told her. "Write down what time I called."

I also called my best friend and we had the same conversation, short and direct. As I hung up, I heard a sound in the hall, then the door to the garage opening.

I went out, and there he was putting his brief case into his car. He straightened without a word, pointed his finger at me, and said, "Pow."

"Drop dead," I told him, shutting the door and committing myself at that moment to the certainty that I would finally leave him.

The question was when.

We had three children, all away at school, but home for the holidays. Our annual family vacation to Hawaii was booked. If I could get through that, send them back to school without incident, get myself off to the residency I was scheduled for immediately after New Year's, I'd have time to figure out how I was going to leave. November, December, and not many hours to dwindle down to a precious few.

I consulted a divorce attorney before we'd left for Hawaii, then asked our office manager to duplicate copies of our tax returns for the past 5 years, at my attorney's suggestion. She could take care of that while we were away.

For years she had been both a loyal friend and a practical woman. As it turned out, she was vital in persuading my husband to produce other documents required by the legal procedures of a divorce. A sort of "office wife" for years, she checked in with me mornings to see what she was getting before he walked into the office: Angry? Happy? Calm? Upset?

Sometime around 5:00 p.m., I'd phone her to ask the same questions. People later asked how it was that I could live with someone so difficult for that long.

When all the dust settled several years after I filed and was finally divorced, I had to ask myself the same hard question. I'd been fortunate.

I play well with others, and thus have many friends. Even our accountant and our stockbroker stuck by me and refused his request to stop representing me.

My accountant encouraged me to get an alarm system in the house I now owned, lights on the driveway and the porch, which I did. Still, there were occasions when I had to call our local sheriff.

About a year or so after our acrimonious divorce, I went to my secret hiding place to take out some jewelry, but when I opened it, every piece of jewelry was gone, save one. Only one box sat in the empty space, fraught with message and intent.

Perhaps years before, maybe as many as 10, I'd thought somehow I'd lost a lovely pin my father had brought me from Israel. Then, I found it beneath the cotton, which had held another pin in that box. It had been there all along.

How my husband mocked me then, and probably then again when my husband-thief took the pin on top, but left the box with my "lost" one so it would be clear about who had taken everything else.

When the sheriff arrived, he dusted for prints, but there were none. I told him my ex-husband was surely involved. "Well," he replied, "this is certainly an inside job. No one could have suspected there'd be anything here." He waved his arm toward the empty space. He volunteered to go to the house where my ex lived and inquire.

I thought of the guns. I knew how desperate and vicious he could be and said "No. Do not contact him. I'm afraid of what he'll do."

When I phoned each of our three children to tell them I'd been robbed, each one of them unbeknownst to each other, asked, "How did he get in?"

I phoned the alarm man who had not quite finished installing security on two of the windows. "I haven't hooked up to the police yet," he confessed. Not until I complete the job. I am really sorry this happened."

I saw a reputable private investigator, well into his 80s. "I know you'd like me to get into his house and look for your jewelry," he said, "but it's illegal. Also, it won't be there. It's either in a safety deposit box, fenced, or stashed somewhere else."

He said in rather a soft voice, "In my experience, these robberies almost always are done by the person the victim thinks did it." Then he asked why I thought my ex had done this.

"He's the only other person who knew of the place, not even our kids knew about it. Also, he's tried to rob me of everything he could. He's bad-mouthed me to our kids, tried to keep me from getting medical coverage, tried to leave me with next to nothing. My good fortune is that we live in a community property state, and my attorney is smart."

Fast-forward several years: my children were having dinner downtown with their grandfather. When my daughter went to the ladies' room, she bumped into her father's new wife there. "You have to come say hello to your father," the woman said. "We're in the little private dining room off to the right. A pharmaceutical company dinner," she added.

My daughter spotted my distinctive emerald and diamond ring on the new wife's hand, waited until she was there in the room with her father and his wife, then took the wife's hand, pulled it close to her own face, and said, "Nice ring, V_."

Her father winked at her and smirked. He said nothing. When she returned almost at once to the table, she told the others what had just happened, and my other daughter said, "I have my camera. I'll go down to say hello. I can take a picture of her wearing your ring." Down she went, but the couple had left within minutes.

It took another decade before he was really gone for good. For several years his health was bad, and then got worse. He had PSP, progressive supranuclear palsy. He had plenty of time to consider what his legacy was going to be; what, beyond pain, he would leave for his kids. The bastard left them nothing. Although it sounds crazy, he *was* crazy, and I can only figure that by leaving them nothing, our children who had tried to stay connected, to visit, to phone, he'd planned to leave me with the responsibility he'd abandoned.

One of our daughters had prohibitively expensive medical expenses with which he refused to help. He and our other daughter hadn't spoken for 10 years. When she sent birthday cards, he sent them back "Return to Sender."

He forged our son's name on a registration form from the DMV transferring sole title on a sports car they had bought together to himself.

Then he transferred our son's savings account to his own account for good measure. Perhaps the disease was partly to blame, but I believe he had a depth of anger all his life that caused pain to almost everyone who knew him.

And I, who had for so many years thought I could manage him, make him smile, even on occasion make him happy? How dumb is that?

Now happily partnered with a man so inclined to happiness and generosity, there's no need for such thinking. Not only very smart, he's wise. He smiles easily, likes my friends and family, and whether we travel with children, his or mine, we love being together, with them or not. Self-sufficient, he shops for our food about half the time, and even more wondrous, picks up his own socks, and changes the toilet paper rolls.

When I consider how so much of my life was spent in despair, it's no wonder that I felt vast relief when my ex-spouse died.

I am not alone, bewailing my outcast state. Surrounded for years by family and friends, a few called to acknowledge his death, but began with, "I know condolences are not in order."

I was told his widow asked that I not attend either the funeral or the memorial service. It would have been unseemly to be visibly happy.

Upon reflection, not revealing my happiness would have been impossible.

Quietly, arrangements made, I did visit the funeral home to view his body privately.

Standing there next to his coffin, finally staring at him without fear, I said, "Rest in peace," then thought, "He's dead and I'm not." I heard myself say to the staff attendant next to me, "He was an extremely difficult man."

My children attended his funeral service, as did two or three close family friends.

Most of those there, they reported, were family of the widow, and next day at the memorial service, the ratio was similar.

Perhaps two or three rows were filled.

This reality was extremely difficult for adult children who must have believed, through all his transgressions and in spite of how difficult he was with our family, their father was highly regarded in the community.

That illusion died too. The spiritual leader who conducted the service was, they reported, balanced in his remarks, acknowledging their father's difficult side as well as his better one. The scant attendance had come as a shock to them. The clergy's candor comforted them.

A week later, I wrote a poem entitled "The Funeral."

The Funeral

And still she wondered if funerals
were like poetry readings: you never knew
who would come, and if they did attend,
whether they came out of love or duty.
Like high school, what you did
mattered such a short time.
Then there was life. Then death.

EPILOGUE

When I was given the message from his widow that I was not to attend either the burial service or the memorial service, per his request, I was not surprised, so accustomed to his mean-spiritedness throughout the years.

I did wish that I could have been there to comfort my children, but they were all over 30, and two long-time family friends called to say they'd be there for them. . . . Their daughter brought sunflowers to lie on the grave, a tribute to his Kansas birth, and fitting, as her parents too were natives of The Sunflower State.

She has been like a big sister to my three, and her father was their father's steady and patient friend. How fortunate to have such friends.

Her father had been a steady friend to me as well. He supported my decision to end the marriage. Nonetheless, in visiting with his daughter last week, she surprised me by saying her father believed that I should have left my husband years earlier than I did.

His was an opinion shared privately by a number of my friends, I learned, including my parents. They all remained tactfully silent until I gathered my strength to file for divorce when I was 50.

Something about 50: you know you will not live forever, and I had no intention of living any longer as I had been.

Fortunately for me, my own life was fairly separate from my husband's. I had always been able to write, teach, volunteer, to spend time with my children when they came home from school. We all had dinner together as a family when their father came home from the office.

Once or twice a year we went on vacation as a family. We led parallel lives in many ways, so being actually alone was something I'd been accustomed to, though I hadn't realized it.

So, some 15 years later, he was dead. How did my friends react? Very few attended the memorial service, and there was no outpouring of feigned sympathy. Rather, their concern was for the children, wanting them to be OK. His death was acknowledged with respect for the sake of my children's feelings.

When I stand back far enough, I see what little respect for him was actually there on the part of many others. I fear that realizing that has been difficult for my kids.

One told me that when she sees a new physician, she braces herself for the inquiry about whether he was her father. Shame, rather than pride, is hard to acknowledge.

Even I experience a kind of shame for staying so much longer than was good for any of us. There's guilt attached to that, perhaps.

But grief? No.

Relief, yes.

He left them nothing, and I am bitter about that. He died wealthy, but destitute of the values that matter. Had my parents not been such positive role models during their lifetime, not only for their children but also for their grandchildren, my children might not have learned that their father was not the norm.

My friends and clergy understood his limitations all too well. At the time of his death, no one pretended he was anyone other than who he was. For me, this is a tribute to the integrity of everyone involved, even if peripherally. The Disenfranchised: that is what we have as survivors.

Each of my children is married now, to people of intelligence and compassion. I see this as a tribute to the man to whom I have been committed for 10 years. He has provided a clear sense of integrity and love by example, as well as genuine interest and a willingness to listen when they have serious questions.

COMMENTARY

For Anonymous (A), many years of verbal abuse, malicious acts, hostility, cruelty, anger, and spitefulness culminated in no feeling of grief when her ex-spouse died. She felt only relief that he was out of her life and could no longer hurt her or her adult children with his unpredictable temper and threats. Under the circumstances her reaction is not unexpected.

One researcher found myriad reasons given by people who reported no grief after the death of their ex-spouse. For example, the ex-spouse had triggered many emotional and/or financial problems for the family even years after the divorce was final, or the relationship was dead long before the divorce. One man wrote, "It has been 19 years. I have made a full and well-adjusted new life." A woman stated her ex-spouse was a physically abusive alcoholic, very manipulative and had turned her children against her (Scott, 2000). Another woman stated she had suffered severe bowel symptoms for many years, the result of anxiety and stress in her marriage. After her ex's death the symptoms disappeared (Scott, 1992).

Billy Graham (2007) has written, "The legacy we leave is not just in our possessions, but in the quality of our lives." Most people want to be remembered by family and friends as being a worthwhile person, someone they could be proud of, someone who loved them or at least cared about them in some way. Certainly the legacy left by A's ex-spouse, both emotional and financial, fell far short of that goal. Instead, he left the children only the shame of knowing that some members of the family, their friends, and even most of his colleagues, did not respect him enough to attend either of the services held in his honor. At the time of his death, A states, no one pretended he was anything other than what he was. She felt that was a tribute to the integrity of everyone involved.

In her Epilogue, A wrote of her feeling of shame for staying so long in her turbulent marriage. Along with shame was a feeling of guilt because of the detrimental effects on her children over all those years. This is a common reaction for a parent who feels she has not protected her children.

Shame is defined as a painful feeling of guilt for something regrettable (*Webster's New World Dictionary,* 2003). It can include embarrassment, humiliation, and a feeling of unworthiness. Shame and guilt can be intrinsic to disenfranchised grief because of the loss of social belonging and connection (Kauffman, 2002). In A's case the inner feeling of shame came from knowing society (in this case, her friends and family) had not approved of her husband's behavior, yet she stayed in the marriage for a very long time. She was fortunate that, despite their disapproval of him, she received continued support and understanding from all of them.

Having been told explicitly that she was not to attend any of the planned rituals, A reports she arranged to visit the funeral home alone. This is not uncommon in situations where an ex-spouse is not welcome or would not feel comfortable attending with others. Funeral directors are fully aware of the special needs people have in divorced and/or alienated families. Part of their responsibility is to take into consideration what can be done to satisfy everyone concerned (*Funeral Homes Guide*, 2010). This is not always easy, but when accomplished it may help reduce the difficulties people have when processing their grief later on.

Part of working through the grief process is being able to establish new relationships. Even though A denied any grief of her own, she was very conscious of her children's grief. In describing her new relationship of 10 years with a man who has all the moral attributes her ex did not, A states he has provided a source of strength, integrity, and love by example to her adult children who have been able to develop healthy marriages of their own. And she has been able to go on with her own very productive life despite having experienced many years of misery.

REFERENCES

Funeral Homes Guide. (2010). Retrieved July 18, 2012, from www.funeralhomesguide.com/funeralplanning.html

Graham, B. (2007). ThinkExist.com. Retrieved August, 11, 2012 from http://thinkexist.com/quotes/billy_graham

Kauffman, J. (2002). The psychology of disenfranchised grief. In K. J. Doka (Ed.), *Disenfranchised grief: New directions, challenges and strategies for practice* (pp. 61-77). Champaign, IL: Research Press.

Scott, S. (1992). Death of a divorced spouse: The survivor's dilemma. In A. Tiemann, B. Danto, & S. Gullo, (Eds.), *Divorce shock: Perspectives on counseling and therapy* (pp. 64-65). Philadelphia, PA: The Charles Press.

Scott, S. (2000). Grief reactions to the death of a divorced spouse revisited. *Omega: Journal of Death and Dying, 41*(3), 207-219.

Webster's New World Dictionary. (2003). (4th ed.). M. Agnes, Editor in Chief. New York, NY: Simon & Schuster.

CHAPTER 8

Missing You

Jean Gant

Preface: I was taking a class at Seattle's Richard Hugo House on writing about loss when I first saw the call for submissions for this anthology. Each week I had left class with an assignment I thought I couldn't possibly do; each week I was able somehow to push through first numbness, then grief to write something around a loss.

The assignment to "address a loved one who has died" felt especially impossible. I had divorced my husband—did I have any right to have such strong feelings of grief for him? The very idea that others might have stories about their deceased ex-spouses was affirming: I was not alone in this circumstance. Being able to write my feelings to my ex-husband was a big step toward healing the grief, and being able to share my story is an enormous step further. Thank you.

❧ ❧ ❧

"I would miss you." Whenever I talked about divorce, about what was missing in our marriage, this was your best response. I wanted to shake you, to scream, "Can't you deal with it at all? We have *problems* to work on!"

Instead, for some reason, I grumbled on for a while and stayed. The spring I asked you to leave, it was unquestionable; it was from fear and necessity. Fitting that I saw the lawyer on April 15th, and asked, "Is there a way I can stay married to him and not be held accountable for his financial actions?"

The short answer, "No," left not much else to say.

The next 2 years I worked hard to stay divorced, to maintain communication with you about our children, to create the image of myself as a single woman, to enjoy my "second childhood" with a succession of strangers. You and I were friends, with only a few lapses into fury.

Your, "Are you trying to get rid of the smell of me?"

My, "Get out of the car, here. Just get out!"

I never missed you, and you agreed it was for the best. Except for the times in the car I sobbed, and bit my hand to keep from screaming. And the times you mentioned casually that when your ship came in you'd buy me a condo.

When you started wearing your underwear on your head and sleeping under the plum tree in the back yard, I helped the kids find resources for your mental illness and went to a support group.

When you were diagnosed with a brain tumor ("invariably fatal,") I was a good friend to you and a strong support for the kids. Our fronts began to crack when I said, "You're dying," and you said, "Kiss me," over and over, one of the short cycles your brain had reduced you to.

The staff at the hospice called me "the wife." I stopped remembering to be divorced, helped you remember to point into the urinal.

After the funeral I was exhausted for months, stuck behind the sense of horror at your illness and death. That fall, I came upon your old sweater, smelled it, and cried all evening, finally missing you.

I began the mourning of my husband, my marriage—reliving 20 years in dream after dream, learning to reminisce with fondness.

Every summer the harvest is richer. The plum tree's branches break with their plenty. I let the raspberries you loved take over the yard and find peace in the hours it takes to pick them, in my new discipline of raspberry-picking meditation. . . .

I notice that the apple tree has hundreds of wormy apples. I remember your delight the year the yield was three, and I vow that next year I'll learn how to spray the tree so we can eat the apples.

I wake up on Sunday mornings and think for a moment you're downstairs in the kitchen cooking breakfast.

My life is full and good, I don't weep for you with loneliness. But I understand, at last, how well you knew what it would be like. I miss you.

EPILOGUE

Twelve years after my ex-husband's death, my perspective on the relationship between our divorce and his death has shifted. "Missing You" tells only part of our story.

When I filed for divorce for financial self-protection, Pat was spending all the money and credit he could get for a strange mission. He and his friend Mark believed that Mark was the reincarnation of Christ, and together they planned to overthrow the Christian church by the year 2000.

My belief when I divorced Pat was that he had joined a cult. Over the next 2 years, his behavior became increasingly bizarre, and he was then diagnosed with a brain tumor. Pat had surgery, but the tumor kept growing aggressively and he died 5 months later.

Pat's doctors said such that such a fast-growing tumor was probably not responsible for his "*folie à deux*" with Mark 2 years earlier. His family and friends have used the tumor to explain his lifetime of eccentricities and emotional difficulties. With time, I find it increasingly easier to conflate the events of those 3 traumatic years and say, "My husband died of a brain tumor."

His eight brothers and sisters, and their spouses and children, now consider me family. For them, I am Pat's widow, not his ex-wife.

After Pat's diagnosis, my children and I had come together around him as family. I was in a relationship with another man, who was supportive of my joining my children in Pat's care. His response was, "How could I be jealous of a dying man?"

My daughter Nora, at 22, was Pat's power of attorney and handled the estate and funeral arrangements. In all other ways, I was included with other family members and friends as a grieving survivor.

Nora and I were with Pat when he died. I took Ben, my 17-year-old son, to the funeral home to see his father's body. The three of us huddled together for emotional survival and support, and in that closeness found a measure of healing.

Over the years since his death I have experienced a wide range of thoughts and feelings about my relationship with Pat and its two tangled endings that I have not sorted out, and maybe never will.

I'm left with a family tightly bound by love and appreciation for each other, above and beyond our roles. For now, this is what matters.

COMMENTARY

Grief is a term that indicates one's reactions to loss (Corr, Nabe, & Corr, 2009). It is an expected, normal, human response to loss. It may be tangible, such as loss of a person to death, loss of a relationship, a body part, a treasured object, a job, or a home. Or it may be symbolic, such as loss of a feeling of security, dreams of what the future might have been, or loss of status in a job or community.

Jean suffered losses on several levels. She lost not only the essence of the man she had loved and married, first to mental illness and then to death, but also she lost the cohesive, happy family she had planned for. Because of the necessity of maintaining the relationship through which she could communicate concerns about the children, and while trying to maintain the image of a single woman, Jean postponed grieving the death of her marriage after the divorce.

Grieving was further postponed when she was drawn into the relationship of being a caregiver and "a good friend [to her ex-husband], and strong support for the children" during her ex-husband's terminal illness. With his death she also lost the friendship she tried to maintain with him after the divorce.

Delayed grief (Worden, 2009) is not uncommon in situations when people have multiple responsibilities such as concerns for their children's grief, plus the stress of maintaining a job and supporting a family.

One woman in the author's study (Scott, 2000) reported she put off grieving in order to give emotional support to her children who were devastated by the death of their father. A year or so later her grief overwhelmed her, but by that time none of her family or friends understood why she was having such a hard time—after all, she had been "doing so well, had been such strong support for her children" since her ex-husband had died. Her grief was disenfranchised. It was not openly acknowledged, publicly mourned or socially supported (Doka, 1989).

Jean was very fortunate that her ex-husband's family and friends included her as a "grieving survivor." Plus the man with whom she currently had a relationship was supportive throughout. This kind of inclusive love and support is what helps grieving people move through their grief work. People who will listen non-judgmentally, will be comfortable with the tears, will call and say, "How are you doing?" or,"Let's have lunch tomorrow," or will be there for the late night call when "I just can't sleep," are essential.

The exhaustion Jean mentions following her ex-husband's death is very common. For her it may have been a combination of the physical stress of being a caregiver plus depression, which is a normal reaction to grief. It often lasts for weeks until something triggers a memory allowing grief to surface. The trigger can be any number of things—a favorite song, a familiar odor, seeing a place or doing something they had enjoyed together. Sometimes the person is not sure what the trigger is. The feelings just are suddenly there, like a giant wave, and may be overwhelming (Schoeneck, 1988).

The experience of finding and smelling her ex-husband's sweater triggered that wave of grief that finally broke the dam of repressed memories allowing her to begin her grief journey at last. She was able to mourn the lost relationship, the many dreams they once shared—to allow herself to "miss him."

REFERENCES

Corr, C. A., Nabe, C. M., & Corr, D. M. (2009). *Death and dying, life and living* (6th ed., p. 213). Belmont, CA: Thompson Wadsworth.

Doka, K. J. (Ed.). (1989). *Disenfranchised grief: Recognizing hidden sorrow.* Lexington, MA: Lexington Press.

Schoeneck, T. (Ed.). (1988). *Hope for the bereaved: A handbook of helpful articles for the bereaved and those who want to help the bereaved.* Syracuse, NY: Family Life Education.

Scott, S. (2000). Grief reactions to the death of a divorced spouse revisited. *Omega: Journal of Death and Dying, 41*(3), 216.

Worden, J. W. (2009). *Grief counseling and grief therapy* (4th ed., p. 140). New York, NY: Springer.

CHAPTER 9

The Ride

Kristina Grey

Preface: A therapist/writer friend of mine shared that she had recently experienced the loss of her ex-spouse and how deeply it had affected her. Coincidentally, my ex-husband had died a few months prior, and I was still mourning that loss. We talked about our feelings and the disenfranchisement of ourselves as ex-spouses. She proposed the idea of forming a group for people in our situation who might want to share their stories. Before this plan could take shape, she sent me the submission call for "Stories by Surviving Ex-Spouses." I was interested, but intimidated. The thought of writing my story, let alone one written "as fiercely, honestly and personally as you can make it" (from the Call for Submissions), seemed overwhelming. But, rather than dismissing the proposal, I let it simmer. I had already expressed my grief by writing a poem. That process had been a release. But on some level, I was aware that I was not finished with the grieving.

Three or four days before the deadline for submissions, I felt compelled to give the writing a try. Having made the decision, I spent whole days at the computer, often typing through tears. Whether or not I submitted the story became irrelevant. I knew once I started that it was something I had to do for myself. It consumed my thoughts. It visited my dreams. I had to see, hear and hold the story in its completion. To say that the experience was cathartic is not honoring its full dimension. At the end, I felt drained and devoid of any remaining resentments. But ultimately, I was moved by the stark realization of the horrific beauty, comedy and tragedy of the human condition.

The unsung hero of my story is Editor, Peggy Sapphire, without whom there would be no collection of stories. Through her sense of the importance, need and value of this topic in our culture today, readers in whatever stage of life can benefit. Her vision, dedication and perseverance to see this project through, deserves the highest praise and admiration.

❧ ❧ ❧

Some of my friends said he looked like James Dean. I was told that I resembled Elizabeth Taylor.

I had no clue of who I was at 17 when I met him. My mother said I looked like a slut and my stepfather called me "cunt."

Try wearing those labels as a self-image. Self-esteem was not on the top of my list. Rather survival and an escape route out of an intolerable home life. Not the best basis for a marriage, but available.

I remember the day of our marriage as if watching it on a black and white screen. It was the black and white stage of my life. I was idealistic and naïve on the one hand, self-loathing and self-pitying on the other.

The night before our wedding, knowing that I was not in love with him, I cried myself to sleep. Marriage, I believed, was one of the few routes out of my home in those repressive days of the 50s.

Although his nature seemed severe, my husband was intelligent, self-confident, sure of his abilities, especially in his element at sail on the sea.

He was inspired by the German philosopher Nietzsche, and aspired to be the super-human.

On the other side of the ledger, he was a man of few words, uncomfortable socially and not physically demonstrative.

We'd met when he was 19 years old. He'd signed on as navigator to sail in a yacht race to Honolulu, and became a crew member on my stepfather's boat. It was no small feat for the two of us to ready the boat. My stepfather was in an alcoholic stupor most of the time.

We bonded as a result of that challenge as well as our mutual love of the sea. We grew to admire each other. I figured admiration and respect were good enough as a foundation for a marriage. Love would come. At the time of our marriage, he had just turned 21 and I had celebrated my 19th birthday 2 weeks earlier.

Eleven months later, I was on the bow of a boat, 3 months pregnant with twins, waving goodbye to him. He was off on yet another yacht race. I was left behind, working. I returned to live with my parents until his return. Our marriage, not surprisingly, had not been bliss.

Newborn twins meant little or no sleeping for me. My husband was going to UCLA and couldn't or wouldn't help. My mother had no interest in helping. I was on my own.

As the years churned away, resentment piled upon resentment. I began to take on my stepfather's abusive and critical attitudes. My husband escaped, giving me the silent treatment, reading (and hiding) porno magazines, sailboat racing, and working.

I realized I'd married my mother: rejecting, criticizing, and abandoning. Verbal abuse became physical abuse. I turned to an old pal, alcohol, to pass away the lonely evenings after the kids were asleep.

Occasionally, he would bring me a bottle, sweeten me up, bring out undies from Frederick's of Hollywood and want me to pose while he took pictures. He would then develop them and proceed to hide them. My mission was to find and destroy.

In the light of day, it was humiliating and degrading to feel like an object. After a near tragic drunk driving incident, I returned to AA for the second time with a resolve to get sober no matter what it took. My husband was against it. He felt threatened, afraid I'd meet someone there.

In spite of his objections, I knew what I had to do for myself and my children. We now had three young sons and I was damned if I was going to continue the alcoholic-parent cycle in which I'd grown up, whether he liked it or not.

As I worked the AA program, life took on meaning. My boys became animated. We did things together. Even my feelings toward my husband changed. I could see how I had played a role in his need to escape. I actively loved him now. I wanted to make amends, but when I went to AA against his wishes, he quit talking to me altogether.

He continued in that mode, but I was confident that if I was kind, loving, and forgiving, he would come around.

Instead, his late hours grew to become even later hours. I became suspicious. One night, I packed the kids in the car and drove the 30 miles (on surface roads in those days) to his work site. I planned to be there at the close of his work. My worst fears were realized as I watched him walk a blond woman to her car and kiss her.

Body shaking, I drove the 30 miles back home in some sort of dissociative emotional panic.

"What am I going to do?" I asked the self that seemed to be standing outside of me. I felt as if my limbs were freewheeling. Nothing seemed connected or attached. Stillness set in. Numbness reigned.

As if out of some metallic megaphone, the accusatory words bellowed out of the mouth on my face like a reverberating foghorn, my ears ringing at the sound.

Blank as fog, he denied everything until I told him what I had witnessed. Then, exposed, he admitted to it and promised it would end. But it did not.

I weighed and re-weighed the marriage, the kids, their futures and mine. No matter how I cut it, the importance of trust weighed the heaviest. There was no way to replace it and I couldn't repair it.

Life as a single parent working with only a 2-year Associate's degree in the early 60s, without resources such as daycare, pre-schools, and so on, was challenging. I'd grown up in times when we called childcare "baby-sitting," which I'd done for my sisters when I was 9, then for neighbors at age 11.

Today, that could be seen as child neglect or worse, but in those days it was common. So it was not surprising that I found baby-sitters among my neighbors and friends as I worked and put myself through the last 2 years of college. Those last 2 years were part-time and took me 5 years to complete.

Looking back, these were some of the hardest times of my life and I don't know how we all got through it.

Oh, I almost forgot to mention the 2-week marriage that I had within that time frame. My romantic illusions had continued to prevail and I married a man from AA whom I'd dated for a year. Shortly after we'd said our "I do's," he figured that meant "I've gotcha," and became abusive to my boys and me.

I'd been in this movie before and I wasn't about to stay for a re-run. I packed my kids and we were out of there.

I'd divorced my twins' father when they were 5 years old, and my youngest was 1 year old. Their father was given monthly visiting rights.

Perhaps because of his continued relationship with the blond woman I'd seen in the parking lot, he wanted to pick up the older boys, but not the baby. My youngest son would stand next to me crying as he saw his father and his older brothers leave. It was heart-wrenching.

One weekend I insisted he take all three children. This demand resulted in his throwing one of the 5-year-old boys against the wall. I called the police. This transition period kept the police busy until some of the passions cooled down.

Rather than continuing the drama, I decided not to make an issue of the fact that he was not paying child support. I was working, making ends meet with a little help from my stepfather. After graduation and a job offer in a northern county, I finally requested back child support.

Generosity was never one of my ex-spouse's strengths. In fact, "cheap" was his middle name. He was as frugal with his money as he was with his emotional availability. Being the creative fellow that he was, he quit his job just before his appearance in court.

"But, your Honor," he'd said, "I have no income." Presto, his child payments were reduced from $300 per child to $300 in total.

Did I mention that he was an engineer?

Oddly, as unfair as it was, I was proud of my own accomplishments and found some satisfaction in being able to provide for my sons. We moved to a rural community north of Los Angeles.

Drugs were prevalent in Los Angeles' junior high schools, and I felt we were fortunate to move out of the area. I bought a house on an acre of land and we played Farmer Jane with all kinds of animals and a pony.

A wonderful Jewish mother with three kids about the same ages as mine lived across the street and adopted us as her extended family. I loved my job as a parole agent working with seriously troubled youth. Life was good.

The boys' father remarried and had another son. He dutifully took our kids along with their half-brother once a month sailing, hiking, or usually something to do in nature.

Once again, he stopped paying child support. Since I was able to support my family, I decided not to rock the boat. We were on good terms, chummy, in fact, and I had become his confidante. I was now hearing about his infidelities and listening to him vilify his wife.

I felt sorry for her and thought I knew the pain she must be experiencing. (He didn't marry the blond.) His wife had children by a previous husband, several sons and one daughter. I cringed one night when he told me how he was lusting after his teenage stepdaughter.

Once he'd loathed me. Now he found me fascinating for having been molested by my stepfather. I told him if he crossed that boundary, he would regret it for the rest of his life. I warned him it would affect his stepdaughter for the rest of hers.

Whether he heeded my warnings, I'll never know. I do know that his stepdaughter has never married and has been diagnosed with lupus. I hate to think what he might have done to her.

A decade passed and his second marriage collapsed. He then married one of the women with whom he'd been having an affair. The marriage took place on a boat in Honolulu and all his sons were invited.

I'll never forget the scene at the airport while waiting for my youngest son's return flight from Honolulu. There sat wife number two waiting for her son. We had always been on friendly terms and sat together. Neither of us had seen wife number three who was also arriving. We were curious, but laughed uproariously at the thought of what she was getting into.

It soon became obvious that he was going to be well guarded by wife number three when none of my calls regarding our kids were returned. Our communication and friendship ended. I rarely saw him. Through the grapevine, I heard she drank too much, was prejudiced against minorities, and thought that she and her children were "hot stuff."

However, she didn't care much for any of her newly acquired stepchildren and let it be known in subtle and not so subtle ways. I also heard that my ex-husband had been diagnosed with Parkinson's disease.

The relationship between my sons and their father became edgy and distant. My youngest son, whose wife is Filipina, took offense to what seemed like a racial slur by his father's new wife and severed their relationship. From the time he'd been abandoned on the front porch as a child, the relationship between my youngest son and his father had been strained.

During my ex-husband's retirement, family became an intellectual pursuit. Unable to relate emotionally, he immersed himself in genealogy, using his meticulous mind and love of history to eke out details of his ancestors' lives. He compiled and presented beautiful books with elaborate family trees and old photographs to each of his sons.

As fate or the Gods would have it, it was our youngest son who had the first and only blood-grandchild. Admirably, our son took the attitude that he did not want to deprive his son of a grandfather and opened communication and his home to his father and stepmother.

Until and throughout the middle stages of his illness, wife number three, a flight attendant, and my ex-husband globetrotted to exotic places. This must've been close to the best of all worlds for him. He loved adventure and traveled almost free. She, sadly, did not like sailing and would not join him on his boat. This had also been the case with wife number two, who had at least made an effort.

Occasionally I would see him at family gatherings, but always with wife number three, who was dedicated to hating me.

His failing health began to show. To my surprise, he showed up, alone, for our grandchild's 8th birthday. That evening, he asked if I would drive him to his motel, stating that he wanted to talk to me.

He began by telling me that he'd been doing a lot of reflecting on the past and had written it all down in a notebook. He showed me a book with the smallest writing imaginable. He wanted to make amends.

I felt so sorry for him. He was beaten down. His once beautifully fit body was no longer the slave at his command. It had taken on a monstrous shape and he had little or no control over its will.

I told him that it was all water under the bridge, that we were young and if we had known better, we would have done better, and that I held no hard feelings toward him. We'd produced three beautiful human beings together and that was good. He told me that he always loved me and I told him the same.

A few months later, I heard that his wife had kicked him out. The story was that he had been having an affair with someone for years and she'd found out by breaking into his personal computer.

I guess she needed an excuse and rationale to get out of her job as his caregiver. She was about 10 years younger than he.

However, the thought of him sleeping with someone, when he couldn't even button his shirt, was ridiculous. Without a place to call home, he stayed on and off with a couple of his sons and on his boat, which was docked in the state of Washington.

This period provided time for him to spend with his sons. He was able, finally, to demonstrate caring. It gave our sons the opportunity to see him as vulnerable and not the superhuman man of their childhood. I think they felt compassion for him.

A few times he stayed with me and we talked regularly on the telephone. I was concerned for him and attempted to help him find an assisted living facility. But ultimately, he was too independent of spirit to consider it seriously.

I spent 2 weeks with him on his boat in Washington the summer before he died. His body had deteriorated to the point that he needed a walker. He was bent at a right angle.

He wanted to sail, but I persuaded him that it would be easier on both of us if we took car trips instead. We drove into Canada and ferried to the islands. His rigid body could not straighten out to lie comfortably in a bed. Mucus poured from his nose into his beard. Food and dribble cascaded out of his mouth and into his whiskers.

People turned from him in disgust. When I first arrived I had to make emergency calls to a friend to ventilate my horror. Finally, I made it a habit to carry a handkerchief to signal him when it was time to attend to his orifices.

He slept quite a bit in the car and we'd pass long distances in silences. But upon entering a new port or city, his young spirit would come alive. He'd become excited and relate some obscure historical fact about where we were.

He died 3 months later, alone on his boat.

His sons planned the memorial. Fittingly, they chartered a boat out of the port of San Pedro where their father had been born. They released his ashes into the lap of his true love, the one to whom he remained faithful his entire life.

I was honored to be there and to witness the celebration of his life with his friends and family. His passing compelled me to write the following poem.

Bon Voyage

A moment ago
You stood on the deck, spread eagle
Lithe of body, senses keen
Trigger-ready for the journey.

Oh, beautiful fair-haired boy,
Warrior of the elements
How the storms took their toll on your poor body,
Ripping through your jacket of pride
Until your chest cracked open
Revealing a mother-lode of moonlight.

Now, you've reached the other side, my old friend,
So, sink into the arms of the Mother
Become the elements
Play the howling winds, the wailing seas
And conduct
Stravinsky sunsets.

EPILOGUE

It has been 5 years since the death of my ex-husband in 2004. As I begin to write this Epilogue, I am surprised by how easily my eyes well with tears as I revisit the happenings and feelings in the wake of his death.

In addition to missing his physical presence and all that he encompassed, I sense that I have mourned the unlived or idealized relationship that dwelled in the parallel under-dream of the flawed life we did live.

The irony for me is that as dysfunctional as the relationship was, I still feel the love.

Fortunately, unlike many ex-spouses, I did attend the memorial with my sons. Word must have spread throughout his family and friends that we'd been in contact at the end of his life. They welcomed me and I felt comfortable at the ceremony.

In contrast, 2 or 3 years prior to my ex-husband's death, while he was still married, his father died. His father and I had had a close and loving relationship, which remained loosely intact after the divorce. When I requested the specifics of my ex-father-in-law's memorial, I was told I was not welcome. My ex-husband's third wife did not want me to attend.

The shock of learning of my ex-husband's death saddened me terribly. I felt loss, but even more so, I felt my sons' losses, all of whom were developing new and compassionate ways of relating to their father. It felt unfair (even though I know life is not fair) that their opportunity for healing and a fuller relationship with him was truncated.

On the other hand, in addition to Parkinson's disease, he was facing back surgery, the results of which were "iffy" at best. Philosophically, we all could agree that perhaps his death was a blessing to him.

Two days after his death, my sons' grief reactions were immediately diverted into an adrenaline state by his third wife's attempt to grab their share of his inheritance. Anger, fear, and their will to survive were the overriding emotions and behaviors that I observed in them and shared on their behalf.

Following the mediation of the case, our middle son (born 17 minutes after his twin brother) began to suffer insomnia and experienced nightmares.

Our eldest twin became obsessed with finishing his father's work of digitalizing family photographs. He spent thousands of dollars doing this. Our youngest son invested all of his inheritance in a business he was starting.

As for me, schooled as an Expressive Arts Therapist, my first instinct was to transform my pain into something concrete with which I could work. Writing the poem for his memorial was very helpful and gave me a feeling of closure.

In addition, I found writing our story to be not only cathartic, but gave me a broader sense of completion in that I could see the beginning, middle, and end. Imperfect and bumpy as our ride was, it has somehow, in retrospect, become okay.

COMMENTARY

The situation of a problem-plagued marriage ended in divorce plus the many continuing losses in her life creates a situation called non-finite loss (Harris, 2010). This phenomenon is defined by the experience of enduring loss characterized by ongoing uncertainty and an undefined, non-finite adjustment or accommodation to the events as they unfold over a period of time. It is not a loss due to physical death, but can include a sense loss such as loss of hope or ideals about what should have been, could have been or might have been (Harris, 2010).

When Kristina learned that her ex-husband had been diagnosed with Parkinson's disease, a progressively deteriorating terminal disease, Kristina involved herself in his care in the last weeks of his life.

During that time her affection for him once again surfaced and they exchanged words of love on their last trip together. This can be another example of non-finite loss as the disease follows an unpredictable course toward finality. Additionally, Kristina experienced disenfranchised grief when she was refused attendance at the memorial services for her ex-husband's father with whom she had maintained a close and loving relationship. Once again, Kristina's emotions were subsumed in the total absence of social acknowledgment by family and friends.

As Kristina's husband continued to humiliate and degrade her, she felt powerless. She turned to her "old pal" alcohol; a common solution sought by people caught in an untenable situation. Some time later, she sought out Alcoholics Anonymous and her life took on new meaning; she felt more empowered, able to think about what was best for herself and her children.

When her ex-husband died, she was spared the emotional wounding that would have come from painful exclusion. Had she been barred from participating in the ritual of the memorial service for her ex-spouse, she would have again been deprived of the necessary rites of participating in marking the finality of her loss. Her loss would have been compounded by the implicit lack of social regard and respect for her feelings. Her inclusion was essential to helping herself begin to work through the grief process.

A ritual is defined as a ceremonial act or series of such acts (Byock, 2004). Rituals have been used for thousands of years in many forms all over the world. They may be part of religious or cultural traditions, or original and spontaneous, created by family and friends who are trying to make sense of what has happened, to find meaning in their loss. Like a life preserver, rituals can provide support when the world seems to be falling apart, when everything seems very confusing (*American Heritage Dictionary*, 2009).

Individuals may create significant rituals as they go through their grieving process. Some examples: visiting the grave site regularly, talking out loud to the deceased every morning, sitting in the loved one's special chair, kissing a picture, saying a prayer, planting a tree or garden, or creating a project to memorialize the loved one (Baird, 2011). Whatever is meaningful to them is appropriate to do.

Kristina mentions several times how much her ex-husband's death has affected her over the years. In her case the continuing bond did not begin right after the divorce but became strong years later. Just as with widowed people, the survivor of a divorced couple often maintains a continuing affection and concern for the deceased (Baird, 2011).

Many years after the death, Kristina states she is surprised that she cries easily as she revisits the memories of their lives. She says she still feels the love, even though there were many times in their dysfunctional relationship when love seemed distant.

In complicated grief such as Kristina's, people often need professional help to sort through the tangles and put to rest some of the hurtful memories (Moss, 1996). For Kristina, writing her story helped put into perspective the bumpy ride that was their relationship. She has gained a sense of completion and made peace with the reality of her unsuccessful marriage.

REFERENCES

American Heritage Dictionary (2009).(4th ed.).

Baird, P. (2011). The role of ritual at the end of life. In K. J. Doka & A. Tucci (Eds.), *Spirituality and end-of-life care: Part of the living with grief series* (pp. 65, 70). Washington, DC: Hospice Foundation of America.

Byock, I. (2004). *The four things that matter most: A book about living* (pp. 40-47). New York, NY: Free Press.

Harris, D. L. (2010). Meaning making and the assumptive world in nondeath loss. In D. L. Harris (Ed.), *Counting our losses: Reflecting on change, loss, and transition in everyday life* (pp. 237-244). New York, NY: Routledge.

Moss, M., & Moss, S. (1996). In D. Klass, P. Silverman, & S. Nickman (Eds.), *Continuing bonds: New understandings of grief* (p. 166). Philadelphia, PA: Taylor & Francis.

Rando, T. (1993). *The treatment of complicated mourning.* Champaign, IL: Research Press.

Tabor's Cyclopedic Medical Dictionary. (2009). (21st ed.).

SECTION 3

". . . A Change of Worlds . . ."

CHAPTER 10

Barking at the Knocks

J. Bradley Brandts

Preface: When my ex-partner, Barbara, passed away, I tried to pick up our conversations where we'd left off, by writing my life story. Part eulogy, part autobiography, the book was to be an outlet for the confusion, grief, and wonderment I was feeling. But I immediately found myself writing at such a distance from my pain that I might as well have been dispassionately composing a phone book.

I kept at it, though, day after day, hoping to do justice to her memory as I sought resolution. After 2½ years of traveling around the country, I had 1,200 pages written. But not one of them was worthy of her, and nothing I'd written had made a dent in my sense of loss.

By the time I learned of this anthology, and its subject of "disenfranchised grief," I had come to understand all too well both its premise and its promise. Barbara wasn't my partner when she died; she wasn't family; and yet she was much more than my friend—which was one reason why I was having such a hard time writing the book, and getting a grip. In not being able to name my grief, I'd struggled to place it into a context that would allow me to fully acknowledge it, express my hurt, and find some peace.

"I'm willing to acknowledge that, in general, life may well be a bowl of cherries," I said when Barbara answered the phone, "but sometimes it's just the pits . . . sticking in my craw."

"Don't you just hate that?" she laughed. "So, what's going on?"

"My back spasmed this morning, and I couldn't get hold of anyone to come help. I spent 8½ hours immobilized on the floor . . . not the place you want to be during a Montana winter."

"Where are you now?"

"In bed," I answered. "I finally reached some folks, and they helped me up onto the mattress . . . but only after they spent 20 minutes arguing with me, insisting that I call an ambulance . . . it kind of pissed me off."

"Were you dressed for success, or did you end up scaring the neighbors?"

"Now there's a positive note," I said, rolling my eyes. "At least I was wearing my boy-clothes. It's kind of an unwritten rule among the gender dysphoric . . . if you're going to come out of the closet, it's best to walk out rather than crawl."

She laughed. "I've heard that. So how are you doing?"

"Besides being blue from hypothermia, and purple from rage, I'd say I'm in the pink . . . but I'd only say that to accessorize my colorful state of being. How are you doing . . . how're you coming with your move?"

"Same as always . . . the U-Haul looks like we loaded it with a bulldozer. . . ."

Cooper, our Great Pyrenees, let out a woof, and then struggled to his feet and headed for the front door, barking all the way. "Hang on a second," I interrupted. Dropping the phone, I hollered, "Cooper! Hush!" And then to whoever had knocked at the front door, I yelled, "It's locked. Go around to the side." Holding the receiver to my mouth again, I said to Barbara, "Sorry. Must be another neighbor got my message."

"It sounds like Cooper's bark is still working okay."

"About the only part of his body that is . . . wouldn't you know it."

"What a guy. So how old is he now . . . 12?"

"Well, we got him when you and I moved to Port Townsend . . . which was 2 years after we met . . . and we were together for 9 years . . ." I answered, staring at the ceiling. ". . . so that's 7. Then you had a couple of years before you got together with Michael . . . and you two have been at it for what? Four years, now? That makes 13."

"He's getting old."

"I know . . . hard to believe. The cancer's eating up his bones, he can't keep anything down but lean hamburger and rice, and he has to pee like a puppy again because he can't lift his leg anymore, but he still insists on barking his authority at anyone approaching the house."

The sound of the back door opening and a tentative "hello" drifted from the kitchen.

"In here," I hollered back. Then to Barbara, I said, "I gotta go."

"Do you need anything? Maybe someone to give you a whole-being Heimlich Maneuver to get rid of the cherry pits?"

"Thanks, but you have enough going on. I'm just going to warm up and see if I can sleep. Bethany, one of the neighbors, said she'd check on me in the morning. How about you? Need any Virgo packing hints?"

"I think it's too late . . . everything is already either busted or buried . . . anyway, we're just going over the hill . . . one way or another we'll be in Sedona by tonight. You have our new number, right?"

"Yeah," I said, listening to the pad of feet coming along the hallway, "I'll call you in the morning and fill you in."

"Okay. Don't take any wooden bedpans."

"Bye."

Barbara and I had met fourteen years earlier, in 1985, while she was working as an astrologer and I was struggling to resolve my issues around gender. One afternoon, a few weeks after she'd moved in with me, I appeared before her in drag. Her response was to compliment me on my dress, and suggest that I up my bra size to match my frame. Which surprised the hell out of me.

Others had reacted to my life story with innocent curiosity, hostile revulsion, or oblivious ignorance, but from the start she saw through my chaotic defensiveness and insisted on addressing my good heart rather than my pained desperation. And over time, because she accepted and loved me for who I was, I came to accept and love myself.

That I felt seen by her was an extraordinary gift, but her enthusiastic willingness to ask questions and try to understand me became an unfolding miracle. Much of my life had been spent engaged in conversations—talking with and listening to people was what I did, what I was good at, and where I felt most comfortable—connection was my default state of being. But it was with Barbara that my aptitude found a kindred tendency. Some days breakfast would run through lunch, or lunch would slide into dinner simply because we each had more to say than could be contained by a single meal. And at night, instead of our minds and bodies drifting toward solitude and quiet, the day's topics would follow us into our dreams and we would continue to work at the conversations in our sleep. It was exhausting, but also completely compelling—no matter how difficult the topic, or how distraught or distracted one or both of us might be, our conversations felt like we were in some way renewing a blessing.

The problem was we found the human condition endlessly fascinating and each other's company to be an irresistible reason to engage, which meant, when we were together, neither of us got any rest. On one occasion, as we talked over the pros and cons of me taking a temporary job in another state, Barbara succinctly summed up our situation, "I say take the job," she said, laughing, "I've got to get me some sleep."

It came to pass that this intensity began to impinge upon our lives. We were as close as ever, but it seemed our time doing what we did, in the way we did it, had come to an end. We talked things over, tried things on, but in the end we agreed we were done—it was time to let go and allow our respective life-changes their due. Cooper stayed with me because I was working on a farm with lots of room, but we kept joint custody and lovingly went our separate ways.

The adjustment was difficult at first, but our decision turned out to be the right one. Living apart, as we continued our daily contact by phone, it became immediately apparent we were much better as friends than as partners. As we went about leading our respective lives, our connection and the full-tilt joy of conversing with one another remained as vibrant and compelling as ever.

By the time I moved to Whitefish, Montana, in 1999, our conversations had become like a fine Napoleonic Brandy—the molecular integrity of our interactions changed as new material was added, but even as our conversations deepened and mellowed they retained traces of all that had come before. So that even life's most ridiculous challenges continued to unfold within a rich, familiar context.

"You're not going to believe this," I blurted, when Barbara picked up the phone the following morning, "they're convinced I'm acting co-dependent, so they've decided to stop helping me until I call an ambulance."

"Who?"

"The entire god-damned neighborhood."

Barbara's laughter resounded from the phone's earpiece and echoed about the room, "Ain't life grand."

"I need to start hanging out with fishermen again...New Age realtors would rather sell off the countryside in the name of the goddess than indulge their humanity."

"So what happened?" Barbara asked, still laughing.

"No one showed up this morning, so I called around. I finally I got hold of Bethany . . . and, since pain and distress turn me into a savant of sorts, I asked her point blank if she wasn't coming over because she thought she was hurting me by helping me. Sure enough, she said that's what it was...the neighborhood had talked it over and decided that as long as they helped me to be comfortable in bed, I wouldn't call the ambulance and go to the hospital."

"Did you tell her about the orthopedic surgeon on Martha's Vineyard?"

"Only a half-dozen times . . . how the doctor did a full set of x-rays, found nothing, and charged me 900 bucks. I kept telling her this wasn't a broken back . . . it was a muscle spasm . . . plain and simple . . . but she wouldn't hear it."

"So what are you going to do now?" Barbara asked.

"Lie here incredulous and agog, and then find a way to crawl out of bed, open the door, and let Cooper out to pee. How'd your move go?"

"I'd probably be hiding under the bed except Ruby beat me to it."

"You should have gotten a goat instead of a cat," I said, ". . . not only would your yard get mowed, but you'd have the hidey-holes all to yourself. But besides that, and being buried in boxes, how is it being out of Prescott?"

"It's fine. I was just unpacking that painting Martin did of me and the hummingbird. . . . I can't believe it's still in one piece after all these years of moving around. So, do you need me to come up early and empty your pee bottle?"

"No, I'll figure something out. Oh, the real estate agent called and said she has two more properties for you to look at. I'll see if I can get myself upright and check them out for you."

"Don't bother. . . . I'll be up there the first of the month anyway," she answered.

"Is Michael coming up?"

"He doesn't think so . . . he has to work."

"Well tell him I have lots of room if he wants to jump on the plane at the last second . . . it'd be great to see him."

"Here, I'll untangle him from his computer cables and you can tell him yourself. . . . I have to go get ready for a reading. . . ."

Barbara, Michael, and I had begun talking about buying a piece of property together, or at least owning properties in the same town. We were growing older and the idea that all of us might finish our days in isolation, scattered about the country in sundry nursing homes seemed too absurd for words. We thought if we chose a place and made a commitment, a sustainable core might form into a connected community of friends and resources.

A few months later, Barbara and Michael bought a place in Whitefish, one street over from me. But then I found out I had chemical sensitivities and realized my back problems were a reaction to airborne toxins. I decided to leave the air-inversions of the Flathead Valley and go looking for a cleaner environment, but the idea of creating a community remained a focus.

Five years later, during the summer of 2005, Barbara and I were still talking 6 days out of 7, and many of the conversations were still about the three of us creating a base somewhere. But the dream remained on hold while I worked with a Naturopath in Sebastopol, California, and while Barbara and Michael settled into their lives in Vancouver, B.C., where they'd moved for Michael's new job.

"Hi," I said when Barbara picked up the phone one morning in July, "how are you doing?"

"I'm exhausted," she answered with a laugh.

"Huh," I said, "how unusual. What's going on?"

"They're doing construction behind the apartment. . . . I tried to tape a reading, but all you could hear was the beep, beep, beeping of trucks backing down the alley."

"That's the problem with being the keepers of each other's history," I said, "there has to be some ongoing history to keep . . . and unfortunately, sometimes that history involves heavy equipment. So, what are you going to do about the apartment?"

"I don't know. My rib's out . . . and I can't sleep. . . ."

"What do you mean your rib's out?"

"It hurts to breathe," she said, "like it's out of joint or something. . . . I need somebody to put it back in place. I'm thinking maybe I'll head to our house in Whitefish for a couple of weeks and see if I can get some help."

I told her what I knew about the chiropractors in the area, and we discussed her options.

Then she asked, "So, what would you do if I had to go?"

We'd talked about death often over the years, and because both of us believed "there is no death, merely a change of worlds," to paraphrase Chief Seattle, I knew by her inflection she was asking what I would do if she was going die. Without missing a beat, I answered, "I'd try to convince you to stay."

"What if I had to go anyway?"

I thought for a moment. "I'd still ask you to stay. But I'd also help you to go if that's what you had to do. . . ."

"Hmm."

"You'd have to try to stay, though," I continued, "even as you were getting ready to go. For Michael's sake . . . for my sake. Me helping you to go, while you're fighting to stay, is the only way to have the whole thing make any sense. It'd be too painful otherwise . . . you know? After all we belong to each other as much as to ourselves."

"Good answer."

"Thanks. So what's going on?"

She paused. "I don't know. Just thinking about it a lot these days. So what are you doing this afternoon?"

The next day, a small earthquake caused my well to go dry. The landlord assured me he'd get the water flowing again, but said it would involve building a road through the property and then doing some drilling. As the heavy equipment moved on site, I began leaving the house each day so as to avoid the diesel exhaust.

Over the course of that week, Barbara's and my conversations became a good deal more sporadic and much less focused than usual. She drove to Whitefish, but still wasn't able to sleep. And the pain in her rib was getting worse. She returned to Vancouver a couple of weeks later, in order to see a chiropractor and a homeopath. But neither of those practitioners were able to discover what was ailing her and she continued to complain of increasing pain and sleeplessness.

"Hi," I said, answering the phone, "how're you doing?"

"I'm exhausted," she said, her laugh almost a whisper.

"Did you call that clinic downtown?" I asked.

"I have an appointment next Tuesday."

"Who'd you get in to see?"

"I forget," she answered.

I opened a file on my computer and read the list of practitioners aloud until she recognized a name. I glanced at the bio and said, "That sounds pretty good. She ought to be able to tell you something. . . ."

"Remember that time you were crawling around the floor in Whitefish . . ." she interrupted, "how you could barely move out of bed because it hurt so much?"

"Yeah," I answered.

"Tell me that story again. I have to believe this will end . . . that things will stop hurting someday."

"Okay," I said, "where do you want me to start?"

"Anywhere . . . wherever you want."

"Alright, so . . . anyway . . . the New Age realtors had left me to my own devices. I was on my back, in bed, and Cooper and I both had to pee.

"I remember it took me, something like 15 minutes to roll onto my stomach, so that by the time I looked over the edge of the mattress, I was soaked from sweat. I'll tell you, no first time parachutist ever felt more trepidation than I did, as I gauged the 18 inches from me to the floor. There was nothing for it, though, so I slid my legs over, tried to kneel . . . and fell.

"Slipping into the few clothes I could find at shoelace level, I inched myself along the floor to the kitchen, found Zip-Lock bags in a lower cupboard, and peed. Then, lying on my back, I looped a belt over the handle of the backdoor, and turn it by friction.

"By the time I'd crawled behind the house to make sure Cooper wouldn't wander off, I was actually feeling pretty cocky. Lying in the snow, I thought to myself, "fuck them all; I can do this."

"Two mornings later, I was again lying out back, when I heard Cooper's muffled bark. Pulling myself through the snow to the lip of the hill, I discovered our dog halfway down, tangled in the brush.

"I crawled to my keys, pulled myself up onto the seat of the car, and drove around the block to the base of the hill. Near as I could figure, Cooper had been pooping in his spot up top, and his legs had given way. He'd rolled down the slope, and everything had kept letting go all over him. By the time I'd untangled him, and we'd slid to the base of the hill, both of us were covered in dog shit.

"I drove him back around to the front of the house, and got him started up along the walk-way. It probably took us 20 minutes, but finally I coaxed him through the backdoor and into the kitchen . . . where both of us collapsed with a 'woof' of pain and submission, half on and half off his bed.

"As I lay beside him, catching my breath, all I could think was, 'this is where I live now . . . here on this dog bed, covered in crap, because at least it's warm, dry, and I don't ever have to move again.'

"But even though I was done in, I wasn't done. So after a bit, I slid out of my coat and pants, grabbed a towel and some bottled water from beneath the sink, and started to wipe the shit from Cooper's coat. He was so wrecked, he wouldn't roll over, so I did his one side and called it good.

"Then, as I was crawling toward the bedroom, someone knocked at the door. And our dog, who couldn't even raise his head while I was toweling him off, answered with a bark and began pulling himself toward the front of the house. Barking like crazy, he dragged himself along, with me in hot pursuit, scraping after him, yelling, 'go around to the side door,' then hollering at Cooper to 'shut up,' and again yelling, 'go around to the side door.'

"Halfway across the room, I realized I was shouting and crawling toward the door, just like Cooper. Which was when it occurred to me that maybe that's all there is to the meaning of life. That you just keep barking at the knocks that come your way until . . . well . . . until you can't anymore."

"It's a good story," Barbara quietly laughed. "Do you miss him?"

"Every day. Remember how he tore into that Seeing Eye dog and the two of them dragged the blind guy into traffic?"

"I forgot about that," she murmured. "He was a terror."

"He was such a terror. Yeah, I miss him . . . miss him a lot."

"That's what big, white dogs are for . . . teaching about love and letting go . . . otherwise the gods would have made it so they live as long as we do."

"Yeah," I answered, before changing the subject, "so what are you going to do until next Tuesday?"

"Hope I feel better. But I've got to drag myself to the bathroom now. I'll talk to you tomorrow."

"Okay, bye."

"Bye."

Early the following morning, I received an e-mail from her, which read, "I'm going to the emergency room." I called, but she and Michael had already left.

The hospital ran some tests and it turned out she had liver, bone, breast, and lung cancer. I talked to Michael and we decided I should act as liaison—people were contacting them, and he didn't have the time to respond. I was truly grateful he had a job for me to do, since I wouldn't be able to tolerate the airborne chemicals in Vancouver, let alone in the hospital. Michael began forwarding the incoming e-mails and phone messages to my place in California, and I intently got to work.

Over the next couple of weeks, I answered e-mails, did research, and disseminated the news from Vancouver, informing and comforting Barbara's and Michael's friends as best I could. At one point it looked like Barbara might improve, then that hope faded. A few mornings later, as I sat typing, a message from Michael appeared. All it said was, "Barbara is free."

Things in me broke. Or rather, those things, which had fractured 3 weeks before when I heard the diagnosis, began to fall away. Sucking it up, I held the pieces in place long enough to talk with Michael, and then to call the hospital to set up a way for people to donate to the palliative care unit. And I continued to hold together as I began typing the 35 individual e-mails to let everyone know what had happened.

That's where I was, a half-an-hour later—sitting at the computer—when a hummingbird flew through the door of the house and landed on the window screen, 2 feet to my left. Motionless, it perched looking at me. And it continued to quietly stare at me, as I took hold of it, carried it to the door, and held out my hands. Looking up from my palm, it continued quiet for a few more moments, then turned and flew away.

The broken pieces inside me tumbled outward, as the magic of "what might be" collided with the ending to "what was." Gazing upon a universe of pain and wonder, I fell apart, collapsing through the infinity of my tears.

During the weeks that followed, I kept thinking about Barbara's and my last conversation and the story I'd told about Cooper, imagining what I would have said or done differently had I known that was to be the last time we'd talk. I couldn't seem to let go of the fact I never got to say goodbye to her. At least not in the way I would have needed to—which would have involved us talking with each other until we were in our late 90s. Only another 40 years or so of conversation and laughter—not too much to ask, I wouldn't have thought.

I also couldn't shake free of the sense that who I was, what I chose, and everything I spoke or wrote in some way reflected the impact she had on my life. Our past had created my present to such an extent that anyone who knew us would be able to see her silhouette within my aura and hear her laughter within my inflections. I owed who I'd become and all the possibilities for my future to the haven she'd offered by her friendship.

Barbara and I had been partners for 9 years and friends for 11. For the whole of that time, our relationship had revolved around the words we'd shared. No matter the challenge or choice I was facing, she'd listen, offer insights, and tease me about taking things too seriously, convincing me in the process that laughing my head off at the sheer wondrous, absurd magic of it all was not only appropriate but practically required. She was the person I called when I found myself crawling in pain about my house—and she was the one I spoke with when I was trying to come to terms with Cooper's passing. So, naturally, she was the person I wanted to talk to about her death. But after 20 years of daily conversations, in which no subject was too trivial or too intense, suddenly there was silence.

It's been 3 years now since her death, and Michael and I have continued to talk and write regularly. But we haven't talked about this—mostly because I would feel like I was being self-indulgent. He's been finding resolution, letting go, and moving on. His needs in this regard, as Barbara's partner, seem to me more important than my own confused grief as someone who was not quite family, but was more than a friend.

But the thing is, neither have I spoken with anyone else. And so, over time, my grief around Barbara's passing has opened a hole at the center of my life. I know I should be talking about this—I'm like Cooper needing to pant on a hot day, only for me it's a desperate need to give voice to my pain so I can begin to let it go. But each time I try, the words don't have anything to latch onto—I wasn't Barbara's husband; I wasn't her sibling—I don't know how to speak about what she meant to me so someone else might understand.

I miss Barbara. I think about her all the time. She was the embodiment of a once-in-a-lifetime encounter that just happened to renew itself every day for a score of years. Despite my efforts to move on, I continue to chronicle my days for her, as if our conversations are merely on hold and we'll be sharing the stories someday. It's like I'm a bereft symbiont, confronting the Zen Koan, "What does it mean to live one half of a continuing dialogue?" When she passed on, others lost their partner, their friend, or their sister, whereas I feel like I lost my tribe.

Even so, I've recently begun to wonder if Barbara's friends and family feel as I do—if they feel her presence, and her absence, as a singular ache that makes them smile. And I wonder if they too continue to carry the imprint of their conversations.

It would be unfair for me to ask them to alchemically transform my grief into a celebration of life the way Barbara could. So, I'm not sure how I would go about speaking to them about this—about how I felt and continue to feel—but it occurs to me maybe the beginning of a conversational bond already exists between us, so maybe I should try.

EPILOGUE

Barbara's and my time together meant a lot to me. I felt completely vulnerable, and yet totally safe with her. And this afforded me the freedom to try things on—to grow and become—without fear of judgment or censure.

Over the years, we came to know each other well, and what we didn't know, we wanted to find out—rather than fear and trepidation, unknowns evoked excitement and curiosity. And this encouraged our shared love of exploration and communication.

In the immediate aftermath of her passing, I felt a lot of things—shock, despair, wonderment, helplessness, numbness, confusion, grief, loneliness, and a sense of unreality—but mostly confusion, grief, and wonderment. The reason I initially had such a hard time writing about my sense of loss, was not due her physical absence—after all, we rarely saw one another, and mostly talked on the phone, during those last years. What threw me was that I didn't know how to carry myself within the silence.

Barbara and I had talked about death many times—ours in particular, and endings in general—so I harbored a conceptual template that might have helped me adjust to her passing. But for some reason, I hadn't considered I might have to work through such a thing without her. Our conversations had been a part of my existence for so long I had no way of dispassionately imagining what life might be like without them—without her.

I have many cherished friends, any one of whom would have helped me in any way I asked. But for the longest time, I had no way to frame the question. The continuity of my days had been broken, in that the person who could understand my reservations, confusions, and pain within the context of her death, just happened to be the one who had died. Having never before experienced the loss of my tribe, and not knowing what that even meant, I had a difficult time sorting through my reactions and re-imagining life.

Thankfully, in the past year or so, I've begun to speak about my grief, as I've worked with an Emotional Freedom Technique (EFT) practitioner. With almost 5 years of unexpressed conversations festering in my psyche, I've had a lot of discharging and processing to do, but the release, the resultant insights, and the ensuing tapping techniques have proven a godsend. As such, I've been feeling more grounded, and less overwhelmed.

I still retain the sense of magic and challenge Barbara's passing engendered. But her absence in my three-dimensional world, as well as her continuing presence in my spiritual and emotional experience, have settled into the background, steadying me in some ways, while impelling me in others. In the widening spaces where the grief once held sway, ways of naming the pain have created new possibilities, and as a result, I've been able to begin talking to my friends about my experience. With their support and understanding, I'm becoming better able to honor Barbara's memory, while moving on with my life.

COMMENTARY

Despite his 2½-year writing odyssey, and the production of 1,200 pages of eulogy, it was still very difficult for Bradley to arrive at the point of allowing himself to begin his grief journey after the death of his partner, Barbara.

Although they had not been living together for many years, their frequent telephone contact had continued after they decided they were better as friends than as partners. Their almost daily conversations were always lengthy and intimate. They never cut the cord of their intense relationship. It was natural that when Barbara died Bradley was devastated. He had lost the one person he felt knew him best, who was non-judgmental, who understood, accepted and explored his gender issues with him. Under the circumstances, it is not unusual that he still had very strong bonds with Barbara. In the book, *Continuing Bonds*, Silverman and Nickman (1996) suggest that many people hold on to the memories of their loved ones for long periods of time, perhaps even forever.

Prior to her death, he had never grieved for the loss of her physical presence in his life for they were always just a phone call away. It was Barbara who was still his confidante when discussing the deeper meanings of his life and philosophy.

Following the cryptic message, "Barbara is free," that told of her death, the symbolism of the hummingbird entering Bradley's room, staring at him and allowing him to carry it out and release it, impacted him tremendously. This allowed his pent up emotions to burst forth in tears and words of grief. He states he still thinks of her whenever he sees a hummingbird. This is a very common reaction.

Many people have reported something they saw, felt, heard or perceived as being a symbol from their loved one that they were happy where they were. Often the experience came at a time when the survivors needed some sign to comfort and reassure them, or to allow them to release their feelings of grief.

In their book, *Hello From Heaven*, the authors report stories from hundreds of people who have had similar experiences. Many were comforted, some were frightened, others were reassured by the thought their loved one was near. For some the experience allowed them to confront their fears of the future allowing them to work through their grief and get on with their lives (Guggenheim & Guggenheim, 1996).

Adding to his grief for Barbara was the fact that she was his source of support following the death of his dog, Cooper. The death of a pet is often disenfranchised.

Family and friends may not understand the depth of feeling we can have for a pet. They may not realize the impact of this loss of a faithful companion, but Barbara understood.

Doka (2002) affirms that the "human-animal bond is strong and resilient enough to tolerate every human defect." This unconditional love exists "nowhere but in the remarkable friendships between animals and people."

In recent years, pet loss has been recognized as causing significant grief not only for the individual, but also for other people and pets in the home (Straub, 2004). After the death of a pet, new losses can bring up many memories and possibly unresolved grief from the past that compounds the grief of the present. Grief from those losses must then be processed to allow the person to go on with other life experiences not colored by the grief reaction (Worden, 2009).

Bradley's extensive travel and eulogy writing is reminiscent of "the travel cure" many people pursue to ease the pain of their grief. It is a way to avoid the sights and sounds that bring on painful memories—to forget. They don't allow themselves to address the "Tasks of Mourning" as described by Worden (2009, pp. 39-53); to accept the reality of the loss, to process the pain of grief, to adjust to a world without the deceased (externally, internally, and spiritually), and to find an enduring connection with the deceased while embarking on a new life.

At the end of their travels, when people finally return home, the grief is still there. They have not allowed the grieving process to take place and now they must face the emotions from which they have been running. It can be more difficult and complicated by that time because they won't have the close support of friends and family to listen to their stories about the deceased, to tolerate the fresh tears when they have long ago processed their personal feelings of grief. They may think the person is crazy for grieving so long when, in reality they have only begun to grieve.

A good example of this is a woman whose two teenage sons were killed in almost identical accidents, a block from home, 1 month apart. The first was just before Thanksgiving; the second just before Christmas. Two weeks after the second death she returned to work but found she could not function in her demanding job. She was fired 2 weeks later and decided to work overseas to get away from the constant reminders of her boys and the pain of seeing the accident site she passed every day.

She functioned pretty well for 3 years and then returned home. Almost immediately her grief, prompted by the familiar sights and sounds, started to overwhelm her again. A perceptive and wise supervisor recognized the source of the problem and advised grief counseling. After a few weeks, the woman was able to gain some understanding of her grief issues. She worked with the counselor to eventually regain some peace within.

Bradley was fortunate to have many friends who were understanding and supportive as he gradually reached out to others and began moving through his delayed grief reaction. He states at the end of his epilogue that Barbara's absence in his three-dimensional world, and her continuous presence in his spiritual and emotional experience have become less intense. Her influence is still there in the background in a positive way, allowing him to honor her memory while moving on with his life.

REFERENCES

Doka, K. J. (Ed.). (2002). *Disenfranchised grief: New directions, challenges and strategies for practice* (p. 252). Champaign, IL: Research Press.

Guggenheim, B., & Guggenheim, J. (1996). *Hello from heaven.* New York, NY: Bantam Books.

Klass, D., Silverman, P. R., & Nickman, S. L. (Eds.). (1996). *Continuing bonds: New understandings of grief* (p. 349). Philadelphia, PA: Taylor & Francis.

Straub, S. (2004). *Pet death.* Amityville, NY: Baywood.

Worden, J. W. (2009). *Grief counseling and grief therapy* (4th ed., pp. 39-53). New York, NY: Springer.

CHAPTER 11

Un-grieving a Death

MM

Preface: When I saw the call for papers for this anthology, my immediate response was "Yes, someone else understands." For years, I had grieved my marriage-turned-divorce the way a widow grieves for a dead husband. My husband was "dead" in a way that was difficult to explain to both strangers and friends, in a way that was difficult to explain even to myself. I mourned heavily for whom he had been and what we had had. In many ways, it was easier inwardly to categorize myself a "widow," but outwardly to present myself as never married. I did not lie; instead, I moved to a different part of the country where I could grieve this loss without the stigma of being a divorcee.

But to me it was a death. Many in this anthology understand that type of pain, that type of secret. In part, writing "Un-grieving a Death" re-scratched wounds. More so, the process of putting words to paper was—as so often is the case—strangely healing. My hope is that these words—that this entire book, with all its histories, sorrows, triumphs, and insights—will become a balm for those who are still "un-grieving a death" on their way to living a life overflowing.

❧ ❧ ❧

My first husband died when I was 26. But not really.

He came and left, came and left. Each time he returned, his arms were full of apologies. Finally, I took what he had given me—the leftover bruises, the moments of nice—packed my car, and drove away into another life.

In my new place of hills and books, no one knew what I didn't tell. I buried his pain-filled love in the back of my brain; let it out only in stanzas and harsh similes typed neatly on a computer screen of words. I told myself he had died and believed it enough to keep myself alive. (It is easier to believe oneself a widow, no matter how metaphorical, than a woman abandoned.)

From the dirt of his grave, I molded myself strong. I gave myself a new set of ribs and took all my broken pieces and bones and polished them into round, flat stones. Some I used as grave markers, grieving away a life I had hoped would be. Others, I piled one on top of another as a lookout for my future.

That first year in the snow-piled landscape of upstate New York, I wrote many poems, like the one below, that both mourned his death and helped resurrect the person I was.

Undressing a Death

February, the click-clink-click of
zipping up the pretend-death I made for you
wakes me. You are not dead enough
not to haunt. Tight in the body
sack of my abstractions (my thin-lipped grief
strapping you to what you are),

you breathe too easily. What I wished, lied, twisted
together into the key that got me here
scrapes now at the zig-zag of

you: my teeth caught in your skin,
in your sheddings, uncoiling of cells,
while you are slipping, none-too-quickly,
into something old.

At times, I'd expect that letter or phone call all spouses dread. But in this version, the person on the other end would tell me, in halting gasps, that my best-friend-turned-stranger had died while experimenting with the latest fashionable drug, while arguing with a new lover, while driving drunk, while . . . ?

What did it matter? The sorrow was in not knowing how I'd respond, having already grieved so long.

Also written during my first year of starting over, the following poem imagines a real death, a real fear, and my response:

Years Later: His Funeral

Children tug at the dark
folds of my skirt,
hands pink with just-autumn air.

    They once huddled behind me,
    hiding from the shadow of your arm raised:
    swoop of a bird too large for the suburbs.

They cry as before they could talk,
for breath, dark, breast, the way we

cluster, move closer, want
to be gone, forget, not to forget
(my reasons, not theirs). Today, I want this dirt

but only to throw away, like ashes,
like confetti from a skyscraper
on a day when the wind can pick every voice from the ghetto,
wind it into the long wail of a hurricane horn,
warning us to go home, gather our loved ones together.

I've cried this day before in wishes,
fear, too long ago to matter. It is morning.
Among the grey, black, navy, someone else here
was your wife. At the prayer, I look for your scorn:
her face.

Although at the time this poem was written I did not have children, I often thought how much harder the escape would have been if there had been others to protect. In a new location, I could begin again slowly, not so if I had been raising little ones and trying to keep all of us safe, while allowing them to visit their father.

With the luxury of time, distance, and singlehood, I could sever all contact with my former spouse. I could wait 7 years to remarry, 4 more to begin a family. I still see this as a great gift.

Nevertheless, over 20 years since my divorce and a lifetime later, when my second husband, two children, and I felt called to join the Catholic Church, I had to re-confront past struggles. Page after page of annulment forms asked about some life I had left behind. I didn't even know where my ex-spouse was or if he were still alive. I still don't know and am glad for that lack of knowledge.

Yet despite all this, the questions unearthed old fears: During the process, would he somehow find me? Would he harm me? Would he harm my family? Similar fears are inherent in "Years Later: His Funeral."

In the end, thanks to some understanding priests, I was not forced to call my former spouse, to write him a letter, or even to find out where and if he was still living.

I am done undressing that death. Will I grieve later when I ever learn of his passing? Dressed now in the warmth of family, it is hard to remember that pain. It is hard to remember that life. Will I mourn for a stranger? For someone known "once-upon-a-time?" I do not know. I do not know.

EPILOGUE

Recently, my husband brought me an old frame he had discovered in the attic. Ironically, he thought I might be able to use it to display a writing award.

"It looks like it's never been used," he explained, wiping off the dust. It still has this fake wedding picture in it."

That's when I looked at the artistic, sepia-toned, fantasy-style wedding photo, took a deep breath and said, "That's me."

The beautifully posed bride, the gentle-seeming groom—they were my life way back when, before I broke free to find the new life in which I am now so comfortably settled.

In that second when my love's eyes dropped, I could see all that he had forgotten. He had pushed it out of his mind. When I claimed the photo as my own, was I being accurate? Hadn't that person disappeared long ago?

"But it was just up there out in the open," he continued. "Anyone could have seen it."

Anyone who was rummaging around in our disorganized attic could have, I thought, and yet I knew exactly what he meant. The framed picture must have fallen out of a box of memorabilia: postcards, snapshots, play tickets, and photos I hadn't looked through for more than a decade. Our children didn't even know that that photo—or that *that* marriage—ever existed.

Now, with my husband, I have new snapshots, new memories. Many of them contain our daughter and son. Some are posed, but most are candid, even silly shots. One of my favorites has my children as toddlers dressed up for Halloween. My daughter has on a long, fluffy wedding veil. Next to her, as a knight, my son wields a sword. Both children are doubled over in laughter, unable to take themselves too seriously. Behind the camera, I was laughing as well.

Although I am not ready to destroy the dusty wedding photo my husband uncovered, I just might reuse the old frame. It is still beautiful and solid. I know the perfect silly shot to fill its emptiness.

COMMENTARY

Many contributors to this anthology express the relief they experienced when they finally were able to write about what happened; to express the pent up emotion they had felt, sometimes for many, many years; to know there are others like themselves whose grief had been hidden but could now be shared. MM states how great the relief was when she knew she was not alone in her grief for an ex-spouse; that her grief would be validated.

MM's situation is a little different than those of other contributors to this book. She states her husband died when she was 26—but not really. After some years of being abandoned frequently only to have him return with apologies, be physically abusive, and leave again, MM packed up and left. However, in the years following, she mourned his "death," and the dreams of the life that she had hoped to have. She wrote out her grief in her poems, and tried to resurrect the person she was.

MM could be the poster person to illustrate disenfranchised grief. She presented herself to the world as never married when she divorced and moved to another part of the country because she did not want the guilt and stigma of being a divorcee. She told only her second husband. Even their children never knew. That was her way of keeping the painful secret of being physically abused and emotionally abandoned. However, her actions denied her the support and understanding of friends that could have helped her progress more easily through her grief (Doka, 2002, p. 11).

Marriage can create a significant part of one's personal identity, self-awareness and sense of self. We are often more bound to our relationship of choice than the family into which we were born. When only one of the partners wants to remain in the partnership, the feelings of abandonment, anger, confusion, grief, and loss can be overwhelming. Something very fundamental is being torn away (Rollin, 1992, p. 7).

If there is a situation of abuse in the marriage, victims are often unable to break the bond for a long time, if at all. There can be fear of leaving; not knowing what would happen to them. How could they cope financially? Would the abuser come after them, catch them and punish with more abuse? Perhaps even kill them? People, both men and women, will seldom leave until the fear of staying is greater than the fear of leaving (Burns, 2007).

Abuse is not simply a mistake, an isolated incident, or a sudden loss of control. It is a persistent pattern of behavior and it is *not* the victim's fault. When one is abused, the perpetrator has an attitude of entitlement and disrespect for the other person. He or she misuses the spouse for selfish reasons and violates his or her dignity and self-determination. The spouse is broken down in spirit, self-worth, and self-confidence (Schaffer, 2010).

For those like MM who decide to leave an abusive and/or violent relationship, there are specific guidelines that can help make it a safer move than it might be without planning. In her article "How to Leave a Violent Relationship," Dr. Joni Johnson (2011) lists seven steps that will help reduce the risk.

MM states she does not know how she will respond if she gets a phone call saying her ex-spouse—her once best friend, turned stranger—has died. As shown in the research, some people were shocked at the news, some unfazed, some sad but not devastated, a few glad, others full of guilt, some overwhelmed (Scott, 2000).

When it is known beforehand that the ex-spouse has a terminal illness, some said they grieved even before the death occurred. This is called anticipatory grief. It is the process of mourning, coping, interacting, planning, and psychosocial reorganization in response to the awareness of the impending loss of a loved one. Even though a person has experienced anticipatory grief there can still be grief, that must be attended after the death.

MM now thrives with a loving, supportive husband and their children, within a fulfilling new life. She still is not ready to destroy the old wedding picture her husband found, though over the years she has created a whole new world for herself.

REFERENCES

Burns, R. (2007). *In the last straw: Domestic violence quotes, motivational quotes and resources in domestic violence.* Retrieved March 2013 from http://thelaststraw.wordpress.com/2007/08/15/quotes-about-domestic-violence/

Doka, K. J. (Ed.). (2002). *Disenfranchised grief: New directions, challenges and strategies for practice.* Champaign, IL: Research Press.

Johnson, J. (2011). The human equation: How to leave a violent relationship. *Psychology Today.* Retrieved 2013 from http://www.psychology today.com/blog/the-human-equation/201107/how-to-leave-violent-relationship

Rollin, B. (1992). Divorce and grief: Some philosophical underpinnings. In A. Tiemann, B. Danto, & S. Gullo (Eds.), *Divorce shock: Perspectives on counseling and therapy.* Philadelphia, PA: The Charles Press.

Schaffer, B. (2010). Emotional abuse: The abuse beneath the abuse. In More than coping. Available at http://morethancoping.wordpress.com2010/04/20/emotional-abuse-the-abuse-beneath-abuse/

Scott, S. (2000). Grief reactions to the death of a divorced spouse revisited. *Omega: Journal of Death and Dying, 41*(3), 10-12.

CHAPTER 12

Chronic and Acute

Marion Cohen

Preface: In my teenage diary I wrote something like, "I believe, logically, that people have the right to look after themselves—that a person has just as much right to do nice things for herself as for other people."

But in our society, it's a kind of taboo to advocate for oneself. We're supposed to be totally "unselfish," martyrs or even masochists, especially if the "other" is someone ill, disabled, or otherwise deified. I discovered this much later in life, when my teenage diary had become my grown-up diary. I was 34, and my then-husband Jeff, 36, was diagnosed with multiple sclerosis.

I have continued to believe that I was as valuable a person and citizen as my physicist husband. I believed my writing and math creations were important to the world, and that my mothering was important to our still young children.

I was unwilling to let somebody ruin my life and the lives of our children, even if that somebody had been my true love.

My teenage musings came in handy, in a world that, it seemed to me, inappropriately encourages self-sacrifice. These musings have driven me, in the face of my family's trials and tribulations, to make the choices I have made, and drive me now to write the things I have written. It has saved me and mine.

❧ ❧ ❧

Before his death 10 years ago, my first husband had multiple sclerosis (MS) for 26 years. All six people in our family suffered in different ways. For the almost 7 years, when his MS was very advanced, my husband was still living at home with me and our four children.

There are three words (not little words but big words . . .) that I tend to use to encapsulate those years: "*nights, lifting*, and *toilet*."

"*Nights*" means Jeff needed to wake me up several times every night, increasingly more often, becoming as many as 30 times as the illness progressed.

"Lifting" means that I lifted him several times daily from wheelchair to toilet and back. If he fell off the wheelchair (because of a spasm), I had to lift him back up, and he weighed more than me.

"*Toilet*" means . . . well use your imagination. (I'll give a hint, though, lifting him off the toilet often "stimulated" him to need to go more, so I would have to put him back on again.)

Here's one of several poems I wrote to expresses extreme anger about "nights":

DEMONSTRATION: APRIL 30, 1992

Take-back-the-night, I want to take back midnight, the night's beginning, when you've almost fallen, almost landed, when you still know but don't know that you know, and I want back 2:30, that single point, the center of turning, sharp as Novocain and I want 3:30, another of the night's many wonderful middles, when you lie in a sphere, tucked into your childhood or your youth or your death, I want the night's middle and I want the night's endings, 4:00, 4:30, those pre-dawnings, pre-awakenings, when you've had enough but are taking more.

And 5:00, and 6:00, give me back my 6:00, and my 7:00, and my 8:00, give me back my mornings, give me back my day.

Give me back my hours, my various hours, quit stalking me, quit jarring me, quit assaulting me, quit raping me; the night is mine, those hours are mine, I want them back, give them back.

During those 6 to 7 years, very few of the health care professionals even mentioned the idea of nursing home. There was also very little help available, because "nights, lifting, and toilet" is not the kind of work that anybody wants to do. (Nor is it well paid. I did it for no pay.)

Jeff was very much afraid of what was happening to him and, of course, that's understandable. However, that fear prevented him from considering what was happening to the kids and me.

I was the one who had to conclude that a nursing home was the only solution, if not to his problem, then to mine. (I knew that I would not survive many more sleepless nights.)

The last chapter of my book, *Dirty Details*, describes my soul-searching, my anger and desperation, and finally it reveals what I had to do to implement my "nursing-home decision."

Here's another of my poems, which expresses my anger at the entire system, the entire world, the entire vague something, which was so responsible for what I had suffered:

THIRTY-FIVE YEARS

What if some serial killer decides, instead of spending his life killing many women
he'll spend his life killing ONE woman?

On the first date he begins.
On the second date he continues.
At the wedding he's halfway through.

Sometimes it hurts and sometimes it doesn't.

And maybe they have children.
And they don't change his mind.

And all that time he has his friends
and he meets them in bars.
"How's it comin' along?" they ask.
"Oh, it's comin' along," he answers.
"It's comin' along good."

Life became infinitely easier for me once Jeff no longer lived at home. But it wasn't easy, or good enough to have him in a nursing home.

Here's a poem that describes what that felt like for me. It's a sequel-poem to "The Misfortune Cookie," from my book *Epsilon Country*.

THE MISFORTUNE COOKIE #2

Help! I'm being held prisoner at 2600 Belmont Avenue.

Help, I'm being beaten by a blow tube
molested by a feeding tube
raped by a suction tube
kidnapped by three wheelchairs converging in the hallway.

Help, I'm an
ambivalence slave.

It's Sunday again and I'm chained to this death
and from my life.

A whole family of professionals
cannot do this together.

I'm not really a prisoner any more.
But help, I have to keep reporting for parole.

By then I was beginning to separate from Jeff emotionally, but only beginning. As the years went by, I began to build a new life in various ways. I wrote *Dirty Details*, found a publisher, and had fun promoting it.

Then I got a fulltime job as a math professor at Drexel University. But I did not build a new romantic life for quite a while. That was another odyssey.

I've just finished a sequel to *Dirty Details*, entitled *Still the End*, after the chronic end during which we all had to stay awake. (No "wake me when it's over.")

One of the things that moved me to build a new life was that Jeff's illness began to get mental. MS sometimes is mental, though that has only recently been discovered, or owned up to by society. Often, in fact, mental symptoms, not only neurological, present long before any other symptoms.

In Jeff's case, he began to get verbally abusive. Once, in front of a social worker, he accused me of stealing his money, a very common symptom of dementia. He also became financially abusive. I'm omitting details here, but our young child Devin and I were harmed, not only hurt. When it was apparent that his verbal abuse would increase, I stopped visiting him.

Here's a poem about that abuse. It's also about the system's denial of that kind of abuse:

The Social Worker Says "The Two Of You Don't Agree"

I'm a very agreeable person.
Very agreeable indeed.
e.g., I'm willing that he have
more money than he needs.

Yes, money he shall surely have,
enough to feel secure.
And I agree that, though I'm suffering
he is suffering more.

But I don't agree he get it all
while the kids and I grow slim.
And I'm sorry but I can't confess
to stealing money from him.

I can't agree that I should suffer
more than I already do.

I'm sorry but I can't agree
to things that aren't true.

When I lost the Drexel job and had to resort to mere part-time jobs, things began to feel very precarious. I was already "up to here" in precariousness, had been for over 10 years.

And when a book of poetry about my passion for math was rejected by the final committee of what would have been a great publisher, when I began dating and fell in love, when that new love turned out to be unworthy, when another incipient romance was thwarted, and about 10 other possibilities went the way of Murphy's Laws, things felt suspicious as well as precarious.

There were just, in the words of my then-therapist, "too many griefs, too many injustices" in my life.

I was not going crazy but I felt as though I might be. And I so fervently wished that, if I couldn't find a full-time job, if I couldn't find a new love, at least Jeff would die the death that was so overdue.

Here's one of my many poems that says it for me:

The Impostor

My life is evil.
It is pretending to be me.
It gets into my conversation, my CV, and my bank account.

It can do this because it occupies the same space and time as me
And because it is believed by most that you are what you live.

But my life is not me and I can prove it.
My life is indecisive and I am not.
My life is aging quickly and I am not.
My life has unresolved baggage and I do not.
My life is kidnapping me.
My life is suffocating me.

I must rescue myself
From my life.

After 2 very bad and sad years, I finally fell in love again, this time with a guy who's very worthy. Eventually he became my husband! I have burst forth in happiness.

And when Jeff acquired an infection in a heart valve, and the antibiotics didn't work, I was on pins and needles, anxiously waiting for him to finally die. I had waited to be free from a kind of slavery in which I'd been living.

Here are two poems about that impatience:

Visiting Him On His Deathbed After Not Visiting Him For Two Years

Difficult private-duty aide thinks she knows what it's like to be a well spouse.
She asks, "Why now after all this time?"
Answer: I can muster now.
I couldn't have mustered all this time.

This Versus It

If this isn't it, then the next this better be it.

If this 'this' isn't it, then the next this better be it.

I hope there aren't too many 'this's' before we get to the 'it'.

How many this's can a soul take?

Of course, then it will probably also be another this.

But it'll be a shorter this.
Maybe a sweet this.
A this destined
to become a that.

Well, it took slightly longer than the doctors thought it would, and Jeff prolonged it as much as possible via his Advance Directive, which stipulated ALL heroics, and no morphine.

But it had to happen. And when it did, I felt more than relief. I felt joy, exhilaration.

It was something to celebrate.

I had already done things like forgive Jeff, get in touch with the sadness of it all, and with any residual sadness that I might be feeling in addition to my exhilaration.

And now my reward was to feel the pure exhilaration.

And here's another poem (perhaps too long) in answer to that "different private-duty aide," who was so judgmental of "the family":

Turn Time Backwards, Bernice

Turn time backwards and you
at first
paid

part time
sit by and with and for him.
And criticize the nurses
who do more than you
who do the things I will do.

Turn time two years backwards
and you suddenly abandon him
and along comes me to the rescue.

I do the things you did
and some things you didn't.
Single-handedly I do
what you and nurses did together.
Turn time five years back
and I'm doing even more.
Five more and it's 24/7.
He lives with me and our four children
not in much better shape than you knew him
more specifically, still dead-weight.
I do lifting (sometimes from the floor).

I do toilet (sometimes diarrhea).
I do nights (every fifteen minutes).
And nights includes toilet.
I do the heroics that you did not do.

And where are you now, as I put ads all over the place begging for help?
Where are you now, as Arin (at fourteen) asks, "When's the government gonna' decide we've had enough and come help us out?"
Where are you now, as Bret (at-thirteen) does nights with Dad?

Where are you now, as Bret (at-twelve) is the one to figure out all the dials on the ventilator and no one but I look upon that tenderly?

Where are you now, in the family bed, as Devin (at two) pretends to sleep because he doesn't want to disturb me more than Dad already does?

Turn time backwards, Bernice, and you not I
have done the abandoning.
Turn time backwards
and you last two

I last twenty-three.
In backwards-time

I rescued him
from you.

And here's one last poem, to end this little piece, for my new love, Jon:

On Getting Engaged The Day After My Husband Dies

October 13, 2003

If the Good Lord disapproved of opposite extremes, he wouldn't keep making them happen.

He wouldn't make bad mail arrive on Saturday.
He wouldn't make people die on their birthdays.
And he wouldn't make a woman, nine months pregnant, give death instead of birth.
If he can dish it out, he can take it.
And you should see the ring. It's so pretty.

EPILOGUE

Jeff and I were married nearly 37 years when we separated, or rather, I separated. By that time he was too sick (with dementia) to make decisions and I think I was compassionate enough not to make a big deal about it with him.

But when his illness and dementia had progressed to the point where he was accusing me of stealing his money, I considered it verbal abuse, correctly, and informed him of that.

After all I'd been through I did not intend to put myself through that. I did not visit him any more.

During the next two or three years, I made exceptions when he was especially sick in the hospital or feeling pain. He always seemed glad to see me.

Sometimes, in his dementia, he'd ask, either during these visits or over the phone, "Why aren't you visiting me any more?" and I'd answer, "Because you accused me of stealing money from you. Remember? You said other verbally abusive things, too, and I don't want to subject myself to that. I'm sorry."

He'd then fall silent. Of course, the whole thing was very sad but I was mostly concerned about protecting myself, and our children. The whole "arrangement" was about as sensible as it could be under the circumstances.

I was the last non-medical person to see him alive. At that time he was probably completely brain-dead, from a heart infection that had not responded to antibiotics or anything else.

My daughter had phoned me that morning, saying, "Mom, I'm not pressuring you but Dad's in really bad shape, and if you want I'll drive us to visit him. . . ."

The two of us were soon standing by his bed, just looking at him, my daughter quite upset, and I glad that the end was near. My husband was apple-red (not beet red), completely unresponsive to anything; there was a sign on his door that said, "No Morphine, Ever," in adherence to his advance directive. I knew that the nurses and doctors were extremely upset by his case.

After my daughter and I had stood there for a while, holding onto each other, and after it was time for us to leave, I said that I wanted to be alone with him for a few minutes. That is when I said my last goodbye to him, both for my own closure and just in case he could hear and understand me in some way. (I've since heard that hearing is the last sense to go, if indeed he was not way beyond that. The infection had spread to his brain.)

The last (one-sided) "conversation" was very satisfying to me. I said something like "I want to thank you for rescuing me from loneliness, a long time ago . . . for the so many good times that we had . . . for our children . . . for the memories which I still have."

Then a longer pause than the others.

". . . And now," I continued, I think that you should *just let go*. You've lived a good life, you've done enough, and you're going to be just fine."

He believed in God. I didn't, but this was for him.

Then, shrugging, I quietly said, "Goodbye," and left the room.

I feel that what I said was just right, for me and perhaps even for him. That night I received the phone call that he had died, and I sometimes wonder whether my farewell words to him somehow helped him to die more quickly, and perhaps more easily, than he otherwise would have.

He had been so determined all those years not to die. I was not the only one who had felt such determination was unwise, given his circumstances.

It had been a long illness, a slow progressive multiple sclerosis. His last 10 years had been spent in a nursing home; for an even longer period of time he had been almost completely paralyzed.

I had participated in his care. "Nights, lifting, and toilet" was the way I described the pre-nursing-home years in my book, *Dirty Details: The Days and Nights of a Well Spouse.*

Although we had been funded for a home health aide 6 hours a day on weekdays, I was on duty during the other 138 hours of the week—including nights.

Moreover, it became increasingly difficult to find home health aides who could lift what is called "dead weight." And we had four children in the house, one of them a toddler, when we started needing home health aides.

During the time Jeff lived in the nursing home, I was still a caregiver, even though freed from "nights, lifting, and toilet." For years I visited him two times a week.

As described in my still-unpublished sequel to *Dirty Details*, I became well-versed in things like suction tubes, feeding tubes, catheters, and relating to other very disabled people (with various types of dementia). I was also responsible for overseeing his relationships with our kids. I was the main family member contact. That last was the easiest part.

Once I stopped visiting him, the hardest part was my worry about whether he would attempt more "financial abuse," as I called it.

I was also worried that we would have to go on Medicaid. (He had almost maxed out on his insurance; it was touch and go, meaning that I fervently hoped that he would die before that happened.)

When the phone call came confirming his death, I whispered, "YES!" Nobody was in the room with me, but on the floor above was my new love, Jon, and on another floor was my youngest son, Devin, aged 17 at the time.

Intellectually, of course, I had known that Jeff had weeks to live. The infection would only keep spreading. Emotionally, the odyssey had lasted 26 years. It seemed amazing and unbelievable that this was the END. That was the disbelief I felt.

Mostly what I felt was relief to the point of extreme happiness. The relief was due, not only to financial matters, but also to my concern for the kids. Now they were free to attain a greater degree of closure.

I had already reached my own closure, years ago, but separating from one's spouse is very different from separating from one's father. Our family had been hanging on quite well despite everything, but now it would have much more going for it, in particular, time and space.

As I said, Jon was upstairs, working at his computer, and I ran to tell him, then to tell Devin. I phoned my sister and good friends, in particular good friends who were Well Spouses.

That entire period was one of the best times of my life, I have to admit. Not quite comparable to when I met Jon, or when I had our babies. But I would definitely describe it as a high.

Jon came with me to the funeral and it was wonderful to see (again) how fine a person he was; it was especially wonderful to see how supportive Jeff's (my ex-spouse's) relatives were for me and for my kids. They were happy for me that I had found new love.

Many went out of their way to tell me they realized what we had all been through, and how they hadn't quite known how to show it during those years. Several friendships developed.

Also, although I was only a part-time (adjunct) college professor, the chairman gave me a week off. I used it to connect, intensely with our kids, and to write about what was happening.

The following week back at work, I gave the poetry reading that I had been scheduled to give at the university. They had kindly told me that, under the circumstances, I could postpone it. But I did not want to.

I had written many more "well-spouse poems," including poems about the latest development. I was very interested in sharing them (as well as the "math poems" I'd become well-known for.

Everybody was extremely supportive and understanding and, again, a couple of friendships developed for me within our math department.

The funeral itself had been very badly done by a rabbi who had barely known Jeff or our family. But the next day, at my house, we had a more meaningful memorial, everybody sharing memories and other thoughts, playing "Dad's" favorite 50s and 60s songs (Jon and I danced to them). I read my "eulogy," which was written in praise of our entire family, not only "the deceased."

In that eulogy, I praised Jeff for our early years, and for his work in physics (General Relativity), and I praised Jeff's family. I told of how much the entire family had struggled, giving some details, and explained why I hadn't visited Jeff regularly during the last 2 years of his life.

I e-mailed copies of that eulogy to those who hadn't been able to attend the memorial.

In summary, the funeral and the memorial were very different in flavor, but my feelings at the time were probably about the same.

Both services brought relief and excitement and allowed any residual closure that I might have needed.

The days, and weeks, and years following the death did not bring on anything negative. No anxiety reaction, no anger, guilt, despair, shock, feelings of depression or helplessness. No fear, no confusion, no hysteria, no loneliness, no hallucinations, no restless over-activity, no irritability, no problems with concentration on my work or anything else, no sense of unreality, no disorientation, no nightmares, certainly no yearning or suicidal thoughts. No physical symptoms, either. "None of the above." Nada.

Indeed, this was a loss with no grieving. Or no grieving at the time of the loss.

The 26 years, in particular the "nights, lifting, and toilet" years, and the dementia years, had given me plenty of "anticipatory grief," plenty of time for me, my subconscious, my therapist, and my new love to accurately and completely assess the situation in its entirety.

There will always be pensiveness, memories, and stuff to sort out with the kids, and I will always be a former well-spouse. But grieving? No.

My children did grieve. And we all talked, again and again. We learned that we all had felt some version of what I had felt: we were all glad, in some way, that it was all over.

I had downplayed my happiness to them, let it out in the small pieces I felt they could handle. Through the years we all became more and more savvy about what we had gone through.

I'm lucky, and I think plucky, to have an understanding and supportive community of friends, audience and readers, my own kids, employers, and Jon.

I'm not an "anniversary type person." That is, I barely notice when the anniversary of the death comes. Usually it comes and goes. Or I remember the next day. Or one of my kids reminds me of it.

I've had one other, more sudden, more unbearable loss in my life, with the death of my newborn at the age of 2 days. That death was a nightmare, but I regained my happiness when I gave birth to our next baby, and 7 years later, another.

Also, my father died when I was 33, my mother when I was 36. Yet I don't notice those anniversaries either. I "merely" write about it all, ad infinitum. I "merely" suffered every bit as much as I hope this and my other writings convey.

COMMENTARY

Over many years Marion was solely responsible for her husband's care after he was diagnosed at age 36 with MS, a slowly progressive disease affecting the brain and spinal cord, leading to generalized nervous system and muscle dysfunction (*The Merck Manual,* 2012). As he became paralyzed and less able to care for himself, Marion became both physically and mentally exhausted. At times she felt she was going crazy, but with strength and courage plus support from others, including her Well Spouse (www.WellSpouse.org) friends, she managed to keep going.

After 16 years of caring for him at home Marion was totally depleted, angry, and resentful. Their children were also adversely affected. Ultimately, Marion's experience of unmitigated and continuous descent into the daily (and nightly) uncertainties of her existence deprived her of any source or sense of well-being. Her belief finally clarified: it was urgently necessary to take care of her needs and her children's for the sake of emotional survival; it was not necessary to be a martyr or masochist. There are many examples of spouses who did not make this move until their own health, physical and mental, was past the breaking point. Such spouses, or any caregivers themselves, become dependent on others for their own care (DeSpelder, 2009).

Life amidst a constant threat of loss, not only of her husband, but of her previously held hopes for her future, is defined as non-finite loss (Bruce & Schultz, 2001). Rather than retaining a core of reasonable expectations for her life and her children's lives, they were instead unremittingly ruled by the crippling effect of uninterrupted loss. In her role as primary caregiver, Marion's hope to somehow retain her sense of "normal" control of her life became tenuous.

As with disenfranchised grief, such non-finite loss is frequently undetected in one's wider personal world. For example, further loss of comfort and nurturing from family and friends often accompanies non-finite loss. The weight of one's intense needs for support is often more than friends and family can provide; thus the divide widens.

Ultimately, these realizations allowed her to place her husband in a nursing home where he lived for another 10 years. This profoundly difficult decision is a measure of Marion's having accommodated to the greatest extent possible for her, and crucially, to recognize her limits. In so doing, Marion grounded herself and began the work of resolving the imminent passage to a future circumstance (Olshanksky, 1962).

There are some people who may think it strange that Marion chose to talk to Jeff when he was in a coma. Even though she knew he might not be aware of her words, Marion felt the need to tell him of her good memories of their earlier life and then to say gently it was time to let go. She said goodbye for the last time.

Sometimes dying people seem to hang on and on, possibly because they are waiting for a special person to arrive from out-of-town, or they are worried about how the family will cope without them, or for any number of other reasons. When an important person in their life gives that permission to let go, death often follows in a short time (Callahan & Kelley, 1993).

The concept of "chronic sorrow" is relevant here, as it defines Marion's role as the primary and long-term caregiver at the last moments of Jeff's life. Chronic sorrow is marked by episodic surges at times of unparalleled intensity, as when Marion understood these last moments were *her* last moments in his presence. Though her final words were not about her grief per se, Marion made peace and found some closure, both essential aspects of the grief process.

In her poem, "This Versus It," Marion clearly portrays her frustration from living on the brink of Jeff's death for so long. When she is finally informed he has died, her exhilaration, joy and relief are palpable. This is something that often happens when there has been a protracted illness, exhausting caretaking duties and difficult relationship issues. One author describes this situation as "an ongoing funeral" for the healthy spouse (Kapust, 1982).

In the following weeks or months some people may start to experience guilt and self-reproach for the happiness they feel, or for what they did or feel they should have done. Family and friends who are unaware of the circumstances may be critical of the behavior but it is, along with a variety of other reactions, a normal response for her situation (Worden, 2009).

Funerals and memorial services are for the living. They help us realize the finality of the death, give an opportunity to express thoughts and feelings about the deceased, can be a reflection on the life of the person who has died and has the effect of drawing together the family's social support network (Corr, Nabe, & Corr, 2009).

For Marion, the funeral for Jeff, conducted by a person who did not know him or the family, was very unsatisfactory. However, the memorial service the following day was a warm, personal sharing of memories and thoughts about Jeff with family and friends in an informal gathering.

Marion wrote the eulogy in praise of all the family members who had struggled over the years. She included praise and thanks for the good man he had been before his illness. It was honest and informative, and offered additional closure for Marion. She thoughtfully mailed a copy to those who were unable to attend the memorial.

For many people the anniversary of a death is a traumatic time, as are the anniversaries of birthdays, holidays, and other special family celebrations when the deceased will not be present, when the loss is particularly poignant. Weeks before the event some people start dreading the day, agonizing about what it will be like, and how they will react. Making a comfortable plan beforehand for what they will do sometimes gives the person a feeling of control over the events of the day. Effective helpers, family and/or friends may need to be available to offer suggestions, but the final arrangements need to be those that satisfy the mourner's wishes (Corr, Nabe, & Corr, 2009).

According to Marion, her life at this point is satisfying and happy with her children and her loving, supportive husband, Jon. She states that she doesn't consciously observe the anniversaries of her many losses; she "merely" writes about them ad infinitum. This seems to work for her as evidenced by presenting her story in this anthology. Writing seems to provide the comfort and resolution she seeks.

REFERENCES

Bruce E. J., & Schultz, C. (2001). *Non-finite loss grief: A psychoeducational approach.* Baltimore, MD: Brooks.

Callahan, M., & Kelley, P. (1993). *Final gifts: Understanding the special awareness, needs and communications of the dying* (pp. 210-237). New York, NY: Bantam Books, Simon Schuster.

Corr, C. A., Nabe, C. M., & Corr, D. M. (2009). *Death and dying, life and living* (6th ed., pp. 235-236, 273). Belmont, CA: Wadsworth.

DeSpelder, L. A., & Strickland, A. L. (2009). *The last dance: Encountering death and dying* (8th ed., pp. 337, 599). Boston, MA: McGraw-Hill.

Kapust, L. R. (1982). Cited in *Handbook of thanatology,* D. Balk (Ed. in Chief). (2007). (p. 170). Northbrook, IL: Association for Death Education and Counseling.

The Merck Manual. (1992). 16th Edition (p. 1488). Berkow, Editor in Chief. Rathway, NY: Merck & Co. Inc.

Olshanksky, S. (1962). Chronic sorrow: A response to having a mentally defective child. *Social Casework, 43*(4), 190-192.

Roos, S., & Neimeyer, R. (2007). Reauthoring the self: Chronic sorrow and posttraumatic stress following the onset of CID. In E. Martz & H. Livneh (Eds.), *Coping with chronic illness and disability.* New York, NY: Springer.

Worden, J. W. (2009). *Grief counseling and grief therapy* (4th ed., pp. 26-31). New York, NY: Springer.

CHAPTER 13

The World Cracking Open—or Living Atop a Cultural, Emotional San Andreas Fault

Deborah Dashow Ruth

Preface: The original reason I submitted to this anthology was simply to try to get more of my poems published. Then Peggy Sapphire contacted me to say that not only had she accepted several of them, but she wanted me to write a narrative to provide a context for the poems.

By the time I'd finished re-re-re-writing my narrative, I realized I'd be publicly revealing aspects of my first marriage that no one ever knew anything about. I briefly considered using an alias—something like Ann Onymus. But then I thought, why not? These difficult things happened to me—and I made poetry out of them!

❧ ❧ ❧

In the mid-60s, the language used for people whose marriages had fallen apart was, "She left him." Or, "They're divorcing."

When my mother heard my first husband tell someone about us, such as "I've left her," she upbraided her soon-to-be-ex-son-in-law by informing him that it was against all codes of polite social behavior for a man to tell people that he had left his wife—even if that was the case—because it was demeaning and degrading to the woman in question.

I never knew if he altered his language accordingly.

For me, the statement "We've split up," solved the problem of who did what to whom.

PROLOGUE to THE AROMATIST'S TALE
(after Chaucer)

Someone tell me, please, what's it about
An old scent that predictably brings out
Old memories in such exquisite details,

The pain that they elicit hardly fails
To stir the mind and make one feel compelled
To visit again old scenes that once repelled.
And yet the possibility of learning
Anew from them makes bearable the burning.
You've heard each Chaucer pilgrim tell a story,
So here's mine. I hope you won't be sorry. . .

With my highly developed olfactory sense, I could detect his Old Spice from across the room. I loved that aftershave, so apparently I was destined to go out with him. And it seemed an ideal summer romance, maybe even good enough to continue after I went back to college in the fall.

My plan was to finish my last two years and graduate before allowing thoughts of marriage to become part of my life's agenda.

His proposal on Labor Day weekend caught me entirely by surprise. I was sorely lacking in self-assurance when it came to the opposite sex. So much so that the way I figured it, if he asked me, then he must be right.

I said "Yes."

But from the beginning, I sensed my too-young marriage would be doomed. I was not conscious of these suspicions, but had a very small nagging sensation somewhere deep in my subconscious. The reason? My groom-to-be was only 4 months older than I was (although he'd been 2 years ahead of me at college).

I had always preferred dating "older men," anywhere from 1 to 5 years older than me. Maybe that was because someone had told me that because boys matured later than girls I shouldn't get involved with guys my own age unless I was prepared to put up with their immaturity.

I thought this 4-month difference in our ages was such a bizarre concern that I couldn't bring myself to mention it to anyone. I figured it was probably pre-wedding nerves. But it never really went away.

And then there was the date we chose for our wedding: July 27. It struck me as a very blah, ordinary date, but I couldn't change it. This had to do with my schedule on the new birth control pills. (Much later I learned I'd been wrong about this and could have chosen virtually any date I wanted.)

So I resigned myself to July 27. No doubt this sounds both weird and petty, but numbers were important to me then, especially numbers associated with special dates. And July 27 didn't sound like much of a special date to me.

Two strikes against this union, and I didn't dare mention them to my 21-year-old fiancé. After all, what could he do about his age?

The third strike far outweighed the other two combined, but I wasn't to know that until the honeymoon. Standing at the altar on that sunny July 27 were two bona-fide virgins. It was 1962, and there wasn't more than a mild whiff of the wildness that decade would ascend (or descend) to, other than the existence of the newly available birth control pills.

Those miraculous pills would free young couples from the worry of an unwanted, unplanned pregnancy. And just as wonderful, or maybe better, there'd be no more of the spontaneity-destroying preparations of donning a condom or inserting a diaphragm. Love-making could be carefree, passionate, and thrilling, with no interruption for birth control precautions.

I had no idea that the aftermath of a double virgin wedding would be so fraught with difficulties.

To make a long and agonizing story short, we remained virgins until the 7th day of our marriage, when we discovered the lubricating property of KY Jelly was the necessary enabler of intercourse.

After that rocky beginning, things didn't get much better, and I figured it was all my fault. Maybe there was something wrong with me. Any conversation about my apparent shortcomings inevitably ended with me in tears and feeling more responsible than ever for our less-than satisfactory sex life.

After 2 years of marriage we moved to California. It was the mid-60s, even before the much-vaunted "Summer of Love." We found a second-floor south Berkeley flat, where the downstairs neighbor's 12-year-old daughter was creating a block-long trail of Beatles posters laid out on the sidewalk to mark the arrival of the Fab Four in the United States.

The ostensible reason for our move to Berkeley was that my husband could then pursue a graduate degree at the University of California. That serious purpose lasted one whole semester before he took an indefinite leave-of-absence from his studies.

Meanwhile, with no experience but much enthusiasm, I had managed to find a job teaching English to 7th and 8th graders at a private school in San Francisco. My minuscule salary, meant originally to supplement what he'd promised would be significant financial assistance from the university, became our sole source of income.

His job searching took a back seat to the excitement of the burgeoning Free Speech Movement on the Berkeley campus, especially when enhanced by the pleasures of marijuana.

I taught every day and spent every evening correcting papers and preparing lesson plans for the next day.

But we spent Sunday nights at concerts at the original Fillmore Auditorium. We had learned that on Sundays, freshly-minted posters for next weekend's program were given out free. Psychedelic art in neon colors, with barely decipherable band names like Jefferson Airplane, Big Brother and The Holding Company, The Sopwith Camel, Richie Havens, The Grateful Dead. At Ken Kesey's "Trips Festival" concerts, we were warned that the punch was laced with something potent, and advised not to drink anything we hadn't opened ourselves.

And then he got a job in San Francisco at a big used book store in North Beach, two doors down from the famous City Lights Bookstore.

**DISCOVERY BOOKSTORE,
SAN FRANCISCO, 1965**

He worked the six to midnight shift
when Fairmont tourists stumbled in
mistaking Discovery for City Lights,
when Vesuvio's Café next door had a sign,
"Booths for Topless Lady Psychiatrists,"
when not yet famous poets, wearing black,
descended like shades from North Beach flats
to trade in books for needed cash,
but he gave them credit for more books instead;
when Richard Farina's stark death by motorcycle
sent widowed Mimi in with books to sell,
and David Meltzer would stop by to chat,
but somehow the six-to-midnight man
always forgot to introduce me.
Retreating alone to the bookless back room,
I would grade homework papers for a couple of hours
then doze on the table till closing time
awaiting our drive home across the Bay.
I lay with my purse wedged under my head,
knowing hardback best-sellers with jackets intact
were being traded as second hand,
and LPs with price tags razored off,
brought in as used were undoubtedly hot.
But the six-to-midnight man stayed cool.
He accepted everything, even
the red-haired jazz-loving belly dancer's phone number
scrawled inside the battered front cover
of a Bullfinch's Mythology he let her trade
for John Coltrane Live at Birdland.

He often went out afterwards with people he met there, but he had to get our car home so that I could leave at 7:30 a.m. to drive to the school where I taught.

His after-work get-togethers grew more and more frequent and he was coming home later and later.

Until the night, or morning, when he arrived home just after 7 a.m. I tried not to let my mind dwell on where he had been or who he'd been with during those hours, and he wasn't offering any explanation.

Although his announcement that we should "separate for a while" knocked me for a loop, I now realize the split was inevitable.

He went off to wander around Europe for a year and returned home with a new English wife-to-be (4 years younger, by the way).

Meanwhile I found a whole new career that paid a lot more money. And I found a whole new man, comfortably older than me—and much more mature than that other one.

After my ex-husband married his young Englishwoman they spent a year in Berkeley, had a child, and then moved back to England.

Four years later I heard that he had died—at the age of 33—but I never did learn the cause. And I was strangely unaffected by the news; our marriage had ended 8 years before, and I'd been happily married to my new husband for 5 years.

Yet I felt as though I should mark this event in some way, so I did several things: I drove over to the other side of Berkeley where I parked across the street from the flat where we'd lived when we first moved to California.

I'd never taken pictures of the house, so I decided to make this my last mental image of the place. But the current owners had planted trees in the front yard, and 8 years of growth had all but obscured the view. Sitting there in the car, gazing through the trees at the rather nondescript two-story wood house, I tried to decipher my feelings, but they seemed scabbed over, covered with a hard shell that sealed in whatever was there—and sealed me out.

I also bought a used copy of James Joyce's *Ulysses*, which my late ex had thought was the greatest piece of literature ever written. I guess I thought that by reading it, I'd be paying tribute to the good times we did have together.

But there was so much other literature I wanted to read that the idea of ploughing through *Ulysses* came to seem like a penance I didn't owe.

It still took another 20 years before I was able to write about that particular period of my life.

ADDRESSING THE DEAD

It's just that I couldn't picture you
having sex with someone else
that time you worked your evening shift
then didn't come home 'til dawn.
My mind might conjure you in bed,
but only having conversation—
Stendahl, Beckett, Proust,
or comparing notes on acid trips
the exploding flowers, bleeding stones.
Tonight, sorting through the past,
I unearthed my Fillmore poster,
a tripped-out grinning Mister Zigzag
from that psychedelic concert,
and through the scrim of smoke, your smile.

I even contemplated writing a novel set in the 60s, loosely based on my own experiences, but I didn't get very far with that plan. Then a friend, who knew that I was blessed (or cursed) with "the rhyming gene," suggested I try a Chaucerian rhymed-couplet parody of the *Canterbury Tales*.

What I discovered was that using the restrictions of "form" poetry enabled me to deal with complex, difficult material, especially emotionally difficult material.

As I wrote, my right brain dizzily dredged up buried memories and details, while my left brain was kept busy setting it all within the strict rules of the form, rather than sternly censoring material it considered taboo. And when I couldn't find a rhyme for something "real," I could make something up, and no one would know the difference. Thus I was able to create a fictionalized account of my first marriage within the arc of a narrative poem.

THE AROMATIST'S TALE

Part I

She rode to Ravinia Park on her old bike
To see the young man she'd begun to like.
He ushered evenings for the symphony,
And in so doing, he could listen free
To music flavoring the summer air,
And savor the exotic atmosphere.
To find herself a possible romance,
She'd decided to engage him in the dance
Whose steps our species early learned, those arts
By which our ancestors first lost their hearts.
Fueled by a force some might define as Fate,
She pedaled swiftly through the employees' gate,
Found him standing at the top of the aisle
Holding a load of programs. With a smile
He greeted her, gave her an empty seat,
Then whispered a suggestion that they meet
Once the orchestra began the Bach.
She waited for him in the parking lot.
Inside his car, they steamed the windows up.
(Both over eighteen—neither was a pup.)
The dusky scent of Old Spice on his face
Was transferred to her skin and left a trace
Of him. That night when she got home, a wisp
Still clung, fragrant reminder of their tryst.
And when he wore his Old Spice to the altar,
It seemed to mean their marriage wouldn't falter.

Part II

While he decided which career to reach
For, she went out, found work, got hired to teach
Pre-teens to write, learn grammar, love great lit,
A job for which her talents nicely fit.
Weekends, they went to Fillmore concerts where
The smell of new-blown grass perfumed the air,
As above each player's bearded long-haired head
In bands like Moby Grape and Grateful Dead,

Wild psychedelic shapes in raucous hues
Oozed and bubbled to rock and roll and blues
Hurled from a wall of amps into the crowd.
The evening passed, the music grew more loud,
They wandered through the rowdy jam-packed room.
She lost him in the sweetly pungent gloom,
Then found him dancing with a strobe-lit girl
In white-fringed buckskin, blonde hair all a-swirl.
The pulsing light around them made it seem
A fantasy—like something in a dream.
Later, he said he'd offered the girl a coke—
She'd laughed, pulled out a joint, gave him a toke.
That was how he started blowing pot.
She tried to smoke it, inhaled, but never got
That rising, floating sense when time runs slow,
When music moves in color to and fro.
He said she held her self-control too tight—
Loosening the reins would give her flight.

Part III

Arriving home from school at three o'clock
One day, she walked right through a wall of rock
And roll to find her husband smiling, stoned
In their dark living room—but not alone.
Three people on the couch, one in the chair,
As pot and throbbing backbeats filled the air.
Dropping a stack of essays on the bed,
She turned and went to join the fun instead.
This time, she vowed, she'd let loose and get high
To join her husband, up there in the sky.
While the others laughed at some dumb joke,
She grabbed a glowing joint for one deep toke
After another, waiting for her mood
To lift. The others were munching out on food.
Afraid of being left behind again,
She took a giant puff and held it in.
The room began to tremble, tilt, and change,
Her mind split from her body—she felt strange,
Like walking slowly down a long dark hall
That echoed with the eerie distant call
Of voices that she didn't recognize.
A dizzy whirling made her close her eyes,
And somehow, somewhere deep inside her head,
She felt a terror-stricken sense of dread:
Her life was just about to end—a plot
Of Fortune that would make her die of pot,
That playful drug, less harmful than a tab

Of acid from a dealer or a lab,
Less toxic tasting than the mescaline
Extracted from peyote, mixed with gin—
Substances her spouse had already tasted,
Experienced truth with visions, then got wasted.
She stumbled to the bedroom and stretched out
Atop the bedspread, gave a frantic shout
To summon her husband from the living room.
Her time was up—she'd heard the trump of doom.
And as her vision and her mind grew dim,
She confessed a hidden truth to him—
That there'd been times she regretted getting married—
Plus other secrets she'd kept deeply buried,
Things she could tell him now that she was dying:
How she'd concealed from him her fear of flying
How sex with him always felt better when
She conjured fantasies of other men,
How pleasuring herself could be more thrilling
Than with him and even more fulfilling.
Her desperate hope was he would understand,
But he just said *"You'll be fine,"* and held her hand,
Told her she should try to go to sleep.
But terror clutched her heart and made her weep.
He dug out a pill that he'd kept socked away
In case this sort of thing happened someday.
He chopped the pilfered tranquilizer up
She swallowed a piece with water from a cup.
Soon she fell asleep and didn't wake
Till sunrise heralded the new day's break.
The memory of her bad trip had her rattled,
Things that, in her panic she had tattled.
But he'd been much too stoned. She could have guessed
He'd not remember all she had confessed.
In days that followed, he'd still get high—she quit.
A few months later, this burdened marriage split.
Then eight years after severing their relations
He died—of drug-related complications.

Part IV

Last week she had some business in the city
On an afternoon that was both warm and pretty.
The crowded elevator closed its doors,
Then started slowly, stopping at all floors.
Suddenly a scent surprised her nose—
A whiff of that old Old Spice curled her toes.
It was as if her ex stood at the back.
Afraid to turn her head to peer through the pack

She froze there, even let her floor go by.
The elevator lifted toward the sky.
Now though the crowd was quickly thinning out
The Old Spice scent persisted like a shout.
At the top floor deciding she would dare
To turn and look she did. No one was there.
How idiotic to think her ex might not. . .
And then she caught a different whiff—of pot.
The empty elevator started down.
Anxious to feel herself on solid ground
She skipped her meeting, went directly home
And at her desk began to write a poem.
My friends you know I'd never lie to you—
Everything here that's not made up is true.
In stories, fact and fiction form a blend—
In fact, I'll tell you straight, I won't pretend:
This story's all about a friend of mine,
Whose life, despite such traumas, turned out fine.
And now my lengthy story's been completed,
I hope there's naught I've left out—or repeated.

AUTHOR'S CAVEAT:
THESIS: Poetry is fiction.
ANTITHESIS: All writing is autobiographical.
SYNTHESIS: Poetry contains both the real and the imagined; only the writer knows which is which.

It was 8 years after my divorce that my mother wrote to tell me my first husband, B, had died in England. I remember feeling stunned, but I have to confess that I can't recall any disturbing sense of personal loss or grief. Mostly I was sad that this 33-year-old man with so much intelligence and promise ended up making his young wife a widow in her late 20s and leaving his infant son fatherless.

By then I was no longer teaching, and thus no longer in contact with any of the people from that time. And the year B split for his European odyssey, I quit teaching high school English and was hired as an administrator at the University of California Berkeley Extension.

All new people—most of whom didn't even know B and I were divorced. The one person with any interest in the untimely death of my first husband was my second husband, Leo, who had seen B only once, in the used record store B operated just off Telegraph Avenue in Berkeley. (Leo didn't identify himself, however.) This was about a year before B had moved to England with his wife and infant son.

So when I shared my mother's letter with Leo, he did exactly what I needed: he folded me silently into his arms for a warm, comforting hug.

I drove over to the Berkeley flat that B and I had lived in for 2 years, and I just sat across the street in the car. I truly can't recall what I was thinking.

What I do know is that my eyes were dry and I was not aware of any sense of emotional (or physical) upheaval. It was as if I were remembering someone from a different lifetime.

I really don't know why B's death had so little significant effect on me. Maybe it was because my life was completely different by then—more stable, happier, less frustrating and fearful, more satisfying and settled than it had ever been with B, either in Chicago or in Berkeley.

EPILOGUE

In thinking about my reaction—or lack of it—I remembered that when President Kennedy was assassinated, it was another graduate student at the U of Chicago (a stranger) who told me the shocking news. I was new to the campus that year and didn't know anybody well enough to have been told about it. In fact, by that time everyone already knew. I felt as though that terrible news was stuck somewhere inside me because there'd been no one I was able to pass it along to. And from then on, I found myself reading everything about the assassination I could put my hands on: JFK life stories, anecdotes, conspiracy theories, the works.

This fascination (or obsession) lasted at least 10 years. I think the main reason was that I'd never been able to get the shock of that news out of me by informing someone else.

However, when I read my mother's letter that B had died, I was immediately able to tell my husband, so I didn't experience the sort of "muffling" that happened with the JFK news.

Still, I had nobody else to tell. I couldn't see myself calling any of the teachers from my previous career—which I had left 6 years before—because how would I react when they expressed their sympathy? What would I say when they asked me how I felt? None of them knew how fragile the marriage had been, and in fact, only one or two of them had ever met B.

So until much later, when I began to make casual references to "my late ex-husband," thoughts of B were virtually absent from my mind. The exact opposite of what happened after the JFK assassination.

Then 10 years later, in 1984, an astrologer (who was highly recommended by several highly intelligent people) showed me on my chart that the year 1973 had been "the end of a big love affair, or similar intense relationship." On impulse, I dug out that letter from my mother referring to B's death. He was only 1 year off. Not bad. Then I re-read her letter. B had died in December 1973. Score one for the astrologer.

I suppose the fact that I couldn't, or didn't, want to write about him, in any form, until 20 years later might be considered a possible after-effect of his death. I hadn't written poetry in 3 decades, and when I resumed, I wrote on dozens of different subjects until I finally tried writing about him. But my unsuccessful attempts were, if not humorous, then wry and world-weary, as if I were writing from a great distance.

Then, during one of the Squaw Valley poetry workshops I attended, I wrote "Discovery Bookstore, San Francisco, 1965," which was eventually published in a poetry journal. That was the first time an experience from my first marriage formed the subject of a completed and successful poem.

Anthology editor Peggy Sapphire sent all of us a questionnaire she thought might be useful. It had been developed by Shirley Scott on the subject of "disenfranchised grief." To all the questions about the amount of grief I had felt and the extent of adverse emotional or physical reactions I had gone through, I answered "None of the above," because these questions simply didn't apply to my own experience of life after the death of my ex-husband.

That day is so long ago.

Sadly enough, in May 2012, Leo died after a brief illness. We were married for 43 years, and his passing has left a gigantic hole in my heart and in my life.

COMMENTARY

In the research report (see Appendix) 22% of participants stated they had no grief reaction when their ex-spouse died. However, many of them checked the physical and emotional symptoms they had experienced that correspond with those typically seen in a normal grief reaction. Other respondents wrote notes and letters indicating their joy, relief or lack of any emotion because they were very happy to be out of the marriage and/or had established new relationships (Scott, 2000). They felt fortunate the person was truly gone from their life.

Deborah states she was stunned when she heard the news of her ex-husband's death, but did not feel a sense of loss or grief. There have been several contributors to this anthology who have expressed they felt no grief. However, most indicated an emotional, physical and/or behavioral reaction that indicated a need for some connection to the person who had once been very close to them.

This is classic attachment behavior (Bowlby, 1969). Whenever there is the death of an attachment figure we are stimulated to connect with others who remind us we are not alone and that we are safe even if the "trappings" (i.e., marriage) are no longer relevant.

Deborah felt a trip to see the flat they had once lived in would be her way to mark B's death. She sat in the car reflecting on the fact that her feelings seemed "scabbed over," not allowing the memories to come out.

Twenty years later she was finally able to write about it. Utilizing the restrictions of "form" poetry she was able to let her right brain dig up the buried memories while her left brain was busy getting words to paper without censorship.

We are all vulnerable in many ways because of our connections with those who die. Some of the causes can be our past experiences, our unfinished business, the lingering effects of a hurtful relationship, being disenfranchised, or facing challenging social circumstances (Attig, 1996).

When Deborah heard about the tragic death of President Kennedy, she had an intense and extended reaction. This may have been a delayed grief reaction (albeit subconscious) to the loss of all she had hoped her first marriage would be, and/or suppression of the pent up frustration and pain caused by the problems with her ex-husband that she had not been able to resolve. She may have buried those unresolved problems and denied the pain of the situation (Worden, 2009). Part of the mourning process is to process the pain of loss so it does not come out later in negative ways that adversely affect the person's life. It may be that years later, intense emotions will be triggered at the time of another meaningful loss (Worden, 2009).

Several people have written about certain odors that remind them of their dead ex-spouse. In her very eloquent and moving poems, Deborah writes of being aware of the fragrance of "Old Spice" when she first met B and throughout the marriage. Years later, after his death, she was in a full elevator when she caught the odor of "Old Spice," but didn't know who it was coming from. It "curled her toes" and triggered strong memories of B. Even when all the people were gone the odor persisted only to be replaced by the odor of pot that was also prominent during her years with B. The experience unnerved her enough that she skipped her meeting and went home where she began to write a poem. Many people would hesitate to relate this experience for fear others would think they had hallucinated, had lost their sense of reality or was going crazy.

Actually, there are many reports of this phenomenon among people all over the world. In their book on "after death communications" (ADCs) Bill and Judy Guggenheim (1995) report the experiences told to them during a 7-year study. One chapter is devoted to olfactory (smelling a fragrance) ADCs, which they say are relatively common. Additional chapters tell of many other types of phenomena such as hearing the deceased's voice, sensing a presence, feeling a touch, seeing the person in the room, hearing a special song from an unknown source, and more. Some people were reported to be fearful of their experience. Many others said they felt a sense of peace and reassurance.

Only 43% of the people who had remarried and participated in the combined 1984–1985 and 1997 research projects reported that their present spouse showed concern and sympathy in the weeks following the death. The others stated their present spouse was jealous, confused by the survivor's sadness and tears, lacked any interest in the event, was angry and/or reacted with silence (Scott, 2000).

Deborah was very fortunate to have had Leo in her life. He was an understanding, loving, supportive husband who helped her through the rough times.

He was the only one she felt she could tell about B's death and he knew intuitively that what she needed was his warm, comforting hug.

REFERENCES

Attig, T. (1996). *How we grieve: Relearning the world* (pp. 76-93). New York/Oxford: Oxford University Press.

Bowlby, J. (1969). *Attachment and loss: Attachment* (Vol. 1). New York, NY: Basic Books.

Guggenheim, B., & Guggenheim, J. (1995). *Hello from heaven!* (Chapter 5, pp. 55-66). Longwood, FL: The ADC Project.

Scott, S. (2000). Grief reactions to the death of a divorced spouse revisited. *Omega: Journal of Death and Dying, 41*(3), 211, 216.

Worden, J. W. (2009). *Grief counseling and grief therapy* (4th ed., pp. 43-46, 140). New York, NY: Springer.

CHAPTER 14

Then, a Deep Silence

Korkut Onaran

Preface: What is death? Is it a kind of silence that is full of unanswered questions? Full of unresolved knots and loads? When we start not answering, turning our eyes away, avoiding conversation, are we starting to die?

Does death have substance? Does it touch us? When we don't feel anything, when no words can reach our hearts, is death touching us?

❧ ❧ ❧

I met my first wife in Ankara, Turkey, where we both grew up. After 4 years of dating during our college years, we got married. A year later, to pursue our doctorate degrees, we moved to Madison, Wisconsin.

Two PhD students in the same field, in the same house, going through the same extended culture shock eventually did not work. In 1996 we finished our dissertations together with our marriage.

After going back to Ankara and teaching a semester, I traveled to this side of the ocean again and started teaching at the University of Colorado. I met my current wife here and made Boulder, Colorado, my home since then.

My first wife stayed in Ankara and remarried. With her new husband, on the way to the airport for a trip to Paris, she had a traffic accident and passed away. I received the news by a phone call.

Early Morning Phone Call From Home

There are times I want to be those few sentences
at the end of that trio in "Cosi Fan Tutte" just to loose
my substance and vibrate in the air. Then,
a deep silence.

Today like a ghost walking through the living,
I lived without touching. I was sealed. Numbed.
I wore a mask. It was a busy day today
at work. There were meetings. Faces talked to each other
of important matters. Death was around.
He always is. He keeps touching us one by one
everyday from all around. You do not realize this
unless he aims at someone who touched you once
in every inch. A touch that stayed with your skin so long
that it went somewhere deep inside, hidden.
But now that she has gone your body reminds you
that that touch was part of something important to you,
something that taught your skin how to see the world.
And you feel guilty because you realize
that she has already been dead in you for years
and now that she has gone her touch wakes you up
and pokes you. It tells you that words not yet spoken
will never be. Then it asks you who you are.
And you hesitate to answer, instead
you want to vibrate in the air and have no substance.

Early in the morning my friend's voice on the phone
spoke to me: "It was a traffic accident," he said,
". . . she died." It sealed my body. Then,
a deep silence.

November 1999
Boulder, Colorado

Mozart's well-loved opera "Cosi Fan Tutte" is about two women deceiving their husbands for some strangers, without knowing that these strangers are actually their own husbands, in disguise.

The husbands, challenged by a friend who claims that all women, when the opportunity arises, are ready for extra-marital adventures, try to prove that their wives are different and loyal. They tell their wives that they are leaving for war. They return in disguise and seduce their wives, successfully proving themselves wrong to their friend.

"What a funny and sexist story," we used to agree. Yet we loved the music. And I still do. Especially the *Trio*, where the two wives depart from their husbands. This part of the opera has always affected me in a deeper way. It is like one of those words that can reach me no matter how down I am, and wake up my senses.

Deception was part of our story too. Not the complete story—our ties to each other were thinning out, but it was the closing chapter. However, I had always thought that there would be a follow-up volume. It would have started with understanding, reconciliation, and forgiveness. This would have followed by a long, lasting friendship. That volume will stay unwritten.

Winter Walk

there are
no stars in the sky
no tables on the sidewalk
there is no warm evening breeze
but a freezing winter wind biting my face
and an ever extending thick white blanket
that sweeps thousands of hours
between now and then and I remember
the face of someone
I've long forgotten
and I start hearing her voice
talking of the concert we've just heard
we are at a crowded foyer yet I hear
only a white silence
her grandfather is the composer
she is particularly critical
all of a sudden
she becomes someone else
somewhere else
talking of something else
that I don't remember even though
I hear her voice
dying she says
is like traveling through air
as an attachment to an email message
that lands on your own blue screen
hearing her
gives me an inexplicable comfort
as if she is here
but she is not
even in the dark
it is white
it has been eight years she says
she doesn't have her face
out of nowhere a memory
of us running on a frozen lake
on a cold late afternoon
reincarnates on my skin
I feel her touch too
it starts snowing again
flakes rush all directions
like minutes confused within
this infinite space called time
remember she says
some die all through life
some use all their dying

at once
the silence is still white
and the blanket is getting thicker.

January 2007
Boulder, Colorado

EPILOGUE

To me, some emotions are like certain words. If they are of unfinished sentences, their puzzled faces stay fresh no matter how much time passes. Sometimes memories come back. So do the unanswered questions.

And her silence surrounds me like a thick blanket. The seconds stretch and I notice certain details on the walls of my memory palace. I discover middle names I never knew I had. I also meet, in between the letters of my name—in those white shadows—speckles of death. They land on my psyche like snowflakes landing on white paper.

COMMENTARY

Sudden, unexpected death usually elicits shock, disbelief, numbness, and/or a sense of unreality. This is often a surprising reaction to a person who thinks that feelings for the ex-spouse are long gone.

Through his poetry Korkut eloquently expresses the depth of his unexpected pain, grief, and regret. In "Early Morning Phone Call From Home," Korkut expresses his immediate desire to escape into nothingness. This often accompanies the unexpected news of the death of someone who was important to us. It is part of the denial we use to protect ourselves from the immediate impact of the awful reality.

Poetry is a vehicle that can give "voice" to loss (Smith, 2006). Poetic self-expression allows the griever to articulate symbolically what he or she may not be able to state plainly (Neimeyer, 1998). For some people, writing letters to the deceased offers a similar way to express their grief feelings when they are reluctant to verbalize them to others. For the survivor of the death of an ex-spouse there can be the fear that people will respond with hostility, rejection, anger, or ridicule. This is the plight of those who experience disenfranchised grief (Doka, 2002).

In addition to the shock of the news, many other factors combined to complicate Korkut's grief process. He did not share his immediate reaction with those around him; he had little or no local support system, an essential ingredient in processing grief; he was unable to attend the memorial or funeral service where he could have shared the memories of her with others who had known them as a couple. Apparently there was no one with whom he felt he could share his grief verbally, another essential ingredient. As Shakespeare wrote, "Give sorrow words. The grief that does not speak whispers the o'erfraught heart, and bids it break." Written or spoken, words allow the normal process of grieving to proceed toward the time when the memory is less painful, as illustrated in Korkut's poem "Winter Walk."

It may be that Korkut had never fully grieved the original loss of the relationship, although he thought he had as he went on with his life. Unfinished emotional business following the final signing of divorce papers is a common scenario. There is often too much bitterness and hate at the time, making it impossible to reconcile anything. Unresolved issues can affect people for months or years (Scott, 2000). With the death of one, the survivor realizes the opportunity to forgive or ask forgiveness, express remorse, or make amends is lost forever.

REFERENCES

Doka, K. J. (Ed.). (2002). *Disenfranchised grief: New directions, challenges and strategies for practice* (p. 11). Champaign, IL: Research Press.

Neimeyer, R. A. (1998). *Lessons of loss: A guide to coping* (pp. 187, 196). New York, NY: McGraw-Hill.

Scott, S. (2000). Grief reactions to the death of a divorced spouse revisited. *Omega: Journal of Death and Dying, 41*(3), 212.

Smith, H. I. (2006). Does my grief count? When ex-family grieve. *Illness, Crisis & Loss, 14*(4), 355-372.

SECTION 4

As the Dust Settles

CHAPTER 15

Geography of a Marriage

Barbara Hoffman

Preface: When I saw the call for poems on dead ex-spouses, I knew I had poems that would fit the anthology. I forgot the narrative part and just sent the poems. Peggy wrote back explaining that the poems had to be within a narrative.

I resisted. I was encouraged. I started writing a narrative. I had to eclipse the marriage into a page or two and put the poems in the order of the narrative. I wrote. I stopped. I was encouraged to finish the narrative and send it in.

Dr. Freud was on my shoulder, urging me to listen to the woman who was putting this ambitious project together. "Finish the narrative. Send your work," he said. Writing the narrative forced me to find the thread of the story. I tried to keep it short, because, well, I'm a poet, and because my adult children will see it. Are they equal reasons? It happened long ago, but it's still in me. It separates my life into before and after, no judgment on either end. The years mute the anger, and sadness remains.

❧ ❧ ❧

The marriage seems like it was 100 years ago. Three children—one-two-three—the first born 11 months after the wedding.

At 35, I woke from the housewife dream. I felt discounted, like last year's clothes. Ignored.

My husband didn't want me to have any other activities but cooking, cleaning, and taking care of the children.

When the children were all in school, I wanted to work. My husband said, "No."

I wanted to go to college at night. He said, "No."

I went anyway.

I curled my hair. He said, "Straighten it."

I wore short skirts. He said, "Cover your legs."

I volunteered to direct programs at the Rosary Society at church. He said, "No, it will take you away from your housework."

I felt as though I were living with a father, not a husband. He refused to go to therapy.

I fell out of love with him.

Soon after I found a lump in my breast. Breast cancer and mastectomy forced me to think of divorce. I thought, ". . . *if* I only have a short time to live, I want to be happy."

Two of my children were in high school, and the youngest in 8th grade.

Catholic guilt set in.

Night Sounds

I remember telling him
I wanted a divorce
I remember his face, stolid
set against feeling it

I remember the look
of his body
as he walked away from me
head up, back straight

in bed that night
in the middle of the night
in quiet darkness
I hear it again
the little boy sound
of my husband
crying in his sleep

I thought not loving my husband anymore was the worst feeling I could have. We were still sleeping together in the double bed, and one night I woke to that heartbreaking sound.

Before the Divorce

I can't bear the sound
of his breathing in bed
I sleep with my daughters
crowded easy sleeps
lulled by their breathing
till they look at me
with sad eyes
and I go back
to the double bed

I set up a cot
for my husband
in the basement

finally I have the better deal
but victory proves bitter
for every time I do the laundry
I see the rumpled cot
and guilt, like an overflow of suds
spills onto the narrow cot
the gray cement floor.

After the breast surgery, I told my husband I wanted a divorce.

He said, "No. Catholics don't get divorced."

I wondered what century he was in. Did he think he could hold me, keep me, like Peter's wife, in a pumpkin shell?

Yes. I thought of how hurt he was. We were supposed to be forever, and he didn't want to let me go. But I had to get out.

Time stretched on. He still refused to consider divorce. He had forbidden me to talk to anyone about our problems. Now I look at the word "forbidden." Who says that word?

Finally, I went to a lawyer. A meeting was set up and I waited for my husband at the lawyer's office.

Fault Line

the appointment is noon
in the lawyer's office
I sit on a brown folding chair
at the top of the stairs
and wait for my husband

the door opens
at the bottom of the stairs
I look down
at his lustrous brown hair
I don't touch anymore

guilt is a great big square
sitting on my chest
pushing me upright

his foot hits the top step
he looks arrow-straight at me
I steel myself against
his drowning eyes

pain splits a chasm
inside us
sorrow moans
up and down the canyon

The divorce and the time leading to it were 2 black years. My depression had piggy-backed upon guilt. I could not fight for myself. I was depleted. I had to get out.

The judge ruled that I'd receive $135 a month for three teenagers and joint custody. The children would remain in the house (owned by my husband), and each of us would live with the children for 6 months and then move to a common apartment for the other 6 months.

The Collaborator

The judge said,
"How can we punish
this woman for wanting
her own life? What price
should she pay?
"We can sentence her
and her children
to live on $135 a month."

"That sounds right,"
said the men
around the mahogany table.

The woman who wanted her own life, said,
"Maybe that's not enough of a punishment."

"You can only live
with them six months
each year," they said.

"Are you sure that's enough
of a punishment for someone
as guilty as I am?" she said.

"No," the judge said,
"if you can't manage
on $135, you lose them."

"I don't know
if I can live without my children," she said.

"Well, for wanting your own life
we don't think that's too much
to give up. In fact,
we might have to take more."

The judge looked around the table
at the men. They all nodded.

"One more thing,"
they said in unison,
looking at her.

She cut out her tongue
and put it on the mahogany table.

How did I ever agree to that? I don't know, but I did. I was the first to move out. I had never lived alone before. It was quiet. So quiet. I missed my children. I cried every day, then picked myself up and went to work.

Moving every 6 months was difficult, and since I still had no college degree, my salary was low. I would need more money to feed the children during the 6 months I lived in the house with them.

Family Court

a year after the divorce
trying to get more money
to feed the kids.
I go to Family Court
they sit me in a cubicle
where I hear the faceless
whispering of the workers

". . . banker's ex," they say
behind their hands
$135 a month for her
and three teenagers

they tsk-tsk
as I fill out papers

just before he gets
the summons

he calls the Court
antes up more money
just enough
to keep us
from going over
the edge
just enough
for food for the kids
just enough
so I can never
buy a lipstick
a blouse
a pair of shoes

Just before the case went to a judge, my husband called and said he would give me more money for the children. It was hard for me not to hate him for having put me through this, for not having cared enough for his children to provide us with enough money for food. Rather, revenge on me seemed his highest motivation.

After 5 years, he remarried. He retired early and moved to Florida.

The children were out of college and working by then. My son was married and had one child. Most of the rancor had disappeared or gone underground. My ex-husband and I were cordial to each other on family occasions. I thought I had detached myself.

He was diagnosed with colon cancer.

Cardiology

on the day
of my ex-husband's
surgery in Florida
I can't breathe
in the city
in the store
on the train
this heavy weight
on my chest

I walk down the stairs
at the train station
drive home
drums beat
inside my head
trying to get out
5 minutes
10, 15
drums still beating
get to the E.R.
nurse pulls me in

pulse 220
bp 240
drums still trying
to leave
through the top
of my head
EKG
morphine
drums stop
I smile
at the cute cardiologist

I want to give him
my heart
say, ". . . fix it.
I've lost something."

After his surgery, my ex-husband had several rounds of chemotherapy. He was okay for a year, but the cancer had spread and soon he was undergoing more chemotherapy. It reached a point where the chemo was not stopping the growth of the tumors. He was dying.

Reprise

the boy I married
years ago
is dying
the hospital bed delivered
to the living room
of his Florida house
I want to call
tell him
I remember
dancing to Fats Domino
Blueberry Hill
the first time we made love
our honeymoon in the Poconos
each baby as it was born
the intimate look across the room
at a party, "Let's go home."

I want to cry at the coldness
that grew between us
the lost kisses
I gave to someone else
I want to cry at the changes
in his body how thin
how close the feel of his bones
under his skin
as I embraced him last time
how like a child he looked

curled up on the couch
hands folded under his cheek
blanket over him on that warm day

soon he will die
what can I say
to close the breach
give him back a kiss

The children went to Florida to be with him at the end. He called me and thanked me for giving him three wonderful children, said he was sorry my life was so difficult. He died soon after.

The Grave

I lay a rose on his casket
wanted to lie down
the length of my body
along the length of his body
along the length of the coffin
my arm curved
over the mahogany
it would be so restful
maybe the only time
I could be restful
next to him
maybe the only way
I could love him.

EPILOGUE

After his death, I didn't think about him. I had already spent 20 years not thinking about him or his life.

Our lives intersected when there was something connecting us with our children or grandchildren. When we were together at family events, I still had to turn away from some of the things he said, his ideas, his prejudices.

I don't remember suffering a depression, just wonderment that he died before I did. At the wake, I was greeted warmly by my ex-husband's business associates and friends.

I did feel displaced at the gravesite, when his second wife sat up front with my grown children.

However, the funeral director made a space for me and beckoned me to come forward. That was one of the most gracious things I experienced during this time, an outside acknowledgment that the life we had together had mattered.

Who can deny blood and bone, the children that we conceived in love? They were that great chunk of our young lives; the busy-ness, his career, my taking care of the children and the house. No time for introspection.

Now if I look back at the young woman I was, the one who, at 19, married that 23-year-old man, it's hard to find her because she has changed.

Nevertheless, in my mind, he is the same: the one I first married, the one I first gave myself to, the one who expected me to stay the same 19-year-old he married. This is the cardboard figure, the one-dimensional folk character that stays with me.

But that is not necessarily the measure of the man. He was more than that to other people.

My life with him was important at the time and it is my responsibility to believe it was important. Those pieces of my life with him will always be with me.

COMMENTARY

During her marriage Barbara likened herself to "Peter's wife in a pumpkin shell": a servant in her own home, she was never allowed any fulfilling activities outside of her home to stimulate her mind and help her grow. As she states, her husband did not want her to change in any way; he wanted her to always remain the 19-year-old girl he had married. For 16 years she tried to change things a little from time to time, but he refused to acquiesce to anything she proposed. He also refused counseling.

This is psychological abuse. There are many behaviors that can fit the category of this term, some of which carry into the realm of violence (National Coalition Against Domestic Violence, 2000). What Barbara experienced was a continuous effort to control her freedom, to keep her at home, forbid her to talk to anyone about their problems, to monitor her appearance, deny her access to friends and employment, and to education which she bravely pursued despite his objection. Her self-confidence was depleted; she was very unhappy.

After her children were teenagers she was diagnosed and had treatment for breast cancer. That was when she decided if she had only a short time to live, she wanted to be happy. She no longer wanted to be controlled, to be a victim of abuse. The only way to do that was to get away from her husband.

One of the worst things in terms of our health, happiness, and deepest values is to live with a resentful, angry, abusive partner. Sometimes we feel we can heal ourselves, restore our personal power, and elevate our self-esteem if only our partner eliminates their abusive behavior. When that does not happen, the only logical decision is to leave the situation if we want to cease being a victim and preserve our mental health (Stosny, 2008).

Barbara told her husband she wanted a divorce. He refused to consider it, said it was against their religious beliefs. He was very hurt and sad that she would even consider such a thing. Over the next 2 very difficult years before the divorce, Barbara became even more depressed as her feelings of guilt mounted.

She may also have been grieving her many losses—the loving relationship she once had, dreams of a forever marriage and a normal home life, loss of a body part from cancer. Depression is a normal part of the grieving process but is more transient and can be exacerbated by feelings of guilt (Worden, 2009). When we are not empowered to obtain the emotional support we need, the result can be increased depression.

Depression is defined as a condition marked by feelings of hopelessness, helplessness, self-doubt, lethargy, crying easily, feeling worthless, and lonely. Depressed people have negative evaluations of themselves, the world and the future. Freud believed that in grief the *world* looks poor and empty, while in depression the *person* feels poor and empty (Worden, 2009).

In one of her powerful, very descriptive poems, "The Collaborator," Barbara details more abuse perpetrated by the men who decided the punitive terms of the divorce. There was financial abuse when adequate money was denied, and more psychological abuse when the threat was made she would lose her children if she could not manage on the small amount of money approved. This added to her depression and fear of the future.

When her ex-spouse remarried and moved away, Barbara felt she had finally detached her emotions from him. However, the day he had surgery for colon cancer, she suffered some heart problems that sent her to the hospital. Was it a coincidence or a strong emotional and physical reaction to the shock of the threat to his life? It is impossible to say, but similar incidents are known to have happened. Our emotions can produce many physical symptoms (Worden, 2009).

In his final days, Barbara's husband called to thank her for giving him three wonderful children, and to say he was sorry her life was so difficult. Whether he was prompted to do this by someone else or it came from a wish to clear his own conscience is unknown. When all else is stripped away and we are dying, we find our most important possessions are our relationships. We cannot change what was, but we can say what needs to be said before it is too late. In his book, *The Four Things That Matter Most* (2004), Dr. Ira Byock states he has seen these four short sentences heal what had been very difficult relationships:

> Please forgive me.
> I forgive you.
> Thank you.
> I love you.

The healing power of these words leaves us better prepared to then say "Goodbye."

REFERENCES

Byock, I. (2004). *The four things that matter most: A book about living* (pp. 3-6). New York, NY: Free Press.

National Coalition Against Domestic Violence. (2000). *Psychological abuse.* Retrieved April 18, 2012, from http://www.ncadv.org/files/PsychologicalAbuse.pdf

Stosny, S. (2008). Effects of emotional abuse. Retrieved April 8, 2012, from http://www.psychologytoday.com/blog/anger-in-the-age-entitlement/200811/emotional-abuse-overcoming-victim-identity

Worden, J. W. (2009). *Grief counseling and grief therapy* (4th ed., pp. 23-24, 32). New York, NY: Springer.

CHAPTER 16

Jake

Denise Handlon

Preface: In the summer of 2005 my dear friend and ex-husband was dying. I was 51, and the reality of no longer having him here was life-changing. My grief following his death was debilitating.

I turned to the tool most often employed in my healing process: writing. Although the story of Jake has been 2½ years in the making, upon its completion, a purging of a deeper, subtler layer of grief assuaged the hole in my heart.

Discovering Ms. Sapphire's request for submissions to this unique anthology has been one more synchronistic event that has happened in my life. I am grateful for her gracious invitation and acceptance of my contribution. At last, the written word has a most appropriate place of rest.

❧ ❧ ❧

This is a story about my journey with grief. A journey that began with the death of a man I had known, and who had known me, for over half of my life. To lose someone who had known me well in all aspects; who understood my moods, tolerated my phases of life, and accepted the changes in my physical appearance, was like losing a part of my own self.

Lest you think that Jake and I shared a storybook romance of happily-ever-after, I tell my story here. The one thing that remained constant throughout my relationship with Jake was that we truly loved and cared for one another. We just couldn't seem to live with each other.

Jake was a large man compared to my diminutiveness. His frame sheltered mine and he frequently commented on how he loved my petite stature. At night, as my body lay encircled within his, he would whisper in awe, touching my shoulder with his rough hand, "your skin is so soft . . . I've never felt anyone's skin as soft as yours." I would reply with good-natured teasing, "It's the olive oil."

During those times I would imagine what it would be like not to feel his arms around me; not to smell the cologne I had come to associate with him . . . the way the scent of Old Spice brought memories of watching my father shave. I knew if ever that day came I would spray his pillow with his cologne and bask in the memory of where he had lain.

I first met Jake in the summer of 1980. It was one of those synchronistic events in which Jake happened to visit his cousin George on the exact night I introduced myself to those same new neighbors. The irony was that Jake had not seen George for 2 years.

Despite my mother's prompting, I had resisted meeting George and Lila, the young couple who had moved to my parents' neighborhood, even though they had a daughter about the ages of my two little girls. I had been hiding away from the world, nursing my self-esteem, so bruised from a painful divorce.

The disintegration of my marriage had shattered my self-confidence and left me shy, broken, and socially withdrawn. Why had I chosen that particular night to move ahead despite my fears? In retrospect I believe it was our destiny to meet.

On this particular warm June evening I found a strength and confidence that propelled me to venture across the street. It was the kind of Midwestern summer night that drew people to their porches in search of a cool evening breeze. I noticed Lila feeding her infant son on the porch step and decided this was the night I would say hello, aware of feeling a peculiar sense of joy, an emotion I hadn't felt in months.

As I approached her house I did not notice the midnight-blue Corvette parked in front of the house adjacent to theirs, nor did I notice the man in the kitchen laughing and joking with Lila's husband. Had I realized all of that I know for certain I would have stayed away, calling for my girls from the safety of my own side of the street.

I had never been impressed with people who flaunted their money on show cars. I considered their owners arrogant and superficial. Back then, life, including finances, was too serious a business for me to involve myself with a man in a fancy car.

But on that night, I sat on Lila's porch sharing stories of motherhood while our daughters played tag on the lawn. I was grateful my girls had found a friend. It had been far too long since I had seen them happy. I was oblivious that Jake was telling his cousin that he was interested in the "cute woman sitting with Lila."

Once we were introduced it didn't take long for Jake to find his way into our hearts. His easy-going manner was a sharp contrast to my ex-husband's high-strung personality.

Initially, my daughters were bashful with this large man and sensitive to his booming laugh. It appeared that everything was funny to him and he was easily amused by the simplest things they did. His infectious laugh eventually taught me to laugh at myself and brought humor to balance my practicality.

Soon enough my daughters learned that he was like a big kid, a natural teacher who enjoyed children. We went on picnics, outdoor concerts, and to drive-in movies.

An avid sports fan, Jake taught them basketball, bowling, and canoeing. But best of all, perceiving their grief for pets left behind in the move, he surprised them with an 8-week-old puppy.

Four years later we were married, with my daughters standing up as our flower girls. Bonded together as family, they were the children he never had. He was no longer their mom's boyfriend. He became their other parent, the man they had grown to love and trust. The night my daughters came to Jake asking permission to call him Dad was one that made his heart swell.

Outsiders could not tell that we were a step-family. My daughters' father lived 800 miles away from them, but their "dad" was right there with them. Life was rich and I felt blessed.

Jake embraced life and loved a good time, but sometimes that good time interfered with better judgment. We were a little like Laurel and Hardy, jumping into situations before thinking through the consequences. He'd screw up his round face afterward and jovially admonish me, "Now look at the fine mess you've gotten us into."

On one of those occasions we were in a hospital elevator on our way to visit my mother. Wanting to show off his prowess, he said to me in his best imitation of the Incredible Hulk, "Watch me open the elevator with my bare hands." Within seconds, we were stuck mere inches from our floor with only a crack left open to peek out and get the attention of the maintenance man. That was the day I discovered that Jake was claustrophobic. Four hours later we were free, but he made me swear never to tell the real reason for the malfunctioned elevator.

Then there was the time he decided he didn't want to ask an employee to bring a ladder to reach the top shelf for a two-by-four while shopping for lumber. As I watched in horror, I could not yell, "Watch out!" fast enough before the domino effect of his yanking on one piece of wood, pinned under another, set off a chain reaction. A smooth, white board torpedoed toward him, sparing his eye but slicing into all layers of his forehead. I could see his skull.

Pushing him down before he passed out, I grabbed the best thing I had in my purse to stop the profuse bleeding—my sanitary pad. Besides an aching head, he nursed a bruised ego as I applied pressure to the wound surrounded by a group of concerned male employees.

This event necessitated a trip to the hospital, which fortunately did not require the use of any elevator to reach the Emergency Department. I stood by his side watching as the resident stitched him up. When it was healed it left a small scar above his left eyebrow as a reminder of his folly.

Although we loved each other deeply, it wasn't easy living with Jake and his financial irresponsibility. There always seemed to be a need to go beyond the established household budget and frequently I would find out too late that bills were left unpaid, and the checkbook not balanced.

My frustration and disappointment grew through the years as I viewed this particular character trait as immature. I felt he was sabotaging our future.

When it finally surfaced that Jake had been gambling, I felt shocked and betrayed by his covertness; saddened that I'd no idea, even after 10 years of marriage.

Although Jake was relieved that I knew at last, he feared I'd leave him, indeed it was an option I contemplated in the following weeks. Understanding that the gambling was a compulsion, and part of a larger problem, I said I wanted us to meet with a therapist to work through our difficulty. I also wanted each of us to attend a support group.

In my group I listened as women discussed their home situations and how the actions of one affected the entire family. Weekly stories were shared as each of us attempted to maintain our own focus of growth.

I wasn't quite sure where I fit into Jake's addiction, but it was suggested that I hold off making any drastic decisions and avoid reacting to his behavior.

Jake refused to attend joint therapy. He explained the origin of his compulsive behavior was due to his childhood, and that he needed to be alone to deal with it.

Respecting his wishes, I retreated and felt a familiar tightening in my gut. Again, my trust issues had been triggered, though for different reasons than in my first marriage. As the problem continued, the effects on our lives as a family persisted as well.

At one point our home went into foreclosure and we solicited the help of relatives to retrieve it. As I struggled to keep us afloat the financial burden lay heavy on my shoulders and Jake's addiction soon wedged itself between us.

Still, Jake refused to include me in his therapy sessions. He soon began missing his appointments and eventually stopped attending altogether.

Gripped by an illness that he did not fully understand, Jake's compulsion was greater than his desire for recovery.

After much soul searching, I divorced Jake after thirteen years of marriage. We were both heartbroken and our families were deeply affected by the breakup.

Our story did not end with our divorce. After much perseverance we successfully moved beyond blame or ill feelings for the dissolution of our marriage.

Our friendship was re-established and grew stronger through the years.

Jointly, we celebrated graduations, marriages (with Jake being the proud father, walking 'his girls' down the aisle), and the births of our grandchildren. We mourned the death of my mother together.

Free of any legal or financial ties to him, I was able to enjoy Jake's other endearing qualities and we relied on each other for comfort and support in ways that only one I'd known intimately could offer me.

Wherever I traveled I could depend on Jake checking up on me to see if I was doing all right. I looked forward to our conversations and hearing his hearty laugh.

Jake was my airport chauffeur whenever I visited family. Our reunion would start with spotting each other through the crowd and end in a huge bear hug, he lifting me off my feet and saying in his deep baritone, "Who loves ya', baby?" I'd giggle like a teenager, happy to be welcomed back so warmly.

He frequently tried to woo me back by telling me we were soul mates destined to be together. I would smile quietly. Who was I to argue? There had been many mysterious, divine moments in my life that went beyond normal explanation. I had learned to accept the place where I was.

In June 2005, Jake was unable to pick me up when I arrived for my annual visit to Michigan, but I met up with him the day before my return to California. Always a hefty man, Jake's appearance was shocking. His skin was ashen and he was holding his pants up with one hand despite the belt he wore. Though he was Italian and enjoyed a lifelong passion for food, I was alarmed that his extreme weight loss was not intentional.

He explained that he had been unable to eat for weeks due to sharp pains in his chest. He had even gone to the Emergency Room to rule out any cardiac problems. I was again alarmed that he had not followed through with a medical appointment and insisted that he make one.

Satisfied that he had explained to the office manager the gravity of the situation, I made him promise to call me following his exam.

There are times in my life when I remember exactly what I was doing when I heard life-changing news. Standing in the frozen food aisle that first Wednesday in July was one of those moments. His voice, still groggy from anesthesia, was heavy in its tone, "They found a tumor in my esophagus," he began.

Unable to move or breathe, I managed to squelch the fear in my voice and said, "Please tell me they did a biopsy. . . ."

Affirming they had, he finished with the news of his appointment with the surgeon in 2 days. I felt helpless and insisted he take our daughters with him to the appointment. He assured me he would.

I trusted that our oldest, now a teacher, and her sister, a nurse, would ask the important questions Jake might not think of.

The news of his cancer came to me from my youngest daughter. I sat crying, barely hearing her words, "cancer . . . inoperable . . . 3 to 12 months . . . additional tests ordered. . . ."

"I'll be home to take care of him," I sobbed, not wanting to think of the incomprehensible news.

I had assisted my father with hospice care for my elderly mother 2 years earlier, but she had been ill with lung cancer and we were prepared for the worst when the cancer reappeared. Not in our wildest imagination could any of us have foreseen Jake's diagnosis. For me one thing was certain: I needed to be by Jake's side.

The next day I phoned Jake. We barely spoke, each of us crying heartfelt tears across the 2,000 miles separating us. I told him I would be with him as soon as possible.

I wish I could say that I left California the next day and that we had those last 12 months, the most optimistic estimate of his prognosis, but it didn't happen that way. Denying the seriousness of the illness and wishing to avoid the inevitable, I found reasons to delay the trip back: my physical rehab appointments from a job injury; my annual mammogram that I'd neglected to schedule, the ongoing saga of a relationship I'd ended weeks before Jake's diagnosis. These were my feeble excuses to stay away.

It was 6 weeks before I saw him again, and I could see the effects of the illness. His skin was jaundiced and his eyes had lost their vitality. He was slipping away and I had allowed my own selfish needs to rob us of our time together.

He was justifiably angry with me and showed it through the cruel way he treated me. It was a side I had not seen in the 25 years I'd known him.

Often choosing silence around me his voice was filled with anger when he did speak.

I observed him discussing his care with our daughters, ignoring any suggestions I offered as if I was invisible. Finally I had to address this issue. I apologized to him for my avoidance in arriving earlier. I explained to him I wanted to be with him, but not if he did not want me there. I told him I understood his disappointment and I would respect his decision either way.

He acknowledged he still wanted me with him and we made arrangements to move into a ground-floor condominium offered by a family member.

Our children and their spouses moved his belongings from his upper level apartment and I made plans to relocate to Michigan. I was well aware of the road ahead both personally and professionally, and I knew that Jake's time would not be long. I continued to push this thought away. It was too overwhelming for me to consider.

All too soon, my brief visit with him was at its end. I felt alone, frightened, and the despair of losing a love I had always relied on was devastating.

My return to California to resign from my job and relocate was filled with sorrow...never to receive his weekly calls, hear his comfort or cheerful message, never to hear the sound of his laughter again. . . .

"What am I going to do without him?" I would sob to myself.

I returned to Michigan quickly this time, as promised. We moved into the condo the day I arrived. Jake was anxious to be alone with me, isolated from the world. Other than his appointments he did not wish to leave our sanctuary.

Grateful for our daughters' tender assistance in caring for their stepfather during the weeks following his initial diagnosis, they had exceeded my expectations in handling the crisis. They diligently found a competent oncologist and accompanied Jake to his first appointments.

With my return they could turn their attention back to their families and work obligations. They'd willingly assisted the man they'd loved for over 2 decades. My return was a relief for these young women who had been thrust prematurely into the world of illness and impending death.

As I made Jake comfortable on the couch that first evening, I sat at his feet and the feelings I had kept inside since the day I received the news of his illness came pouring out. I cried as if my heart was breaking, for indeed it was. He patted my head in attempts to console me.

"Jake," I said choking on my sobs, "I will never find anyone who has loved me the way you have."

His old self returned and he laughed the familiar laugh when he was amused by something I had said, and said, "Oh, yes you will."

I looked deeply into his eyes, "No, it's true," I said. "I've never been loved by anyone so completely. You have loved me unconditionally. That isn't something that happens often. I'm so sorry I've stayed away. I don't want you to die. What am I going to do without you?" And that produced fresh tears.

Jake reminded me of the love letter he had given me 9 years earlier and asked if I still had it. I nodded. I kept it with the journal I had written during the time of our divorce.

"Then, not to worry . . . I will find you again, in another lifetime. You are my soul mate . . . we are meant to be together," he told me with a twinkle in his eye.

Originally, Jake had put up a valiant front, and expressed a desire that all his friends and family gather in a celebration—a living wake.

It was an unrealistic expectation given the ferocity of the cancer. Early additional tests had revealed cancer cells had already infiltrated the liver. Although his appetite would diminish with time, a stent had been placed to offset the stenosis of the esophagus created by the tumor, allowing him to receive liquid nourishment. Palliative care was all that the medical personnel could offer and his prognosis had been decreased to a possible 3 to 6 months. He reassured me that he was not afraid; he had made his peace with death.

As a hospice nurse, I'd learned that death comes in subtle, predictable stages revealing the progress of the terminally ill patient in that process. As Jake's days of alertness began to wane, I carefully monitored the minute details as his condition changed, reporting to the doctor and adjusting his medications.

He withdrew from everyone except his immediate family and one friend who would visit to relay news to Jake's other friends. Soon, he was withdrawing from me as well, and I would observe him as he meditated and dozed for longer periods of time.

Jake had three wishes on his journey toward death. He wanted to be pain-free and to die at home surrounded by loved ones. His third wish was that we remarry.

Miraculously, I was able to honor all three wishes. One week before his death we remarried, with our daughters standing by our sides once more, no longer flower girls, but grown women witnessing our union.

The marriage ceremony was a mere formality, for we had remained loving friends, committed in ways we had been unable to achieve as a married couple. Our deepened relationship surpassed time, distance and commitments to other relationships, and now surpassed terminal illness and death.

Remarkably I had changed from one who had begun the journey frightened and more concerned for my own imminent loss to one who was fully present and in service to what had been unfolding throughout our time together. A spiritual presence provided me with strength, calm, and acceptance more powerful than my emotions. We were in a state of grace, he and I, and I was in reverence to that. I provided him with whatever he needed for a loving transition.

In preparation for the finality, I'd notified Jake's mother and siblings to come to his bedside. The priest had already given Jake the blessing of last rites and his death was impending.

We discussed the option of hospice and Jake agreed. The hospice nurse arrived the Wednesday prior to his death, assessed him, and honored our request that they remain in the background until further notice.

The following day I asked Jake for permission to open the doors to visitors. Alert, but weak, he was no longer plagued by the symptoms that had kept his friends at bay. I reminded him that it was a desire he had expressed to me 12 weeks ago when we first began this walk with cancer. It was the right time for his living wake to be honored.

He trusted me with this decision. We began calling friends and relatives who had waited in prayerful support for a chance to meet with him. Now it was their turn to tell him how much he meant to them.

Gifts of food and drink were brought in as word spread among his large circle of friends and relatives. People shared their thoughts, hugged and kissed him goodbye, or sometimes just sat silently and held his hand.

The dining and living rooms overflowed as people gathered in communion and support the Thursday evening preceding his death. The living wake that he'd envisioned materialized.

After the last visitor left, Jake slipped into a deep sleep, his loud breathing filling the room. Jake's sister, our daughters and I set up camp that night on the floor surrounding his bed, while his mother rested in the adjacent bedroom.

The next morning Jake remained unresponsive. I continued with my usual routine and made him comfortable as I lightly washed his face and spoke to him softly. Suddenly, Jake's eyes flew wide open and he smiled. He beamed as if he had awakened from a beautiful dream that he wished to share. I urged my daughter, who had been with me in the room, to run and get the others.

The room filled with a warm, golden presence as we supported him in this last important phase of surrender. As the five of us sat around his bed he turned to look directly at each of us, and openly received our words of love.

We told him how much he meant to us, reassured him we would be fine, and though we'd be left behind, we didn't want him to worry. We offered him a safe journey into the light and God's love.

When the last person was finished, he closed his eyes and sighed, still smiling; then he returned to the deep, unresponsive place he had experienced earlier. He remained that way for the rest of the day and into the night, with periods of restlessness. Late that evening, following a family discussion, we notified hospice and the on-call nurse returned to adjust his medications.

For the second night in a row we lay vigilant around his bed, his loud breathing rhythmically reverberating through the room. I drifted to sleep around 2:00 a.m. and awoke an hour later to stillness. Moving to his bedside I kissed his cheek, feeling the remaining warmth of his skin. I checked for a pulse. He died the first Saturday in October, sometime after all of us had fallen asleep.

In the early morning, before the dawn broke the skyline and the first morning birds greeted the day, I sat holding Jake's hand in mine, talked softly to him and gently stroked his head. It was my time to be alone with him before the reality of his death was known to the others and the clamor to care for the body started.

I savor the significance of that time. For so many years Jake had cajoled me to grow old with him. Now my life with Jake had come to an end. He'd moved ahead without me. It was a precious moment that I cherish.

Jake's body was cremated according to his wishes, and a memorial service offering support to those left grieving for him. We selected a holy card of a white dove spreading its wings against a sky blue heaven and had his poem printed on the back, in remembrance of him.

I have a favorite photo that is dear to my heart. It's an old photo of a much younger me sitting on Jake's lap. A frozen still-shot of a happy couple. His chipmunk cheeks puff into fleshy mounds with his beaming smile, pressing them up and into the orbital cavities, making it difficult to detect his sensitive, brown eyes. My long, brown hair cascades down my shoulders as I sit smiling, while his strong arms embrace me in love and support.

Jake's arms were one of his physical features I loved most. When he wrapped his arms around me I felt safe and protected. His arms lifted my daughters onto his shoulders for views above crowds when they were little girls.

My daughters were just 3 and 5 when Jake and I met. He'd become our knight in shining armor, safe, reliable, and adventurous. Instead of a white steed, he drove a shiny, blue Corvette, which he willingly traded for a more practical car to hold the four of us. His adoration for his "ready-made family" bridged all concern and confusion. A bond of love was created for the big man with the big heart.

I had watched those arms lift, move, chop, and dribble. While I silently mourned the muscle atrophy that robbed him of his strength, I was grateful for the memories of him paddling our canoe, throwing hoop shots with friends, and tossing Frisbees to our dog. Proudly, those arms offered his daughters a steady hand as each young woman walked into the arms of her beloved. His arms tenderly held our newborn grandchildren as his eyes filled with joy.

Whatever he did, whether it was his passion for cooking, or wrestling with the kids, training the dog, or mowing the lawn, he was gruff, rough, and tender all in one man.

Jake's laughter, his love for his family will be remembered and greatly missed. As time moves forward there will always be a space in my heart that is Jake's.

EPILOGUE

Jake's diagnosis of esophageal cancer, in the summer of 2005, made every remaining moment crucial. In the 12 weeks preceding his death, we lived as a family and went through a roller coaster of emotions.

His request for me to move in with him and do hospice care was a bittersweet gift for which I shall always be grateful. Despite ongoing conflicts with his mother, Jake's wishes were honored and took precedence over everything and everyone else.

Jake had pre-planned many details of his funeral so the anguish of decision-making was reduced. One of the most personal decisions that my daughters and I made was our selection of a holy card to present to funeral attendees. To honor his unpretentiousness and spiritual freedom we selected a simple winged dove taking flight against a vivid, blue sky.

Replacing the traditional prayers printed on the back of these cards, we offered the poem he had written just weeks before his death.

In his simple way, he implored those left behind not to grieve for him, but to rejoice and find the joy that he had anticipated in his meeting with God.

In the midst of the emotionally charged meeting with the funeral director, Jake's humor and presence came to light one last time. In a moment of fatigue I said aloud, "I am getting really hungry. I hope we can wrap this up pretty soon." Within seconds, much like the story of Manna from heaven, a pretzel stick dropped to my side out of nowhere. We sat there stunned for a moment before bursting into hysterical laughter. I looked around dumbfounded and could only conclude it had been "hidden" between the leaves of the plant I sat next to, waiting for this particular moment to make itself known.

The funeral itself was difficult. While my family stood by my side, including a younger brother and my widowed father, I was well aware of the animosity that many of Jake's family members had for me, in particular his mother. She did not miss any opportunity to attempt to put me, or my daughters "in our place." It distressed her tremendously to know that Jake and I had reunited in a simple matrimonial ceremony just 1 week prior to his death.

In the days that followed the funeral, I fell into a robotic routine of taking care of the business of moving from his mother's condo and into my daughter's guest room.

I had made a quick move from California to Michigan to care for him, leaving behind my job and spiritual work. All of my worldly possessions were locked up in a tiny storage unit while my daughter graciously opened her home to me.

Insomnia plagued me at night and crying spells followed me throughout the day. I marked time through the family's routine, spending days caring for my grandson who turned 2 as autumn moved toward winter.

Although my daughters were patiently supportive during this time period, after 4 months of grieving they encouraged me to move forward. Yet, the deep despair I felt was so debilitating that I had neither interest nor capacity to imagine returning to work, much less seek employment.

One evening, staring out at the December moon, a realization hit me: I am homeless, unemployed, and my dearest friend was gone forever. I missed Jake's reassuring phone calls and booming laughter when he'd ask, "Who loves ya' baby?" His presence had brought me an irreplaceable peace. In that moment, I experienced a raw wound in my heart center and sensed a dark void. I felt I could cry forever.

After 6 months, I took a job as a travel nurse, finding my first assignment in the same location of California I had recently left. Despite the familiarity of the locale, the reality of my loss weighed me down. I cried constantly, but somehow managed to get through the first 13 weeks without Jake.

My next assignment was closer to family and the exact opposite of the first in every way. Where San Francisco had been a short drive from me, this second assignment was in a rural town with a population under 5,000. I found the seclusion a welcome retreat and spent days moving through a healing process, writing and visiting with family.

It has been 4 years since Jake's death. I am nearing yet another anniversary month as fall returns. However, it is not the September marital anniversary, or the October passing that brings a tear to my eye.

My anguish has returned regularly in the month of August—the month I moved in with him and watched the light leave his eyes.

I never seem to recall this cycle unless I make a tearful phone call to my youngest daughter. Her gentle reminder of this time period brings it back into focus for me.

With that realization I am able to allow for the mourning once again, then set it aside and move on. I have accepted that it may always be this way. I am okay with that.

In the meantime, in my thoughts and in my heart, I let him know how proud he would be of "his girls" and our grandchildren.

COMMENTARY

It is not surprising that Denise experienced an overwhelming grief reaction after her ex-spouse/spouse died. Even though they could not live together, they never really broke the emotional ties of their relationship. As Denise states, they always truly loved and cared about each other whether they were divorced or not. The fact that they married again just a week before he died shows the strength of their attachment. Her overwhelming grief was a normal reaction to the death of someone she loved deeply.

Research has shown that 29% of respondents reported either a severe (21%) or overwhelming (8%) grief reaction (Scott, 2000). One woman reported she and her ex-spouse planned to meet for lunch to talk about getting back together when he was killed in an automobile accident on his way to the restaurant. They had been divorced less than 2 months. The shock of his sudden, unexpected death, exacerbated by the dashed hopes for a future together, contributed to what she called an overwhelming grief reaction.

The symptoms Denise experienced in the days and months following Jake's death can be part of the normal process of grieving: insomnia, crying spells, deep despair, moving robotically through the days, and depression.

There can be many physical, emotional, and behavioral symptoms of normal grief (Worden, 2009). Physical symptoms may include tightness in the chest and/or throat, heart palpitations, nausea, shortness of breath, lack of appetite, listlessness, weakness, constant fatigue, headache, backache, dry mouth, and an empty feeling. Increased severity of chronic health problems such as allergies, asthma, arthritis, hypertension, heart, and gastric disease is common. It is wise for people to be evaluated by a physician if they have questions about what is happening to them physically and/or emotionally.

Many people, including Denise, have found that writing their thoughts, feelings, and the kaleidoscope of reactions they are experiencing in a journal provides a good outlet (Corr, Nabe, & Corr, 2009).

However, for some the idea of journaling seems daunting. One woman said "I'm not a writer! I don't know what to write. That blank page is too intimidating!" It was explained that she didn't have to buy a notebook; she could use any available scrap of paper. She didn't need to worry about spelling, punctuation, sentence construction, or penmanship, and no one would ever read it unless she gave permission. She could write anytime, but it might be helpful if she set aside some special time each day.

The instructions were to just write whatever she was thinking and/or feeling at the time, to let it flow onto the paper any way it came out. She agreed to try. Over time the result was over 80 pages on odds and ends of different kinds of paper, some written in crayons of different colors, many hardly legible except to her. She said that getting it out of her head, breaking the sleep-robbing circular thinking, expressing the craziness that was going on in her thoughts had freed her to concentrate on the many good memories she had, to start the process of adjusting to her loss and begin to heal (Scott, personal communication, 2006).

Grief is likened to a deep wound in the body: it has to heal from the bottom up. A scar will still be there but the pain will be diminished. If a wound is allowed to close over at the top with no healing below, in time it will fester. The infection beneath will eventually burst out. When grief is held in, never acknowledged or tended to, it will eventually burst forth in negative ways such as inappropriate behavior and anger. This can lead to complicated mourning, including continued denial and the inability to relinquish the deceased, despite the sufficient passage of time for that process to have begun (Rando, 1993). The manifestation of this complicated mourning becomes the person's persistent inability to live a happy, productive life.

Denise was very quick to say she would take care of Jake in his final illness, but her denial of the seriousness of his situation kept her from going to him for 6 weeks. His anger, when she did arrive, was predictable. To their credit, they addressed the conflict openly and were able to spend the remainder of his life in a peaceful, loving, supportive relationship.

At Jake's request, Denise arranged a living wake so he could be with some of his family and friends for the last time (Albom, 1997). A living wake, or living funeral, is a celebration of a person's life before they die so they can hear the affirmations of the life they have lived, know they are loved and respected. This occasion has become more accepted in recent years and can be held anywhere the person wishes; a home, nursing home, church, ballroom, park, theater, or other location. It can be a ceremony, celebration, and/or party. Attendees often find the event awe-inspiring (Carson, 2012).

For Jake, it was the last goodbye. Although he was conscious and aware at times during the next 2 nights while the family members sat with him, his communication was limited to an occasional smile and looking directly at them to receive their loving words. He finally died peacefully when everyone was asleep. Denise had kept her promise to care for him to the end.

REFERENCES

Albom, M. (1997). *Tuesdays with Morrie: An old man, a young man, life's greatest lessons.* New York, NY: Random House, Inc.

Carson, D. (2012). *Living funeral: The grandest list celebration.* Retrieved May 8, 2012, from http://celebration2life.com/2012/04/living-funeral-the-grandest-life-celebration/

Corr, C. A., Nabe, C. M., & Corr, D. M. (2009). *Death and dying, life and living* (6th ed., pp. 235-236, 273). Belmont, CA: Wadsworth.

Rando, T. (1993). *Treatment of complicated mourning* (p. 149). Champain, IL: Research Press.

Scott, S. (2000). Grief reactions to the death of a divorced spouse revisited. *Omega: Journal of Death and Dying, 41*(3), 210.

Worden, J. W. (2009). *Grief counseling and grief therapy* (4th ed., pp. 18-31). New York, NY: Springer.

CHAPTER 17

How I Survived

Penelope Scambly Schott

Preface: When I saw a call for writing about dead ex-spouses, I thought immediately of a poem I had written some years ago, about my children's father. I sent it to Peggy, who urged me to write my "story" around the poem.

The experience of re-explaining what happened has served to put it at a more comfortable distance than ever before. As my Army veteran, (now husband) said for both of us, after he went back to Vietnam as a tourist, "I have developed compassion for my younger self."

PART ONE

The poor man has been dead for almost a quarter of a century.

I can say it: he wasn't a nice person. Or maybe, in some other situation, he was. Maybe with others he was charming and helpful. In which case, let me re-phrase it: he wasn't a nice husband.

With me, he was controlling and nasty. He was lazy and self-centered. If he didn't get what he wanted when he wanted it and exactly how he wanted it, he pouted. He mocked and criticized me in front of the children.

He had been stricken with juvenile diabetes at age 11 and grew up feeling the world owed him. It wasn't a chip he carried on his shoulder, it was a boulder.

He did have a beautiful singing voice and he loved good literature. Every so often, he could be very witty. I try to remember clever remarks he made so I can tell them to our children.

I met him at a literary tea party at the university, at a time when I was desperate for an escape from having to be brilliant. I was tired of trying to be perfect, getting straight A's, being wonderful enough to avoid my mother's disapproval.

He was almost done with his PhD in Psychology. (I didn't know then how many nutty people want to be psychotherapists.) In short, he was the first person I might date who was ready to get married and start a family. I could drop out and play house. I wouldn't have to get grants and go to graduate school. I wouldn't have to shine in a star career. I could sew curtains and bake bread.

Although I wasn't physically attracted to him, he was entirely presentable and he really did appreciate poetry. He quoted Yeats with enthusiasm.

Before then, I'd fallen hard for a couple of callow young men and it hadn't worked out. My choice was very calculated now: this man was about as well as I would do in the husband-and-father department.

I was in a big hurry to get pregnant. I'd had an abortion as a teenager, and the doctor had said to me (I realize now, vindictively), "You know this means you may never be able to have a baby."

The sweet guys I dated were too young to get married. Therefore, it would have to be this Yeats fan, this Pygmalion who had read my poetry and decided I had possibilities that he could cultivate.

In the months before we got married, all the clues were there. I worked hard at ignoring them. I let him be patronizing. I let him tell me what to think. I let him humiliate me. I let him separate me from my friends. I was totally trapped by my own rush to be married.

I wanted to die. At one point, after an attempt to assert myself only to have him skewer me to the point of despair, I took an overdose of pills and, to save my life, had my stomach pumped.

He talked the hospital out of calling the police and we moved up the wedding date. I no longer expressed any opinion that differed from his. I no longer dared have opinions. A year later I had a fat and happy baby boy.

After two children and 7 years, my husband had an affair.

I didn't know or care whether it was his first. I had gone to graduate school after all, and my husband's brother had predicted that the man would leave me before I finished my PhD. I was mid-dissertation when he left.

I wouldn't have left him, thinking it wouldn't have been fair to the children. And, I thought, ". . . as you make your bed, so shall you lie in it." But I was delighted to see him go.

He and I each remarried twice after our divorce. I had been his second wife, and numbers three and four were also young college students.

The Pygmalion urge never left him. He wanted a young, pretty, bright girl whom he could shape.

He left a very young widow.

My second marriage was a disaster. I was broke and said "Yes" to a guy who claimed he loved kids.

As it turned out, he loved vodka more. Two weeks after I agreed to marry him, I got a full-time teaching job at a good university, but it took me several years to escape from that marriage.

For me, in the marriage department, three has been the lucky number. I call Eric "my third and final husband." We've been married for years and years, and we hope for many years more.

We were already together when my first husband died at the age of 49. It was complications from diabetes that finally killed him. He had a long, horrible death, had both feet amputated, almost went blind, and finally died of a stroke.

No matter how badly he had treated me, his last 3 years were much worse than anything I would ever have wished for him.

PART TWO

I'm a compulsive reader. I will read anything—cereal boxes, graffiti, and wall posters. I have always been addicted to those signs outside churches where ministers post slogans to attract the attention of passer-bys. Mostly the signs are pious or corny, sometimes funny.

The one that made me pull over and stop my car was, "How Do The Guilty Survive?" Parked on the side of the road, I wrote that down. The words came at me with an intense immediacy.

Though I am a born and bred atheist, I almost considered attending that church the next Sunday, just to find out how the guilty do survive. What shocked me about my reaction was that, until I'd read that sign, I'd never thought of myself as "guilty."

Suddenly I knew I had done something terrible. I'd married a man I didn't love. He *chose* me and I *made do* with him. My children's father had been dead for many years, and yet not until I'd read that sign did I realize I'd done him wrong.

My whole life roared back at me; the reality of the marriage, the circumstances of the separation, everything that had happened since.

I remembered him physically and thought of his body rotting in the ground. I thought about him toe to head, feet still missing, eyeballs now dried up and shrunken. I thought about the pallor of his skin. I thought about his penis. I thought about how I'd never liked him to touch me.

From there, I went on to recall all the worst public atrocities of the time, everything in the big world and the small. I remembered raising my kids alone and without money. I thought about how the divorce had damaged them.

For the first time, I stopped feeling like a victim and knew I was guilty.

On the same scrap of paper where I'd scribbled the church board message, I started jotting pieces of a poem. Here's the final version, finished quite a while later:

How Do The Guilty Survive?
E.F.K. 1935-1984

1

How? In the mouths of the innocent
who ignore me,

by the embraces of the wicked
who cherish me,

for the lust of the virtuous
who envy me.

What rots first: **OCCULUS**
or **PHALLUS?**

2

Of the full dozen men
I've squeezed in my nether hand,

yours is (I think) the only
penis deceased.

You gave me no pleasure.
I was too young and hated

my mother.
If you loved me, I'm sorry.

3

It was after Hiroshima,
it was before Pol Pot,

it was before Chernobyl,
it was 1968 but we had two kids

so I missed the show.
It was the night before

you left me;
I was so glad.

4

Afterwards, I was poor
and wanted symmetry:

I sat her with pigtails
in a ladder back chair,

her golden brother
has a slow leak in his soul.

How do the Guilty survive?

5

For years, I took
anything I was offered:

a gallant came by with sickle pears
and yellow jackets for my tongue.

Thank you, I said.
Thank you, for permission.

Please carve on my tombstone:
SHE TRIED VERY HARD.

6

Both our children are adults.
I fed them and fed them.

When I finally had time
to look, nothing made sense;

I wanted to ask the birds:
Why do you keep laying eggs?

Our children wink
with your four brown eyes.

PART THREE

And then, as a different person, I went on with my life.

It's been years since I saw that church sign, but I continue to read it at the back of my own eyes. I try to be a kind person, but I no longer think I am a good person. I have become more honest. I have become more compassionate. I'm hard on myself for my own errors, but I tend to give other people a break.

I also have a different sense of the world. I still don't know why birds go on laying eggs, but I know they did it before I was hatched, and they will continue to do it when I'm gone.

My daughter's amazing hair is no longer in pigtails. Like me, she tries too hard.

My son is making a good life despite the leak in his soul. His little boy has brown eyes. This child is likely to see new variations on Chernobyl and Pol Pot.

So that's everything I know about how the guilty survive. The guilty just go on. Like the rest of us. Like all of us. Or they don't.

Given my family history and my current health, I may survive to be very old. My children's father died too young.

Maybe it's my job to preserve him as a young man so I can hold a part of him alive for his graying children. I try to hold the good parts.

EPILOGUE

By the time my ex-husband died, I had married and divorced an alcoholic, and was remarried to the good man with whom I am now growing old. My ex-husband's death mattered to me only as it affected our children.

We got a call in the morning from his soon-to-be-widow saying he had suffered another stroke, and I spent the day with my teenage daughter waiting for the phone call to tell us it was over.

I then started phoning all over several states trying to track down my son who was doing his post-college road trip thing. (This was, of course, pre-cell phone.) My son drove home in time to fly to the funeral with his sister. I helped him choose a necktie and drove them to the airport but never considered going with them.

The strongest sadness I ever had about my ex-husband occurred a couple of years before his death when his diabetes led to amputations, first one foot and some months later, the other. I had never found his body appealing, and this was too awful to deal with.

Or the only way I knew how to deal was through poetry. Here's what I wrote then:

The Poor Dead Feet of My First Husband

The smell crawls through the phone
as you speak your unspeakable news:

Disease, that eager bride,
has swamped you with dank embrace,
sucks all night at the stumps.

I see in this close air
how the slick knobs of your bones
in their separate cold pieces
lie wedged between wall and headboard,

each piece leaking.

My fingers splotch on the phone:
they will not touch again
that unresilient skin,
yellowy-white and shiny
like the fat on old meat.

In those years your damp flesh
lay on mine like a blight,
I moved away from my skin
and inside my fresh nightgown
I slept in a circle of air.

Somebody kind should gather
these small pieces of your death;
somebody kind should murmur
How sad; somebody kind,
somebody else.

I think that phrase "somebody else" sums up my feeling of disconnection. I had never loved the man, I had done him an injustice by marrying him, and he had done me many injustices in the 7 years of our marriage.

When he left me, our kids were 6 and 3, and although I would struggle as a single mother, marry too quickly a man who claimed to love my children. I remained grateful that my first husband had left. Out of sheer decency, I would have felt obliged to stay with him. I had always tried to behave decently toward him, if only for the sake of our children. After he got sick, I stopped taking any child support.

I have recently given each of the children art objects that their father selected many years ago. Every now and then I remember something funny he said and then I have a story to give my children.

My son's young son knows that he had another grandfather who died years ago, but my present husband is Grandpa.

COMMENTARY

Guilt is the feeling of self-reproach from believing one has done a wrong (*Webster's New World Dictionary*, 2003). It is a common response to the death of a loved one in the early days of grief. There are always those things we remember that can make us feel guilty. Perhaps we should have, would have or could have done or said something that might have made a difference in the relationship or situation in some way.

Continued guilt may be realistic and well-founded or unrealistic and unjustified (Stearns, 1985). It is typically associated with lowered self-esteem, heightened by self-blame, and a feeling one should make some retribution for the supposed wrong (Corr, Nabe, & Corr, 2006). Over a 7-year period, Penelope was the victim of emotional abuse from a bully who battered her self-esteem at every turn. She was delighted when he left. She had never thought of herself as being guilty until she saw the church sign many years later asking, "How Do The Guilty Survive?" She was shocked by her reaction of no longer feeling she was a victim. All the bad memories from the past came roaring back to her along with all the horrors of the world's tragedies. Suddenly she "knew she was guilty."

Guilt can be rational or irrational. Either way it is very real to the person involved. It must be attended and addressed if the person is to move on to a productive and happier life.

There can be many sources from which guilt arises. In Penelope's case, she felt guilty because she thought she had not been fair to either of her ex-husbands. She knew she had not been honest in telling them why she had married them.

At a very young age she married her first husband to get away from having to be perfect for her otherwise disapproving mother. She had never loved him. She never considered attending his funeral and she states his death matters to her only as it affected their children.

Her second husband was an alcoholic. She rushed to marry him because he said he loved her children, and she needed his financial support. That marriage soon ended in divorce. In light of her mother's early demands for perfection, she had again failed miserably. The guilt mounted when she thought about the damage she knew her children had suffered.

Penelope apparently buried her guilt feelings for many years until she saw the church sign. Over the time it took for her to write the poem, "How Do the Guilty Survive?" she was able to review all the hurt and guilt of the past. Ultimately she came to some resolution of the facts that provided her with a different sense of the world. She tried to be a kind person but still did not see herself as a good person, even though she was more compassionate and did many kind things for others. Ultimately she decided her job was to preserve memories of her ex-husband as a young man in order to keep a part of him alive for his adult children.

At some point guilt must be resolved to enable us to live our lives fully. Continuous feelings of guilt consume too much of the energy we could apply to living a more productive and happier life. Eventually it is necessary to give ourselves permission to say, "I did the best I could with what I had to work with at the time." Sometimes it takes the help of an experienced grief counselor to get to this point.

Penelope's third husband, an Army veteran, said on his return from visiting Vietnam as a tourist, "I have developed compassion for my younger self." Perhaps it would help all of us to reflect on this, forgive ourselves for perceived or actual transgressions, and move on with our lives.

REFERENCES

Corr, C. A., Nabe, C. M., & Corr, D. M. (2006). *Death and dying, life and living* (5th ed., p. 205). Belmont, CA: Thompson Wadsworth.

Stearns, A. K. (1985). Cited in C. A. Corr, C. M. Nabe, & D. M. Corr (2006). *Death and dying, life and living* (5th ed., p. 405). Belmont, CA: Thompson Wadsworth.

Webster's new world dictionary. (2003). M. Agnes, Editor in Chief. New York, NY: Simon & Schuster.

CHAPTER 18

Postmortem

Joyce Lombard

Preface: The work of grief is no stranger to my life. My internship as a family therapist was with a hospice, and it has been my professional specialty for 25 years.

I have listened to women who have discovered an unknown love-child after a spouse's death, and women who have discovered they may have never been legally married.

Yet, sitting with their lonely experiences was not enough as I anticipated, from afar, my ex-husband's days of slow dying, then his death, and then—gone. Like those searching for the deceased as part of grief work, I searched for meaning, and for community. I went to a conference about grief, where disenfranchised grief was not discussed.

I sought references, which led me to the Kenneth Doka book, *Disenfranchised Grief,* and went straight to Chapter 10, "A Later Loss: The Grief of Ex-Spouses," which I read again and again . . . yet those 11 pages were not enough.

Information and acknowledgment of the disenfranchisement are vital, yet my story, linked with others is what takes this isolating life experience out of the closet. This process gives my voice a place, and like the little fish who finds her place in the body of a big fish (really made up of lots of little fish swimming together) in the Leo Lionni children's book *Swimmy*, together we create community, where healing can begin.

Foretelling Dream of August Ninth: I am in a house with many women. After a while I focus on a bed in my bedroom. I notice the headboard has a sun-like medallion in curve at the top. At the bottom, in the precise middle, I know I will pin ribbons, in rainbow pattern, the length of the bed.

The pinning of ribbons is a ritual to ward off the serious illness of my husband.

I remember back to how my first husband and I created a sculpture with candles to form an altar in our church as we came to grips with his cancer diagnosis. The children were then 4 and 7.

I know I've done a ritual act before. Now I secure a bright purple cord in the middle, at the top of the headboard, then weigh whether to ask the woman whose bed this is, if I can use a strong upholstery tack at the bottom. Then I'll be ready to tack the other colors, first on the left, then to the right. A balanced pattern.

❧ ❧ ❧

I write the dream the next afternoon and search for meaning. As far as I know, my husband Tim is in good health. Yes, my former husband Paul and I did create a sculpture at the time of his first cancer diagnosis 41 years ago.

A few hours later the phone rings and it is Jenny, my eldest daughter, saying her dad is seriously ill.

"He has 4 to 6 months to live," she tells me.

I am stunned. My gut knows this is a crossroads.

I have been divorced 24 years, the precise number of years our marriage lasted. Many times I thought I was finished with all that. And I was finished. For then.

But this is now.

Near the end of his last 4 months, his final days came during winter blizzards and holidays. My two adult daughters, Jenny and Anne, flew from different parts of the country to be with him and his young wife. Their father had remarried 8 years ago to a woman they barely knew.

I was raw with the separation from my daughters, feeling yet another effect that divorce has on families, remembering the time I wrote these lines in my poem

How It Sometimes Goes

the children dream the wildest dream
of a mom and dad
who love each other fiercely
and on whose laps dreams are mounded into clay
they dig eager fingers into.

Beyond that, I was now a non-entity, and what he had said many times rang true during the 10 bad years of our marriage. "This is not about you. It is about me."

I combed my dream for meaning deep within my psyche: it is my bedroom, yet not my bed. In the dream I waffle briefly between asking the owner of the bed for permission to make my mark with a strong tack. Then I just do it.

I ask myself, is the long-divorced, ill husband, still a psychological husband? Do I still have work to do?

As he is dying and I hear my daughters' voices over the long distance between us, rivers of tears pour from my body, and my gentle husband Tim holds me, bears witness to this discharge.

Paul is dead.

First comes the rawness of emotion, the chasm of separation from daughters, the invisibility of my grief. No one speaks of it; there is no ritual or community for closure. The obituary holds no clue to my existence through 24 years of marriage, two children, and 6 years of putting him through school, career changes, and endless moves criss-crossing the country.

It makes me nauseous to read in the formal notation that "he wishes to thank all those who have loved and cared for him through the years."

And then I get busy with the tools I know best—pens, paper, and paint. I didn't know where this was going as I began writing, pouring emotion out the dark broad pen in circles, waves, and staccato lines on large sheets of shiny paper. Words need to be expelled from my being, need to exist, yet that is not all. Like scribbled words on old wallpaper before pasting over with new, I write, then comb them over with brilliant colors of paste paper, leaving the words there as I transform the page. No internal censor, no diary to be re-read or found, just each precise moment moving into the next. Now I am at the paper cutter with my third sheet. The sound of the blade slicing through paint-covered words satisfies my instincts, as well as my need to take action.

Clean, precise, intentional, this is a contrast to how I felt when I wrote all over these pages days before. I chop sheets in half, then in vertical and horizontal strips. The image of the wood chopper scene from the movie *Fargo* enters my brain. There is something gut level satisfying about sound.

I then weave these strips together to make new cloth from old. The process is interior. All the betrayals, confusion, destabilizations, denials spilled out on page after page.

Seven months later I pick up the clinical scalpel of dissection. I see this is not just about you, Paul, but also about me. As I tease apart the fibers of our lives I see what we were both looking for when we were so young.

You lost your hero-father, a test pilot for the Navy. Then you lost your mother when she sent you to the military academy at age 6. She was "the world's best mother to our little soldier," your father had earlier inscribed in a book he'd given her.

As Gail Sheehy writes in *Passages*, you were on the runway, ready to take off, just behind our children after all my good mothering. You were an emotional teenager hotly seeking yourself and love in all the wrong places.

And me, product of the 1950s, well-prepped to be the good mother with an unknown hidden agenda.

My mother's mother died when she was 9. I was told my mother would surely die by the time I was 10. Fiercely and blindly I would keep a family intact for the 20 years it takes to complete that task.

Only later could I write.

As I search my files, I find more poems than I remember writing on the material of my marriage, with lines such as these:

> "You want too much," he says, when we arrive at this familiar place.
> She says, "Does the small boy now grown in your mirror
> want too much, the one whose father fell from the sky?"
> There are men of a certain age who don't know how to change their lives,
> so they stash wives like yesterday's newspaper.
> There are women of a certain age
> who want to change the arrangement,
> having married the man's potential.
>
> and
>
> Does my once best friend drape her long red hair
> over the dots penned by the radiologist on your chest?
> Are your wedding rings stains on the rented dresser?
>
> and
>
> The time has come for you to leave.
> I see it in the silent gatherings of your belongings,
> your speech frozen beyond the silent door.
>
> and
>
> Husband gone, children claiming their own walls,
> I spend a year painting whatever pleases me,
> all over the inside of my house.
> The coming out of this woman took thirty years.

As I do the work of grief, I move out of the interior, solitary part of moving pen, paint, and paper around into new configurations for its own sake.

For myself, and for those who experience disenfranchised grief, I work my way to having a public voice. Like the 13th fairy who was not invited to the christening in *The Sleeping Beauty,* I was deleted from the script through poignant oversight, but I will have my say.

At this time, 8 months after Paul's death, after working on the draft of this essay, I dream that I am in the back seat of a car with him. His body is heavy with depression and despair, and he says he can't do anything, go anywhere, even if he wants to. I notice I am not driving the car during this night journey.

But I am in charge of my vehicle when I speak up, and as I sit next to him in that car, I say "I am getting out of here!"

EPILOGUE

Now, 3 years later, I have some perspective on the grief process for myself. I can look back on not only what I felt, but what I did in the years after his death.

Perhaps because I have had scant support around the death and my despair from anyone except from my husband, Tim.

I've gone to the venue which historically sanctions the unacceptable, disenfranchised, shadow side of life: the arts.

My isolation and disorientation went right into a black foam core marionette-like, 12-inch character, arms and legs of varying lengths, squiggly rubbery snakes, and colored pom-poms from my kids' arts drawer plus other juicy stuff decorating her body. The cracked glass face and google-eyes in this double-sided piece reeked of vital, raw energy. It hung in my studio for 2 years before I was done with it.

Then I placed it, limbs akimbo, on a cracked glass surface within a simple frame, titled it "Discombobulated Me," entered it in an art show where many women were stopped in their tracks. It sold.

That animated image stays alive in the world and moves on. It takes time.

The creative process in my Life Toolbox found socially supported and public outlets through my poetry. "Never Over" was published in a journal and I attended the publication reading in a distant city. Later I read it at a local poetry reading titled "Women With Wings."

Finally, I framed the writing and art piece I'd chopped up and wove and inserted my poem for exhibit at a gallery. Men and women attending the exhibit met me eye to eye, with words, tears, and clasped hands in recognition.

I find that putting feelings through a creative process distills, transforms, and communicates like nothing else: I feel seen and heard in community with others who have their own unspoken grief.

I tell my daughters what I am doing is grief work, but do not share the content with them. If they would ask I would tell, but they don't.

They share with each other and tell me they miss their father.

Beginning with his final illness and throughout the death and funeral, they do not ask about me.

Nor does anyone in my large extended family ask, "How are you?"

For whatever reasons, in the 24 years since the marriage ended, our daughters Jenny and Anne (now in their mid- to-late 40s), or my successful now long remarriage, no one seems to connect me to the man I fell in love with when I was 17.

I have continued to dream of Paul. I've wondered what unresolved issues from that long ago marriage were piggy-backed onto my death response, especially since I had remarried 3 years later.

It didn't matter that we seldom talked or saw each other due to both physical distance and our emotional cut-offs.

One day, while looking for something else in my attic, I came across letters languishing for 24 years in a cardboard box. With time and distance, and significant active grief work under my belt, I read them.

In that hour, I moved from anger and confusion to sadness and understanding, as tears released the bond of attachment that was always much stronger on my part than his.

Then I shredded the letters and guess what: no more dreams!

At this point, I feel released. No more art or writing waits in the wings.

And I know some things about my grief: I am done . . . for now. And I will never again disregard the feelings and experiences of another person, as I admit I have, as they have faced the death of their ex-spouse.

COMMENTARY

Everyone has their own way of expressing and working through their grief. At one time it was thought that men and women grieved in very different ways.

Men in general were thought to focus on their feelings of guilt and anger, to repress or hide their feelings of vulnerability and not seek help or share their grief. They might attend to solving the practical problems, be strong for others, bury themselves in work and/or engage in physical actions. They might *think* about the loss but not let the *feelings* emerge (Corr, Nabe, & Corr, 2006). On the other hand, women in general were thought to more freely express their emotions, reach out to family, friends, and/or support groups, tell their grief story over and over, and gradually work through the pain of their grief.

More recently it has been pointed out that individuals, whether male or female, have their own grieving style. It may be "intuitive," with emphasis on experiencing and expressing emotion. Or it may be "instrumental," focusing on practical matters and problem-solving (Doka & Martin, 2010).

Men and women have been socialized by their different backgrounds, family influences, personalities, and lifestyles. As a result, regardless of gender, they will grieve their loss in their own way, which may include parts of both styles. Joyce illustrates this point very well as she successfully uses a combination of styles to work through her grief.

It was very fortunate that Joyce could share her deep grief with her very supportive second husband, something that frequently does not happen. Often the new spouse does not understand, is jealous, just doesn't care, or is angry and/or confused by the emotional outbursts (Scott, 2000).

Despite this support, Joyce felt cut off, isolated from her daughters, friends, and community. There was no ritual to share; no public acknowledgment of her participation in his life; no mention of being the mother of their two daughters. No one asked about how she was doing.

In an effort to express her continuing grief and despair, she turned to an activity she describes as one which "sanctions the unacceptable, disenfranchised, shadow side of life: the arts." Through the physical process of producing art that expressed her "Discombobulated Me" persona, she connected with and emotionally affected those who viewed it.

Joyce's immersion in her creative process exemplifies what is possible when the urgency of unremitting grief so compromises our life functions that nothing short of fundamental change is required. Through her art work, Joyce discovered the power of "meaning making" (Harris, 2010), the work of re-envisioning trauma as a catalyst for gaining life-renewing insights of ourselves.

Additionally, such a catalytic process can help us to enlarge our world by reaching out to find community where none was thought to exist. In this world Joyce found the necessary acceptance and social support that had previously been denied. And she vowed never again to disregard the feelings and experiences of others who have faced the death of their ex-spouse.

Joyce's commitment to such a deliberately enlightened awareness of other's grief marked her parallel commitment to self-awareness and the promise to change. Janoff-Bulman (1992) offers the concept of "shattered assumptions." This concept rests on people's capacity for restoring hope to their lives, which had seemingly lost its potential for hope. Janoff-Bulman has essentially proposed a challenge to the grief-stricken; that in order to come to terms with a new reality, it is necessary to discard prior core beliefs, the foundational anchors that have guided us so far.

For Joyce, the final act of breaking the bonds that had held her in such pain was accomplished when she reread the old letters. It was a grief ritual of remembering that allowed her to do this in great depth and awareness. She was then able to understand the ramifications of what had gone before. Memories, both good and bad, were reviewed in a new light that allowed her to move out of anger and confusion into understanding. Then the tears came easily to release her from the past. The act of shredding the letters closed the door on disturbing dreams that had plagued her for years.

REFERENCES

Corr, C. A., Nabe, C. M., & Corr, D. M. (2006). *Death and dying, life and living* (5th ed., p. 227). Belmont, CA: Thompson Wadsworth.

Doka, K., & Martin, T. (2010). *Grieving beyond gender: Understanding the ways men and women mourn.* New York, NY: Routledge Taylor & Francis.

Harris, D. (2010). *Counting our losses: Reflecting on change, loss and transition in everyday life* (p. 240). New York, NY: Routledge Taylor & Francis Group.

Janoff-Bulman, R. (1992). *Shattered assumptions: Towards a new psychology of trauma.* New York, NY: Free Press.

Scott, S. (2000). Grief reactions to the death of a divorced spouse revisited. *Omega: Journal of Death and Dying, 41*(3), 216.

CHAPTER 19

Ex-humation: Digging Up The Past

Mary Kolada Scott

Preface: After my son sent a letter from prison requesting a copy of his father's obituary, I realized I would be the caretaker of mementoes and memories I would pass on to him. In this account, I have tried to be fair and to gain acceptance of circumstances and people beyond my control.

I wrote this essay for closure, but the past resists absolute resolution. My ex-husband's youngest daughter re-entered my life after a separation of many years.

After serving his sentence, my son is working to stay clean and out of trouble.

Along with his father's obituary, I will have this record for him. No doubt, he will have his own story to tell.

❧ ❧ ❧

"Please send a copy of my father's obituary just so I can have it with me," our son wrote from jail last year.

His father had died 4 years earlier, and Ryan had lost the original I had given him. My son is a meth addict who has bounced between jail and the streets. He has lost many things over the years: his belongings, a car impounded after one of his arrests, his father. He loses touch with me, unless he needs something. Like now.

My son counts on me to save his father's obit, as I have kept every scrap of his life. I'm his father's historian, the guardian of memories. I have scrapbooks and journals and poems that capture his life.

So I have rummaged through my hope chest looking for the one thing his father left behind.

I wrote a poem about this excavation.

Exhuming My Ex

October 2006

My son writes from jail.
Please send a copy
of my father's obituary
just so I can have it with me.
He has lost the original
I gave him four years ago
after my ex-husband died.

My son lost it on the streets
or during numerous jail stays
or maybe left it in the impounded car
my son never reclaimed,
all his possessions reduced
to the contents of his pockets.

So my son counts on me to save
the obit as I have every scrap
of his life. His historian,
guardian of his memories.
I have to find it first, buried
within the boxes and papers vaulted
in closets and drawers.

After half an hour, I unearth it
from my hope chest
beneath my son's baby book
that recorded every milestone,
first holiday, each baby tooth crowning.
Meth has claimed his permanent ones.

I retrieve the yellowed clipping.
My ex is smiling, youthful and carefree,
released from these confines.
I imagined divorce had relieved me
of connection but I bury him again and again
only to have him rise up.

I close the hope chest, no longer
the container for a bride's dreams.
The lid shuts with a shudder,
like a coffin lid lowered against
a past that the future never reconciled.

I found out my ex-husband had died the day before his obituary was published. My present husband is a copy editor at the newspaper where I also work. When he came across Doug's obituary in the stack of listings to proofread, he came to my desk to tell me Doug had died.

Doug's best friend had promised to let me know, but he'd never called.

I called my son at work and broke the news. We had been expecting Doug's death any day, and I'd offered to take Ryan to the hospital to see his father one last time, but Ryan had declined. He cried when I told him his father was gone, but he didn't want me to come and console him. He also refused my offer to accompany him to the funeral.

I didn't go, and I don't know whether Doug's other two ex-wives attended either.

I suspected bad blood between Ryan and his half-siblings, the four children from Doug's first marriage, but Ryan didn't say much when I asked him.

I heard that Doug had been evicted from his senior assisted living apartment just before his death because Ryan had been living there illegally. I didn't know that story first-hand. My son's life in his father's house has always been sketchy. Doug tried to protect me from Ryan's activities, so I probed the Sheriff's website and discovered that my son was a felon.

The odds had always been great that Doug would die before me. He was 17 years older than me. He was 67 when he died of esophageal cancer, which had originated as prostate cancer.

Typical of his fear of doctors, Doug had resisted getting medical care long after blood had appeared in his urine and the diagnosis was grim.

Doug had told me he was fighting cancer, but as the months progressed, it was clear he was losing the battle.

On one of my birthdays, he called from a convalescence home to wish me a happy birthday. He apologized for his behavior during our relationship. We made amends throughout his remaining days.

I wrote a poem following this conversation:

Another Chapter

From a convalescent home
where you're recovering from cancer,
you call on my birthday as you have
every year since our divorce,
any excuse to make a connection.

I thought we'd closed this book before—
in a judge's chambers finalizing the decree,
across thresholds of separate households,
at weddings we didn't attend.

An old story: tears, cold words spitting like hail.
I'm sorry, we blurt out after details of betrayal
have blurred like images printed off-register.
We've mastered reading between the lines.

It's a mystery how our saga will end.
I tuck away this conversation like a bookmark
slipped between pages of text recording our lives,
moving it forward to a new spot
as the complex plot unfolds.

It takes two to make a marriage, good or bad, but Doug rightfully accepted most of the blame for the demise of ours. I was 23 when we met, he was 40, already the father of four children, and he should have known better.

I wanted a family and security, and rushed into marriage with a man who seemed mature because he was older. We were mismatched from the start; he was a Republican Mormon and avid sportsman. I had been raised a liberal Catholic girl who preferred intellectual pursuits.

Fourteen years later, Doug went through a mid-life crisis, quit his prominent position at a corporation, and divorced me.

The housing market was in a slump, so our large house in the suburbs was on the market for 1½ years, during which time we still lived together with our son.

It was torture trying to move on as an unmarried woman, but we made the arrangement work. Friends and neighbors commented on how well we got along and that we should stay together. The venom had dissipated, but the wounds hadn't healed yet.

After I finally moved to a nearby condo, my son called me at work to tell me his father had rented an apartment across the street from our complex.

"Just think of it as a street running between your parents' bedrooms," I told my son.

Ryan lived with me briefly, but moved in with his father when he was 13, because he needed a male role model and guidance.

I eventually moved to a city 35 miles away but had frequent visits with Ryan.

Doug had remarried, to a woman with six children. (I declined his invitation to the wedding. I knew how the last one turned out.)

I was hopeful the large family would help Ryan heal. His alcohol and drug use was probably engaged in full gear at this time.

I married a wonderful, supportive man who tried to help me with my strained relationship with Ryan (and Doug).

One day we arrived at Doug's house to find Melissa, Doug's wife, crying and assembling packing cartons. We dropped to our knees and began helping her make boxes for moving out. She poured out her anger and frustration.

I had been where she was now. I packed in silence. Words were superfluous.

In their divorce fallout, Doug gave me their washer and dryer for safekeeping. My husband and I still have them. They're old but they work. I prefer substance over image.

A few months after Doug's death, a friend gave me a psychic reading for my birthday. I was skeptical, but agreed to do it as a novelty. I was awestruck by the psychic's observations (my friend had not prompted her in advance). She told me I had a son; but that I hadn't given birth to him (Doug and I had adopted Ryan as a newborn). She said Ryan would flop around for a while. "Let him," she advised.

She mentioned Doug, my dead ex-husband. The psychic said Doug had a message for me.

"You can call on him anytime," she said.

Her words were chilling. Doug had told me repeatedly after our divorce to call him if I needed anything. He had helped me move my belongings when I had left a boyfriend. He had offered to pick me up if I had car trouble. The psychic's words echoed his expression of concern.

Much as I like to think that we severed ties at divorce or when "death did us part," there is some distant connection.

There is no permanent closure, only periods of serenity when I accept that that part of my life is over. Doug rattles around in my consciousness like a hanger in an over-crowded closet. I don't notice it, but sometimes it pokes me when I'm rooting around for something else.

Now our son sits in another facility. He has "advanced" to state prison. He writes and asks for a copy of his father's obit again. I knew he had lost the last copy I'd sent him a year ago.

I'd claimed his belongings before he was transferred to the pen, and it was not in his wallet. He knows I will have the original. He knows I will send another copy. There will always be this connection, our son demanding that I review our relationship.

My son is the one who grieves most and needs closure. He's lost his father, who enabled his addiction, rescuing him while I practiced tough love.

Now it is left to me to handle Ryan, who didn't attend his father's funeral, who has fretted about where his father's remains ended up.

I've advised him to call the mortuary, which he did. He learned his father had been cremated (not in keeping with Mormon tradition, but Doug had died penniless), and the cremains given to Ryan's brother.

I have offered to perform some ritual with Ryan that would create closure, but he has resisted.

As I write this, it's September 11, 2007. Today is my father's 87th birthday. Today is the 6th anniversary of 9/11. Doug and I were married on September 11, 1976. I recall this as an afterthought now, no longer on my reality screen. Our son will be 28 tomorrow.

I resent that I'm left to pick up the pieces of the mess Doug left behind. I'd had to tell our son by myself that we were getting divorced. I'd put the house on the market because Doug said he couldn't face it.

Divorced at the age of 40, I'd lost my marriage, our big house in the hills, a family (I no longer hear from Doug's children), my faith (I had converted), and my dreams of finishing school when Ryan was older, before re-entering the workforce.

I hate that I still know things about Doug I should have forgotten. He loved Hank Williams Jr. and wore white patent leather shoes just like his idol Pat Boone. He favored gingerbread, Necco wafers and Abba-Zabas. He was a sports fanatic with several television sets tuned to different sports events. He read the National Enquirer until I refused to buy it anymore.

He always told his kids to "watch out for the fox" as Geppeto admonished Pinocchio when they left the house.

People advise you to ". . . not speak ill of the dead . . ." but writing this stirs up pain that still haunts my dreams. Doug's control and disapproval still echoes—I was never sporty, blond, or petite enough.

Doug had bought me a new sewing machine as a wedding gift, but gouged its cabinet getting it into the van. Three decades later, it still mars my enjoyment when I sew.

Before our 1st anniversary, he begged me for an annulment, because his children and I had conflicts. In my defense, I was 24 and had an 18-year-old and a 16-year-old living with us just after our honeymoon. We later got physical custody of the younger kids when they became teenagers with problems.

Doug was a perfectionist who obsessed over his hair, plastering it until it became a stiff helmet of hairspray. If it failed to conform, he threw the brush, hit himself, or punched holes in the walls. Whenever Doug flew into rages, our small son wet his pants in fear.

When my family visited, Doug hid in the bedroom to watch TV. One Thanksgiving, a friend and her husband stopped by and waited 2 hours for Doug's return. He'd gone to buy butter but was sidetracked by the golf course between our house and Alpha Beta and decided to hit balls instead of entertaining friends.

He delighted in hiding behind furniture or in closets and jumping out at me when I came home.

When I won a prestigious award at college, I attended the honors ceremony alone. He never went to any of my poetry readings (never mind the golf tournaments, church activities, and work-related events I went to on his behalf).

When my mother died, Doug was absent from the funeral, and I let people think that his friend, who did attend, was my husband.

And there is regret. I'm sorry that I never loved Doug the way everyone deserves to be loved. He missed the drama and aftermath of 9/11.

Doug didn't see his beloved Angels win the World Series in 2002.

When my son regains his life, Doug won't be there to witness Ryan achieve, get married, or raise his own children.

And he will never read my obituary and fill in the blanks as only he could. As I wrestle in his absence now, I'm left standing, holding the pieces.

For my son's sake, I keep track of them. Someday he may ask me for them.

EPILOGUE

An excerpt from my journal about 2 weeks after my ex-husband's death:

> I dreamed last night that my son had died, not Doug, and I was heartbroken. I realized yesterday that my relationship with Doug is finally over—I no longer need to keep working on it (I always did most of the work anyway).

It was difficult to determine if I was grieving Doug's death or suffering from other stresses, such as menopause and my son's drug addiction. My doctor prescribed blood pressure medicine, hormone replacement therapy, and sleeping pills. Supportive friends sent notes reassuring me I was entitled to grieve.

Over the ensuing years, I was angry that I was left to handle my son's troubles alone, to be the tough parent. Family secrets and lies surfaced after Doug's death that altered my perception of our life together. I felt cheated. I had trusted a man I didn't really know.

I have reconnected with my former stepchildren and enjoy having them in my life again.

Our son served a prison sentence, and he has been clean and employed since his release 2 years ago. Ryan presented his fiancée with the diamond ring I had flung at his father in anger during our divorce. It's bittersweet to see it gleam on her finger. My first grandchild will be born in the fall, and it feels strange to celebrate the milestones in my son's life without Doug.

Ryan no longer asks me for copies of his father's obituary. He had a memorial tattooed across his chest: his father's name and birth and death dates indelibly inked over his heart.

COMMENTARY

Mary shows a capacity for understanding how grief lingers on; that closure is an end, a closing, or a finish (*Webster's New World Dictionary*, 2003), but may never be completely achieved. Several times throughout her narrative she repeats, in different ways, that the past resists resolution.

Other contributors have expressed the same view. However, if they have allowed themselves to grieve, they find the pain lessens over time even though painful memories come back intermittently. This happens to those who have allowed themselves to accept the reality of the many ramifications of their loss, to adjust over time to the way things are, to develop new skills and gain control over what happens to them, and to move on with their lives (Worden, 2009). In order not to get stuck in the past it is necessary to allow ourselves to grieve.

In her poem, "Choosing Life Again," Rachel Naomi Remen, MD (2011) puts it another way. She states that grieving is not about forgetting, but is about remembering with love, not pain. Grieving allows us to heal. We go through a sorting process, let go of things that are gone and mourn for them. Then we can take hold of things that have become a part of who we are and build again.

Some readers may be surprised that Mary's son has a memorial tattoo placed over his heart. This is very common according to tattoo artists who frequently design special tattoos to honor the memory of family members, friends, pets, even some national tragedies such as 9/11 (to honor first responders). The designs may be very ornate, fierce looking, or sweet and full of delicate flowers. They may contain lightning strikes, birds, armed forces symbols, or babies. Some may contain a quote with very stylized letters (Memorial tattoos, 2011; Hohnny, 2011). For Ryan, the tattoo seemed to take the place of his father's obituary from which he apparently drew much comfort. Best of all, the tattoo could not be lost.

In her epilogue, Mary tells of other stresses in her life that affected her grieving process. Even after so many years she has some anger about having to "still take care of everything alone" just as she had always done.

But in spite of all the ups and downs she has gone through she has finally reconnected with her former stepchildren. Her son has stayed free of drugs and been employed for a significant time. Seeing her diamond ring on the finger of Ryan's fiancée is bittersweet, but she is looking forward to the birth of her first grandchild with pleasure. Yet it still feels strange to her to be celebrating the milestones in her son's life without Doug.

Through many tumultuous years Mary has worked hard to finally get to the point where she can begin to look forward to more peace and serenity as the dust settles.

REFERENCES

Memorial tattoos. (2011). http://pinterest.com/remembrance/memorial-tattos/

Tattoo Hohnny (2011). http://www.tattoojohnny.com/search/ memorial?K-memorial,

Remen, R. N. (2011). *Choosing life again.* Retrieved October 4, 2011, from http://www.reclaimyourlifefrompain.com/choose_life.html

Webster's New World Dictionary. (2003). M. Agnes, Editor in Chief. New York, NY: Simon & Schuster.

Worden, J. W. (2009). *Grief counseling and grief therapy* (4th ed., pp. 39-53). New York, NY: Springer.

Afterword

Peggy Sapphire

What is left to you, the reader of these stories? What is their impact? Where do your thoughts linger? What would you say if asked to describe this anthology?

Given that there is no parallel of existing work against which to measure whether this collection matched its objective, I had to question whether a cohesive fabric was achieved, a coherent theme threading its way through each and every story: was disenfranchised grief synthesized here in the voices of the disenfranchised? So far, only questions.

The very fact of having received submissions at all must not be underestimated. It became apparent, as related in the majority of contributors' prefaces, that each felt the strong presence of trepidation, even dread, as they approached revealing *and* submitting their stories. The telling would become an unearthing, and once begun, would gain momentum the writers chose not to staunch.

If there is one overriding impression I hold as editor, it is that each story seemed to hold the gravity of an epitaph, marking the death of someone long ago, now deliberately excised. Personal ground needed excavating, intimate feelings required exhumation. All this without precedence, without the certainty of acceptance, in the literary or social sense. Perhaps that is why there are no precursors to this collection.

I am struck by the immediacy of the memories, none of which are recent. They are expressed with extreme clarity of images, un-prettified telling of marital miseries, domestic abuse and violence, alcoholism and the solitary life of a spouse caught in that particular cycle of punitive manipulation. All this is told from the perspective of individuals who first suffered the death of their marriage, who now revisit from the survivor's perspective on the physical death of that ex-spouse.

I am moved by that which could not be detailed, not because it is beyond the reach of the writer but because it lies between the lines, deep in the writers' viscera, powerful by the absence of particulars.

Death of the ex-spouse brought recall previously either frozen or abandoned in time, of paralyzing loneliness, the unyielding grip of anger, of guilt, and the resulting sense of spiritual captivity. This particular grief, shrouded and silenced in disenfranchisement, now transcends its previously unacknowledged state, I believe, and achieves acceptance in the wider world.

The contributors in this anthology give confirmation to the findings of Tedeschi and Calhoun (2004), that transcending the alienating, isolating experience of disenfranchised grief *can* be achieved, even in the face of "seismic" nature of their losses.

I am moved by those whose love for their ex survives the physical death and endures as eternal friendship. They seem to tell us it will live with them as long as breath allows. All this told within the confines of disenfranchised grief, unfamiliar to all but the seasoned practitioner, researcher, or scholar.

On another level, I am left with an overriding sense of the injustice meted out at the hands of those who would shun an ex-spouse: judges, clergy (save one uncommonly compassionate minister remembered here), friends, family, certain social services, and society as a whole. How can it be, given the shelves of books on grief and bereavement, on spiritual healing and inspiration, that there still remains a growing segment of our population which can find little or no "mainstream solace?" Another question.

In the face of conclusive evidence that grief reactions are most formidable if the ex-spouse's death closely follows the divorce, I find what I call the *indelibility effect*. That is, no matter how distant the actual death, the memories seem urgent. Stories here were decades old in the minds of the contributors, yet unrecorded. None in this anthology had their story in their "Done" folder.

In their willingness to finally commit them to paper, what seems to remain is the discrete language of each couple. Many recountings are no less than reprises of couples' distinct styles of humor, snippets and extended dialogues. Each contributor's story has endured like lyrics to well-known love songs, or vintage blues.

It is a well-understood phenomenon that the toll of unreliability within intimate relationships is more painful than the finality of death. The long-term, long-lived effect of such unreliability reverberates for a number of contributors, and perhaps may have inhibited the forming of wished-for intimate relationships. That remains unclear, and presents another question. Whether in the form of solitary anniversaries, recurring, unpleasant dreams, wisps of fragrance, unbidden chards of memory, contributors tell of these persistent echoes of their loss. It is instructive that ritual is revealed here as a healing act, as is the process of creating art, whether writing, poetry, sculptural, or visual arts.

A good number of these contributors have achieved, finally, what was beyond reach but not beyond hope: remarriage or recommitment to a life partner. Such a passage is a likely result of disenfranchised grief's well-earned, hard-won resolution, recognition and acknowledgment. I sense, for those contributors who have chosen not to reveal whether or not they have found a life partner, that there is peaceful equilibrium.

The children of a deceased, divorced parent will necessarily need to successfully navigate their own grief process. Significantly, contributors relate their need for their children's support and presence. Contributors speak of their continued vigilance for their children's (including adult children) emotional health. None has asked that their children "know" what caused the death of their parents' marriage. But the contributors have drawn needed comfort from their children as they too marked the physical death of their parent, in all of its manifestations.

As the process of compiling this anthology continued over the years, there have been many instances where direct contact between myself and individual contributors occurred. Our communications increasingly gave me a sense of their warm rapport, of people wanting to be engaged in a mutual effort. Their commitment to the goal was obvious. As editor I have sensed their solidarity, and it seems to have transcended the fact that the contributors remained unknown to each other. I grew to recognize the presence of an undeclared community by the time this project was bound for publication. I decided to poll the contributors as to whether or not each would give permission to share their contact information with each other, so they might, if they chose, begin knowing each other independently. The result was a quick and unanimous "Yes."

My thoughts linger where the passion lies . . . in the form of utterly fearless and discomforting disclosure through prose, and in the poetry which speaks of irrepressible relief and renewal, some with soaring, playful wit, some with an unsparing shining-of-the-light on their loneliness and longing. And there is the quiet, spare eloquence of what is left unsaid.

What lingers, for me, are thoughts about our communal nature, our human capacity to achieve personal peace in the face of pain, to regain one's wounded personal dignity in the face of the isolating impact of disenfranchisement.

Leaves me to myself, to plumb my own depths.

REFERENCE

Tedeschi, R. G., & Calhoun, L. G. (2004). Postraumatic growth: Conceptual foundation and empirical evidence. *Psychological Inquiry, 15,* 1-18.

APPENDIX

Grief Reactons to the Death of a Divorced Spouse

QUESTIONNAIRE

How long were you married before you were divorced? ________________

How long were you divorced before your ex-spouse died?________________

How would you describe the quality of your relationship with your divorced spouse in the year or so prior to the death? Non-existent ___ Loving ___ Friendly ___ Harmonious ___ Respectful ___ Helpful ___ Hostile ___ Bitter ___ Spiteful ___ Antagonistic ___ Unfriendly ___ Other ________________

Rate your last conversation with your divorced spouse. Pleasant ___ An angry confrontation ___ Helpful in settling some financial or emotional business ___ Tension filled ___ Too long ago to remember ___ Other ________________

What caused the death of your divorced spouse? An accident ___ What kind ___ Alcoholism ___ Suicide ___ Murder ___ Other ________________
Did you participate in his/her care during the illness? Yes ___ No ___
If yes, in what way? ________________

How did you find out your divorced spouse had died? By telephone __ Yes __ No __ Who told you? ____________ Who was with you at the time? ____________

What was your reaction to the news? Shock __ Disbelief __ Surprise __ Anger __ Numbness __ Guilt __ Hysteria __ Relief __ Laughter __ Tears _ _ Other ______

If you viewed the body of the deceased, what were your feelings at the time?

____

If you attended the funeral, what were your feelings at the time? ____________

____

Were you comfortable being there? Yes ___ No ___ Why? ________________

____

If you did not attend the funeral, why did you stay away?________________

____

In the days and weeks following the death of your divorced spouse, which of the following did you experience? Anxiety ___ Anger ___ Guilt ___ Relief ___ Despair ___ Happiness ___ Shock ___ Helplessness ___ Depression __ Fear ___

Numbness ___ Confusion ___ Hysteria ___ Loneliness ___ Hallucinations ___ Restless overactivity ___ Irritability ___ Lack of Concentration ___ Sense of unreality ___ Disorientation ___ Nightmares ___ Isolation ___ Suicidal thoughts ___ Tearfulness ___ Yearning ___ Disorganization ___ None of the above ___ Other ____________________

In the days and weeks following the death of your divorced spouse, which of the following physical symptoms did you experience? Faintness ___ Heart palpatations ___ Headaches ___ Increased blood pressure ___ Neck pain ___ Back pain ___ Oversensitivity to noise ___ Fatigue ___ Tightness in chest ___ Tightness in throat ___ Nervousness ___ Sleeplessness ___ Skin disorders ___ Lack of appetite ___ Compulsive overeating ___ Bad cold or flu ___ Difficulty in swallowing ___ Stomach upset ___ Flare-up of stomach ulcers ___ Heartburn ___ Vomiting ___ Diarrhea ___ Constipation ___ Allergic reactions ___ Asthma attack ___ Arthritis flare-up ___ Dry mouth ___ None of the above ___ Other ____________________

In the weeks and months following the death of your divorced spouse, did you experience an increased use of the following? Alcohol ___ Tobacco (in any form) ___ Tranquilizers (Valium, Librium, etc.) ___ Sedatives (sleeping pills) ___ Stimulants (caffeine, amphetamine, "diet pills") ___ Anti-depressants (Elavil, Tofranil, etc.) ___ Marijuana ___ Cocaine ___ None of the above ___ Other ____________________
How long did this increase continue? ____________________

Please list all medications you were taking regularly during the weeks and months following the death of your divorced spouse.____________________
____

In the <u>first year</u> following the death of your divorced spouse, which of the following did you experience? Any minor accidents ___ A major accident ___ Sudden onset of a severe illness ___ Unanticipated surgery ___ Other ___ None of the above ___ What kind of accident, illness, or surgery did you have?____________________

Do you feel you had a grief reaction to the death of your divorced spouse? Yes ___ No ___. If yes, how would you describe your grief reactions? Slight ___ Moderate ___ Severe ___ Overwhelming ___ Other ____________
Why do you think you experienced a grief reaction to the death of your divorced spouse? Unresolved emotional conflicts ___ Residual guilt concerning the final illness ___ Continued affection or love for the deceased ___ Realization of the finality of the loss of the relationship ___ Concern about unresolved financial problems ___ Unresolved anger ___ Other ____________________

If you have remarried, how did your present spouse react to your expressions of grief? With concern for you ___ Jealousy ___ Sympathy ___ Anger ___ Resentment ___ Silence ___ Lack of interest ___ Confusion ___ Other _______

How did your children react to your grief?________________________________

How did your friends react to your grief? Did not know about the death ___
Knew, but never mentioned it ___ Thought you were being foolish ___
Were supportive and sympathetic ___ None of the above ___ Other _________

Do you think other people understood how you were feeling? Yes ___ No ___
If no, what would have been most helpful during the grief reaction?
Family support and sympathy ___ Friends' support and sympathy ___
Sympathy cards and letters ___ Talking with a friend ___ Talking with a clergyman ___ Professional counseling ___ Other ____________________

On the anniversary of the death which of the following do you experience?
Depression ___ Tearfulness ___ Remorse ___ Pleasure ___ Anger ___ Guilt ___
Sadness ___ Happiness ___ Regret ___ None of the above ___ Other ________

Have you experienced the death(s) of any other significant people in your life?
Yes ___ No ___. If yes, how would you rate your grief reaction to their death(s) compared to your grief reaction to the death of your divorced spouse?
Much less severe ___ Less severe ___ The same ___ More severe ___
Much more severe ___

THANK YOU FOR TAKING THE TIME TO
ANSWER THIS QUESTIONNAIRE

GRIEF REACTIONS TO THE DEATH OF A DIVORCED SPOUSE: RESEARCH RESULTS

Shirley Scott

Please Note: The following is a condensed report of the combined results of two studies. The first research projected was done in 1984–1985, the second in 1997. Both used the same materials and procedures.

A report of this research study was given in Washington, D.C., June 27, 1997, at the combined meetings of the 19th Annual International Conference of the Association for Death Education and Counseling, and the 5th International Conference on Grief and Bereavement in Contemporary Society.

* * *

Seventy-eight percent of the respondents reported they did have a grief reaction following the death of a divorced spouse. Of these, 23% stated the reaction was slight, 48% stated it was moderate, 21% stated it was severe, and 8% stated they experienced overwhelming grief. When reporting the cause of death, 67% listed unexpected deaths such as: heart attack (44%), accident (13%), suicide (7%), and murder (3%).

In relating why they thought this grief reaction occurred, "realization of the finality of the loss of the relationship" was checked by 34%, "continued affection or love for the deceased" 28%, the "unresolved emotional conflicts" 20%. For this group that experienced a grief reaction, the least time between the divorce and the death of the ex-spouse was six weeks, the most 40 years. In general, the shorter the time between the divorce and the death, the stronger the grief reaction reported.

For the 22% who reported no grief reaction, the reasons given ranged from "it was such a great relief" (when the ex-spouse had triggered many emotional and/or financial problems for the family even years after the divorce was final), to "the relationship was dead long before the divorce", and "it had been 19 years. I have made a full and well-adjusted new life." For this group, the least time between the divorce and the death of the ex-spouse was one year, and most, 33 years.

Immediate reactions to the news of the death were similar to those reported in the grief literature. Shock, tears, disbelief, surprise and numbness topped the list. Even many of those who reported no grief reaction listed the above. Some of these people also listed "relief."

The age of the respondents ranged from the mid-20s (1.3%) to the mid-80s (1.5%). The largest group (33%) was from 51 to 60 years old. The next largest groups were from 61 to 65 years of age (20.5%), and from 41 to 50 years of age (19%). Women consisted of 88.5% of the respondents, 11.5% men. Sixty percent of all respondents attended the funeral of their ex-spouse. Only 56% of those felt comfortable being there, and 9% checked both "Yes" and "No," indicating ambivalence in their feelings.

Responding to the question of whether family and friends understood the survivor's feelings, 52% checked "Yes," 48% checked "No," or were ambivalent. It appears that almost half the respondents received little or no understanding and sympathy from people who would usually be 100% supportive in response to the death of a significant person in the life of the survivor. Lack of understanding also affected those who experienced no grief. They reported some people were shocked and angry when told the survivor felt no grief and/or great relief.

Overall, respondents checked emotional and physical responses to the grief reaction in patterns similar to those established in accepted grief literature. Tearfulness, depression, relief, guilt, sense of unreality, and loneliness were checked most often. Of the physical responses, sleeplessness, fatigue, nervousness and lack of appetite were checked most often. In most instances, the more responses people checked, the greater the degree of grief reported.

In those cases where remarriage had taken place, only 43% of the present spouses showed concern and sympathy for the survivor, 15% reacted with jealousy, 15% showed lack of interest, 7% showed confusion regarding the survivor's reaction, 4% reacted with silence and 3% showed anger.

When comparing the grief reaction to the death of other significant people in their lives to the grief reaction experienced after the death of their divorced spouse, 34% indicated they felt a "much more severe" grief reaction to the death of other significant people. Twenty-four percent felt a "more severe" reaction, 22% felt the degree of severity was "the same," 14% checked "less severe," and 6% checked "much less severe.

Some of the conclusions that may be drawn from this study are:

1. A grief reaction to the death of a divorced spouse is a common occurrence.
2. Family and friends frequently do not understand the feelings of the survivor.
3. The grief reaction to the death of a divorced spouse is frequently not as severe as that following the death of another significant person. This may be due in part to the time lapse between the divorce and the death, and/or the degree to which the survivor has already grieved loss of the relationship.
4. Since the divorce rate hovers around 50% and more people are living to an older age than ever before, there will be a growing number of people in the future who will experience the death of a divorced spouse.
5. The survivor needs to be reassured this is a normal grief reaction to the death of a person who has been significant in his/her life.
6. Society in general, and caregivers in particular, must be aware of the need these people have for understanding and support.

Further Readings

CREATIVE ARTS

Atchity, K. (1986). *A writer's time: A guide to the creative process from vision through revision.* New York, NY: W. W. Norton & Company.

Bettelheim, B. (2010). *The uses of enchantment: The meaning and importance of fairy tales.* New York, NY: Random House.

Cameron, J. (2002). *The artist's way.* New York, NY: Penguin Putnam.

Chodron, P. (2000). *When things fall apart: Heart advice for difficult times.* Boston, MA: Shambala Publications.

Edwards, B. (1986). *Drawing on the artist within: A guide to innovation, invention, imagination and creativity.* New York, NY: Simon and Schuster.

Erikson, J. M. (1991). *Wisdom and the senses: The way of creativity.* New York, NY: W. W. Norton & Company.

Gioia, D. (1992). *Can poetry matter?* Saint Paul, MN: Graywolf Press.

Goldberg, N. (2010). *Writing down the bones: Freeing the writer within.* Boston, MA: Shambhala Publications.

Gray, D. R. (1998). *Soul between the lines: Freeing your creative spirit through writing.* New York, NY: Avon Books.

Mills, J. C., & Crowley, R. J. (2001). *Therapeutic metaphors for children and the child within.* New York, NY: Brunner/Mazel.

Moustakas, C., & Moustakas, K. (2004). *Loneliness, creativity & love: Awakening meanings in life.* Philadelphia, PA: XLibris.

Progoff, I. (1992). *At a journal workshop.* New York, NY: Dialogue House Library.

Selling, B. (1997). *Writing from within: A guide to creativity and life story writing.* Alameda, CA: Hunter House.

Stillman, P. R. (1998). *Families writing.* Cincinnati, OH: Writer's Digest.

Tiberghien, S. (2007). *One year to a writing life: Twelve lessons to deepen every writer's art and craft.* New York, NY: Marlowe & Company.

Ueland, B. (2007). *If you want to write: A book about art, independence and spirit.* Minneapolis, MN: Graywolf Press.

BEREAVEMENT LITERATURE

Abrams, M. S. (2001). Resilience in ambiguous loss. *American Journal of Psychotherapy, 55*(2), 283-291.

Afifi, T. D., & Keith, S. (2004). A risk and resiliency model of ambiguous loss in post-divorce stepfamilies. *Journal of Family Communication, 4*(2), 65-98. doi: 10.1207/s15327698jfc0402_1

Agllias, K. (2011). No longer on speaking terms: The losses associated with family estrangement at the end of life. *Families in Society: The Journal of Contemporary Social Services, 92*(1), 107-113. doi: 10.1606/1044-3894.4055

Attig, T. (2004). Disenfranchised grief revisited: Discounting hope and love. *Omega: Journal of Death and Dying, 49*(3), 197-215. doi: 10.2190/P4TT-J3BF-KFDR-5JB1

Beder, J. (2004). *Voices of bereavement: A casebook for grief counselors.* New York, NY: Brunner-Routledge.

Berzoff, J. (2006). Narratives of grief and their potential for transformation. *Palliative and Supportive Care, 4*(2), 121-127. doi: 10.1017/S1478951506060172

Boss, P. (1999). Insights: Ambiguous loss: Living with frozen grief. *The Harvard Mental Health Letter, Harvard Medical School, 16*(5), 4.

Boss, P. (2002). Ambiguous loss in families of the missing. *Lancet, 360,* s39-s40. doi: 10.1016/S0140-6736(02)11815-0

Boss, P. (2006). Ambiguous loss: Preventive interventions for family professionals. *Journal of Family and Consumer Sciences, 98*(2), 8.

Boss, P. (2007). Ambiguous loss theory: Challenges for scholars and practitioners. *Family Relations, 56*(2), 105-110.

Boss, P. (2010). The trauma and complicated grief of ambiguous loss. *Pastoral Psychology, 59*(2), 137-145. doi: 10.1007/s11089-009-0264-0

Bruce, E. J., & Schultz, C. L. (2001). *Non-finite loss and grief: A psychoeducational approach.* Baltimore, MD: Paul H. Brookes Pub.

Carroll, J. S. (2007). Family boundary ambiguity: A 30-year review of theory, research, and measurement. *Family Relations, 56*(2), 210-230.

Cole, A. L., & Cole, C. L. (1999). Boundary ambiguities that bind former spouses together after the children leave home in post-divorce families. *Family Relations, 48*(3), 271-272.

Corr, C. (1998). Enhancing the concept of disenfranchised grief. *Omega: Journal of Death and Dying, 38*(1), 1-20.

Davidson, H. (2010). *A review of the literature on three types of disenfranchised grief: Grandparent grief, grief of birthmothers following adoption, and the grief of ex-spouses* (Master's thesis). Retrieved from http://www2.uwstout.edu/content/lib/thesis/2010/2010davidsonh.pdf

Doka, K. J. (1989). *Disenfranchised grief: Recognizing hidden sorrow.* Toronto, Canada: Lexington.

Doka, K. J. (2002). *Disenfranchised grief: New directions, challenges, and strategies for practice.* Champaign, IL: Research Press.

Faber, A. J., Willerton, E., Clymer, S. R., MacDermid, S. M., & Weiss, H. M. (2008). Ambiguous absence, ambiguous presence: A qualitative study of military reserve families in wartime. *Journal of Family Psychology, 22*(2), 222-230. doi: 10.1037/0893-3200.22.2.222

Fireman, K., & Poole, C. (2012). I wouldn't shed a tear: A caregiver's complicated grief following the death of the abusive cancer patient. *Psycho-Oncology, 21,* 42-43.

Foltyn, J. (2012). Sojourn, transformative: Emotion and identity in the dying, death and disposal of an ex-spouse. In D. J. Davies & C. W. Park (Eds.), *Emotion identity and mortality across disciplines* (pp. 85-98). Burlington, VT: Ashgate Publishing.

Gilbert, K. R. (1996/2007). *Unit 9—Ambiguous loss and disenfranchised grief: Grief in a family context.* Retrieved from http://www.indiana.edu/~famlygrf/units/ambiguous.html

Hill, E. (2012). Coping with ambiguous loss. *Lancet Neurology, 11*(3), 215-215. doi: 10.1016/S1474-4422(12)70036-4

Kalich, D., & Brabant, S. (2006). A continued look at Doka's grieving rules: Deviance and anomie as clinical tools. *Omega: Journal of Death and Dying, 53*(3), 227-241.

Kamerman, J. (1993). Latent functions of enfranchising the disenfranchised griever. *Death Studies, 17*(3), 281-287.

Kauffman, J. (2010). *The shame of death, grief, and trauma.* New York, NY: Brunner-Routledge.

King, D. A., & Wynne, L. C. (2004). The emergence of "family integrity" in later life. *Family Process, 43*(1), 7-21. doi: 10.1111/j.1545-5300.2004.04301003.x

Lenhardt, A. M. C. (1997). Grieving disenfranchised losses: Background and strategies for counselors. *Journal of Humanistic Education and Development, 35*(4), 208-216.

Madden-Derdich, D. A., & Arditti, J. (1999). The ties that bind: Attachment between former spouses. *Family Relations, 48*(3), 243-249.

Morgan, E. (2004). *The loss of a life partner: Narratives of the bereaved.* Malden, MA: Wiley-Blackwell.

Moss, M. S., Moss, S. Z., Rubinstein, R. L., & Black, H. K. (2003). The metaphor of "family" in staff communication about dying and death. *The Journals of Gerontology. Series B, Psychological Sciences and Social Sciences, 58*(5), S290-S296. doi: 10.1093/geronb/58.5.S290

Moules, N. J. (1998). Legitimizing grief: Challenging beliefs that constrain. *Journal of Family Nursing, 4*(2), 142-166. doi: 10.1177/107484079800400203

Neimeyer, R. A. (2001). Reauthoring life narratives: Grief therapy as meaning reconstruction. *The Israel Journal of Psychiatry and Related Sciences, 38*(3-4), 171-183.

Reidmann, A. (1998). Ex-wife at the funeral. In M. J. Deegan (Ed.), *The American ritual tapestry: Social rules and cultural meanings.* Westport, CT: Greenwood Press.

Robak, R. W., & Weitzman, S. P. (1995). Grieving the loss of romantic relationships in young adults: An empirical study of disenfranchised grief. *Omega: Journal of Death and Dying, 30*(4), 269-281.

Rothaupt, J. W., & Becker, K. (2007). A literature review of western bereavement theory: From decathecting to continuing bonds. *The Family Journal, 15*(1), 6-15. doi: 10.1177/1066480706294031

Scott, S. (2000). Grief reactions to the death of a spouse revisited. *Omega: Journal of Death and Dying, 41*(3), 207-219.

Silverman, W. B., & Cinnamon, K. (1994). *When mourning comes: A book of comfort for the grieving.* Northvale, NJ: Jason Aronson.

Sinnott, J. (2008). Spirituality and resilience in the face of ambiguous loss. *Gerontologist, 48,* 160-160.

Smith, H. I. (2006). Does my grief count? When ex-family grieve. *Illness, Crisis & Loss, 14*(4), 355-372.

Thomson, L., & McArthur, M. (2009). Who's in our family? An application of the theory of family boundary ambiguity to the experiences of former foster carers. *Adoption & Fostering Journal, 33*(1), 68-79.

Thorngren, J. M., & Betz, G. (2006). Ambiguous loss and the family grieving process. *The Family Journal, 14*(4), 359-365. doi: 10.1177/1066480706290052

Tubbs, C. Y., & Boss, P. (2000). Dealing with ambiguous loss. *Family Relations, 49*(3), 285-286.

Tubbs, C. Y., & Boss, P. (2000). An essay for practitioners dealing with ambiguous loss. *Family Relations, 49*(3), 285-286. doi: 10.1111/j.1741-3729.2000.00285.x

Visher, E., & Visher, J. (1991). *How to win as a step family* (2nd ed.). New York, NY: Brunner-Routledge.

Wolfelt, A. (1983). *Helping children cope with grief: For caregivers.* Levittown, PA: Taylor & Francis.

Wright, N. (2011). *Helping those in grief: A guide to help you care for others.* Ventura, CA: Regal.

Yalom, V. (2010). *Kenneth Doka on grief counseling and psychotherapy.* Retrieved from http://www.psychotherapy.net/interview/grief-counseling-doka

Zonnebelt-Smeenge, S., & DeVries, R. (2010). *From we to me: Embracing life again after death or divorce of a spouse.* Grand Rapids: MI. Baker Books.

Zupanick, C. E. (1994). Adult children of dysfunctional families: Treatment from a disenfranchised grief perspective. *Death Studies, 18*(2), 183-195. doi: 10.1080/07481189408252650

OTHER RESOURCES

Websites

Grief Net – http://griefnet.org/index.shtml
Grief Share – http://www.griefshare.org/
Grief Watch – http://www.griefwatch.com/resources.html
Healing Story Alliance – http://healingstory.org/rrr/links
Hospice of the Valley – http://www.hov.org/
Legacy.com – http://www.connect.legacy.com/
Legacy.com – Grief Poetry: Poems of Death and Murning (n.d.). Retrieved from http://www.connect.legacy.com/page/grief-poetry-poems-of-death
Open to Hope – http://www.opentohope.com/
Tragedy assistance program for survivors (TAPS) – http://www.taps.org/

Online Grief Support Groups for Ex-Spouses

Hospice of the Valley - http://hovforum.ipbhost.com/index.php?showtopic=175
Legacy.com - http://www.connect.legacy.com/
Loss of an ex-spouse forum
http://www.onlinegriefsupport.com/group/traumaticsuddenloss/forum/topics/loss-of-an-ex-spouse?xg_source=activity
The Well Spouse Association – http://www.wellspouse.org

Articles in the Media

Bielski, Z. (2009, July 9). The death of an ex-spouse raises wrenching questions. *The Globe and Mail.* Retrieved from http://www.theglobeandmail.com/life/relationships/love/divorce/the-death-of-an-ex-spouse-raises-wrenching-questions/article1212738/

Divorce Info (n.d.). Retrieved from http://www.divorceinfo.com/deathafterdivorce.htm

Glazer, M. (n.d.). How do you mourn and ex-spouse. Retrieved from http://ezinearticles.com/?How-Do-You-Mourn-An-Ex-Spouse?&id=459347

Isaacs, F. (n.d.). *What to say when an Ex dies.* Retrieved from http://www.connect.legacy.com/inspire/page/show?id=1984035%3APage%3A5817

Primo, J. (2008, April 29). Grieving another's grief. *New Jersey Local News.* Retrieved from http://www.nj.com/helpinghands/goodgrief/index.ssf/2008/04/grieving_anothers_grief.html

Sheehy, L. (n.d.). The death of Dan—or how to deal with the death of an ex-spouse. Retrieved from http://ezinearticles.com/?The-Death-Of-Dan—Or-How-To-Deal-With-The-Death-Of-An Ex-Spouse&id=664183

Tousley, M. (2012). Death of an ex-spouse. Retrieved from http://www.opentohope.com/?post=death-of-an-ex-spouse

Contributors

ANONYMOUS lives in Northern California, has co-founded and leads poetry workshops and participates in Sixteen Rivers Press, a poetry collective dedicated to publication of poets in the San Francisco Bay area. A graduate of Wellesley College, she received her MFA from Warren Wilson Program for Writers. Anonymous is Professor at University of San Francisco's Fromm Institute. Her fiction and poetry have appeared in *Kenyon Review, Nimrod, Ploughshares, Missouri Review* and *Runes.*

ANNE BOWER lives in rural Vermont with her partner, Jim Rose, writing, gardening, teaching t'ai chi, and bemoaning the state of the world, while simultaneously celebrating friends and family relationships. Anne holds a PhD, English from West Virginia University, and has taught American Literature and Composition at West Virginia University, Waynesburg College, Ohio State University. Her previous publications include books and articles on food, culture, pedagogy, and literary topics.

J. BRADLEY BRANDTS has degrees in Psychology and Education, which are sources of pride but not income, and for that he feels blessed. He has had two short stories published in Gray's *Sporting Journal,* and a third is forthcoming. He has published several non-fiction articles. The myriad unrelated jobs, from teacher to commercial fishing captain to house-builder, and years of random travel that resulted, opened the way to treasured friendships, amazing conversations.

MARION COHEN holds both an MA and PhD in Math, Wesleyan University. Marion's spousal care-giving memoir, *Dirty Details: The Days and Nights of a Well Spouse,* Temple University Press. She has taught at Temple University, Drexel University, University of the Sciences in Philadelphia, and the University of Pennsylvania. She has published 19 books of poetry and non-fiction. Her latest full-length poetry collection is *Crossing The Equal Sign* (about the experience of mathematics). She currently teaches Math at Arcadia University in Glenside, Pennsylvania.

JEAN GANT lives in Seattle, Washington, in the family home she shared with her ex-husband and their two children until their divorce in the mid-1990s. Jean holds a MEd in Early Childhood Education, University of Michigan, and MA in Counseling from Seattle University. Jean's career spans

40 years as a teacher, autism specialist, and child mental health therapist, and attempts to make sense of her world through writing. Her children live in the neighborhood and visit often. She has published numerous essays and non-fiction articles.

KRISTINA GREY received an Art scholarship from Santa Monica College, and holds a BA Social Science/Art from California University at Long Beach, MA in Counseling Psychology from University Without Walls, and is a Certified Expressive Arts Therapist. She lives in California where she enjoys working as a counselor and expressive arts therapist with high-risk youth within the juvenile justice system. She is also a painter and sculptor.

DENISE HANDLON, 54, is a writer and registered nurse, with particular focus in the Behavioral Health field. Denise has written short fiction and children's stories, won several awards for various articles, and writes for *Hubpages*, online (http://hubpages.com/profile/Denise+Handlon) and http://hubpages.com/hub/Unresolved-Grief. Denise is the proud mother of two married daughters and four grandchildren living in Michigan. She currently resides in North Carolina.

BARBARA HOFFMAN holds an MA in English/Creative Writing, SUNY Stony Brook. She has taught Journalism AP in collaboration with Adelphi College. Chapbook: Lilacs From The Truck. Publications in the United States and abroad include *Minnesota Review, Blue Mesa Review, Beloit Poetry Journal, Pots On, Slipstream, Ekphrasis, Fan, Margie, Fulva Flava, The Seventh Quarry (Wales)* and other poetry journals, as well as non-fiction articles in *The New York Times* and *Newsday*. Awarded Fellowship to VCCA (Virginia Center for Creative Arts), Sweetbriar, Virginia, 1995. She was awarded a Fellowship to SUNY Stony Brook, National Writing Project.

ELIZABETH KERLIKOWSKE holds a PhD in English, Western Michigan University, lives in Michigan's palm and is a Professor at Kellogg Community College. Her fifth book, *Dominant Hand*, was published by Mayapple Press. She has published five poetry chapbooks, one anthology of children's stories and two poetry collections. She has had hundreds of publications in journals and small press. Elizabeth is President of Friends of Poetry, which runs "*The Poems That Ate Our Ears*" contest for kids.

JOYCE LOMBARD is a psychotherapist, artist, and poet. She loves to have her work in anthologies, where her voice becomes part of a larger vision. She has been published in two Papier Maché Press anthologies. She also exhibits and has won awards with her eco-spiritual mixed media sculptures.

MM has published eight poetry books and over 350 poems, stories, and essays in journals and anthologies. She is the author of two children's books and the recipient of numerous awards. She directs a creative writing program at a state university.

JAMES MCGRATH, from Santa Fe, New Mexico, holds an MA in Art & Humanities from the University of New Mexico. He has two books of poetry, published by Sunstone Press, *At The Edgelessness of Light*, 2005 and *Speaking With Magpies*, 2007. Jim has taught Art and been the Director and Dean of the College at the Institute of American Indian Arts. James has been poet/artist-in-residence with USIS (United States Information Service), Arts America in Yemen, Republic of the Congo and the Kingdom of Saudi Arabia.

KORKUT ONARAN holds a PhD in Environmental Studies, University of Wisconsin. He is originally from Turkey where he earned an MS in Architecture. Korkut now lives in Boulder, Colorado, where he is a Principal in the practice of architecture and urban design, Wolf-Lyon Architects. Publication credits include the First Prize in Cervena Barva Press 2007 Chapbook Contest and Second Prize in 2006 Baltimore Review Poetry Competition. His poetry has been published in journals such as *Penumbra, Rhino, Peralta, Colere, Writer's Journal, White Pelican Review, Crucible, City Works Literary Journal, Water–Stone, Review, Atlanta Review,* and *Baltimore Review.*

DEBORAH DASHOW RUTH holds an MA, University of Chicago, English Language & Literature. After Deborah Dashow Ruth attended the life-changing Squaw Valley Poetry Workshop, her poems began appearing in such publications as *Comstock Review, California Quarterly* and several anthologies. Two poems received nomination for the Pushcart Prize. She is working on a poetry collection and a series of short plays set in the 1950s.

PENELOPE SCAMBLY SCOTT received her PhD, Late Medieval English Literature, from the Graduate Center of CUNY, NYC. She is a professor of Literature and Creative Writing. Penelope has published six books of poetry, most recently a verse biography, *A Is For Anne: Mistress Hutchinson Disturbs the Commonwealth*, and a lyric collection, *May Generations Die in the Right Order.* She has been married for well over 20 years to her third and final husband.

MARY KOLADA SCOTT lives with her second husband in Ventura, California, holds an AA degree in Journalism. She has been Editorial Operations Manager of the Ventura County Star newspaper for 19 years. Her poems, fiction and non-fiction have been widely published in literary journals and poetry anthologies for the last 45 years. A visual artist, Mary exhibits her watercolors and linocuts at local art shows and galleries.

BARBARA TRAYNOR is a freelance journalist, professional volunteer, educator and author of the non-fiction *Second Career Volunteer.* She has published travel articles and political Op-Eds, and memoir, *Treasured Pleasure* (OASIS Journal). Barbara is the founder of "*Pen Lights,*" a critique writing group.

LINDE GRACE WHITE is the author of *Dollbaby: Triumph Over Childhood Sexual Abuse*, Cedar House. Linde holds a BA in English/Humanities, MEd from Xavier University in Guidance and Counseling. She is a 25-year veteran of public school teaching and counseling with severely emotionally disturbed children, has taught in and conducted the Counseling Program at Southern Ohio College. Linde is the author of a poetry collection, non-fiction, short fiction, is an avid reader, knitter, musician and grandma.

ROSEMARY WYMAN resides in Floyd, Virginia, and provides end-of-life care services and hospice support. Her passion is End of Life Development©. She integrates her creative abilities as an artist and writer to bring her community to greater awareness of the value of consciously supporting life's concluding chapter.

Biographies

Peggy Sapphire

Peggy Sapphire, MS Lehman College, CUNY (City University of New York), educator/counselor in New York State public schools, specialized in issues of single parent families, children of divorced parents, and has presented numerous workshops for educators related to these concerns. As an Adjunct instructor, she taught graduate and undergraduate courses in Educational Psychology and Counseling. She is a member of ADEC, Association for Death Education and Counseling.

Sapphire is author of two poetry collections, *A Possible Explanation*, Partisan Press, 2006, and *In The End A Circle*, Antrim House, 2009. Her non-fiction appears in *Education Digest* on the subject of school violence and its relevancy to student disenfranchisement. www.PeggySapphire.com

Kenneth J. Doka

Dr. Kenneth J. Doka, PhD, is a Professor of Gerontology, The Graduate School at the College of New Rochelle, New York, and Senior Consultant to the Hospice Foundation of America. Dr. Doka is a prolific author and editor (www.drkendoka.com). His books include *Disenfranchised Grief: New Directions, Challenges and Strategies for Practice*. He is editor of *Omega: Journal of Death and Dying,* and *Journeys: A Newsletter for the Bereaved.* He has been President of the Association for Death Education and Counseling.

Shirley Scott

Shirley Scott, MS in Health Science, Columbia Pacific University and a BSN, Magna Cum Laude, Florida Southern College. She is a Registered Nurse, Grief Counselor and Certified Thanatologist (CT). As a researcher, her commentaries in this anthology illustrate the issues and patterns reflected within each narrative. Her work is cited in Dr. Kenneth Doka's book, *Disenfranchised Grief: New Directions, Challenges, and Strategies for Practice.* For over 30 years Ms. Scott has presented workshops at state, national and international conferences on grief counseling, palliative care concepts, and end-of-life care decision-making. Her work on grief when an ex-spouse dies appeared in *Omega: Journal of Death and Dying*, 2000.Her work has also appeared in *The American Journal of Nursing* (2010). Scott was presented the 1996 Annual Service Award by the Association for Death Education and Counseling.

Index

AA. *See* Alcoholics Anonymous
Abuse, 107, 153
ADCs. *See* after death communications
Addressing the Dead (Ruth), 127
Advance Directive, 53
After death communications (ADCs), 134
Alcoholics Anonymous (AA), 79, 85
Ambiguous loss, 62
Ambivalence, 1, 24, 202
Anger and Confusion After Death (McGrath), 38–39
Anniversary of death, 121
Annulled (Kerlikowske), 31
"Anonymous," 65–72
  accountant, 67
  children, 66–70
  divorce, 67, 70
  divorce attorney, 66–67
  ex-spouse death, funeral, 69–72
  ex-spouse health, 68
  ex-spouse's legacy, 71
  new relationships, 68, 72
  relief, 70–71
  robbery, 76–68
  threats, 65–66
Another Chapter (Scott), 189
Anticipatory grief, 107–108
Aromatist's Tale, The (Ruth), 128–131
Artist's Way, The (Cameron), xv
Association for Death Education and Counseling (ADEC), xviii
Attachment behavior, 133

"B"
  Leo, 131, 134–135
  marriage, 124–125
["B"]
  memories, event marking, 127, 131–133
  move to California, 125
  news of, reaction to death, 127, 131–133
  separation, 126
  Sunday night concerts, 125
Barbara
  cancer, death, 96
  Cooper dog, 90–92, 95, 98–99
  grief, 97–100
  last conversation, 95–96
  Michael, 92–93, 96–97
  relationship with, 97–98
  resolution, 89
  separation, 91
  symbols, 96, 99
  talks about death, 98
Barbara Traynor's ex-spouse
  absentee father, 57–58, 61
  children, 57–63
  divorce, 60
  forgiveness, 63
  grief process, 61–63
  illness, 58–59
  love and hate, 63
  resentment, 62
Before the Divorce (Hoffman), 146–147
Bon Voyage (Grey), 83
Bower, Anne, 13–25
Brandts, J. Bradley, 89–101
Byock, Ira, 154

Cameron, Julie, xiv
Can Poetry Matter? (Gioia), xiv
Cardiology (Hoffman), 149–151
Children of divorce, 197, xi–xii

Choosing Life Again (Remen), 193
Chronic sorrow, 120
Closure, 193
Cohen, Marion, 109–121
Collaborator, The (Hoffman), 148–149, 154
Color of Ice Melting, The (McGrath), 37–38
Complicated mourning, 166–167
Continuing Bonds (Klass, Silverman, Nickman), 99

Delayed grief, 76, 134
Demonstration (Cohen), 110
Depression, 153–154
Dirty Details: The Days and Nights of a Well Spouse (Cohen), 111
Discovery Bookstore, San Francisco, 1965 (Ruth), 126, 133
Disenfranchised grief, 1–2, xi–xv, xvii
Disenfranchised Grief (Doka), 179
Divorce rate, 1, xii, xviii
Doka, Kenneth, 1–2, 100, xvii–xviii
Doug
- distant connection, 191
- illness, 189
- living with, 192
- making amends, 189
- marriage, 190
- Melissa, 190
- obituary, 187–189
- psychic reading, 190–191
- son Ryan, 187, 189–191, 193–194

Dream research, 24

Early Morning Phone Call From Home (Onaran), 137–138
EFT. *See* Emotional Freedom Technique
Eliot, T. S., xv
Emotional Freedom Technique (EFT), 98
Epitaph (Kerlikowske), 31–32
Epsilon Country (Cohen), 111
Exhaustion, 76
Exhuming My Ex (Scot), 188

Family Court (Hoffman), 149
Fault Line (Hoffman), 147
First Marriage: Going for Broke (Kerlikowske), 2–29
Five Wishes document, 53
Forgiveness, 10–12
Four Things That Matter Most, The (Byock), 154
Funeral, The (anonymous), 69
Funerals, memorial services, 121

Gant, Jean, 73–76
Gemini Under Glass, 2003 (Kerlikowske), 30
Gioia, Dana, xiv
Graham, Billy, 71
Grave, The (Hoffman), 149–151
Grey, Kristina, 77–86
Grief reactions, xvii–xix
- attachment and, 34
- children and, 35
- death of divorced spouse, questionnaire, 199–201
- death of divorced spouse, research results, 133, 210–202
- men *vs.* women, 184
- mourning, 24
- symptoms, 35

Guggenheim, B., 99, 134
Guggenheim, J., 99, 134
Guilt, 175–176

Handlon, Denise, 155–167
Harold
- anger, relief about, 9
- children's grief, support, 10
- daughter's wedding, 10
- death of, 5–6
- dreams about, 10
- negativity, forgiveness, 6
- parents, grandparents, 9
- Rosemary's anger, forgiveness, 9–12
- sadness about, 9
- shadow return, 5
- struggles, 6

Hate After Twenty Years (Kerlikowske), 31–32
Hello From Heaven (Guggenheim, Guggenheim), 99, 134

Herb
  California state law and, 48, 51
  children, 47–50, 54
  death, 47–48
  divorce, 50
  end-of-life care, 53
  funeral, 49, 51–53
  Mary Kay, 47–50, 53
  resentment, 51–52
Hoffman, Barbara, 145–154
How Do the Guilty Survive (Schott), 172–173
How It Sometimes Goes (Lombard), 180
"How to Leave a Violent Relationship" (Johnson), 107

Immediate reactions, 202
Impostor, The (Cohen), 113
Indelibility effect, 196
Intensive Journal Workshop (Progoff), xv

Jake
  arms, 163
  daughters and, 156, 160
  death, 163
  divorce, 158
  friendship reestablished, 158–159
  funeral, 164
  gambling addiction, 158
  hospice, 161, 164
  illness, 159–161
  laughter, 156, 163, 165
  life after, 165
  living wake, 167
  living with, 155–157
  love for, 161
  overwhelming grief, 155, 160–161, 164–165
  remarriage, 162
  visitors at end, 161
  wishes on journey towards death, 161
Jean
  anger, 40–42
  daughters, 38–40
  death, 38
  grief, 40–42
  marriage, divorce, 38
  memories of, 37, 39, 42
[Jean]
  mourning, 41–42
  reconciliation, 42
Jeff
  abuse, dementia, 112, 116
  Advanced Directive, 114, 116
  children, 116, 119
  death, 116–117
  eulogy, 118, 121
  funeral, 118
  home health care, 117
  last conversation, 116
  multiple sclerosis (MS), 109–110, 112, 119
  separation, 115
Johnson, Joni, 107
Journaling, 166
Joyce, James, 127

Kerlikowske, Elizabeth, 27–35
King, Martin Luther Jr., 63
Klass, D., 99
Kristina's ex-spouse
  child support, 80
  children, 79–81, 84
  divorce, 80
  failing health, death, 82–83
  grief, 83
  marriage, 78
  memorial, 83–85
  memories, 85–86
  resentment, 77–78
  second marriage, 81

Lee
  Anne's concern for children, 24–25
  Anne's friends, family support, 24
  arguments with, 16–17
  Autumn 1993, 21–22
  cancer, surgery, 17–18
  chemo therapy, 21
  children, 23
  death of, 22
  divorce, remarriage, 19–20
  dogs, 20–21
  dreams of, 22–24
  January 1981, 17–19
  memories of, 23–24

[Lee]
moods of, 15–17
November 1987, 19–20
Rose and, 20–22
sadness over death, 22
Spring 1973, 13–17
warm day in 1991, 20–21
Living wake, 167
Living Will, 53
Lombard, Joyce, 179–185, xiv
Lunch After Twenty Years (Kerlikowske), 28–30, 35

Matthews, Dave, 9–10
McGrath, James, 37–42
Meaning making, 184–185
Memories, 37, 195
Misfortune Cookie, The (Cohen), 111
"MM," 103–108
MM's ex-spouse
anticipatory grief, 107–108
death, 102
marriage, divorce, 102
wedding photo, 106, 108

Never Over (Lombard), 183
Nickman, S. L., 99
Nietzsche, Friedrich, 62, 78
Night Sounds (Hoffman), 146
Non-finite loss, 84–85, 120

Odors, 134
On Getting Engaged The Day After My Husband Dies (Cohen), 114–115
Onaran, Korkut, 137–141
Ongoing funeral, 120
Online grief support for ex-spouses, 208
Overwhelming grief, 164–165

Parents, 12
Passages (Sheehy), 181
Pat
children, 75–76
death, funeral, 74–75
divorce, 73–74
friends, family, 75–76
[Pat]
grief, grieving, 75–76
missing you, 73–74
mourning, 74
Paul
daughters, 180
death, 180
foretelling dream of August Ninth, 179
grief process, 179, 181–185
rituals, 179–180
Penelope's ex-spouse
disconnection, 175
as husband, 169–170
remarriage, 170
sadness over, 174–175
Pet loss, 99–100
Peter Pan Falling (Wyman), 7–9
Poetry, 140, xiv–xv
Progoff, Ira, xv
Prologue to the Aromatist's Tale (Ruth), 123–124
Psychological abuse, 153

Rando, Therese, xiv
Remarriage, 134
Remen, Rachel Naomi, 193
Reprise (Hoffman), 149–151
Rituals, 85, 179–180
Ruth, Deborah Dashow, 123–135

Schott, Penelope Scambly, 169–176
Scott, Mary Kolada, 187–195
Scott, Shirley, 201–203, xvii–xix
Searching for a Reflection (McGrath), 38–39
Selected Slides, Kerlikowske
daughter, 28–29, 34
divorce, 27
ex-husbands death, 27–28, 33–34
ex's legacy, 28
ex's wife, 28, 34
reconciliation, 34–35
Self-advocacy, 109
Shame, 71
Shattered assumptions concept, 185
Shaw, George Bernard, 63
Sheehy, Gail, 181
Silverman, P. R., 99

Social Worker Says "The Two Of You Don't Agree," The (Cohen), 112
Stereotyping, 47
Still the End (Cohen), 111
Stone, Ruth, xiv
Support groups, 54
Symbols from loved ones, 96, 99, 134

Tasks of Mourning, 42, 100
The Doughy Center: The National Center for Grieving Children and Families, 54
The Poor Dead Feet of My First Husband (Schott), 174–175
Thirty-Five Years (Cohen), 110–110
This Versus It (Cohen), 113, 120
Travel cure, 100
Traynor, Barbara, 57–63
Treatment of the Complicated Mourning (Rando), xiv
Turn Time Backwards, Bernice (Cohen), 114–115

Ulysses (Joyce), 127
Undressing a Death (MM), 104
Unreliability, 196
Unresolved issues, 140–141
Uses of Poetry and the Use of Criticism, The (Eliot), xv

Visiting Him On His Deathbed After Not Visiting Him For Two Years (Cohen), 113–114

Websites, 208
Well Spouse, 117, 119
White, Linde Grace, 47–44
Winter Walk (Onaran), 139–140
Wyman, Rosemary, 5–12

Years Later: His Funeral (MM), 104
You Never Know (Matthews), 9

In Praise

This book is engaging, informative, and inspirational. Whether you have experienced the death of an ex-spouse or seek to support someone who has, you will find this book illuminating. The deeply personal stories of the contributors, so frankly told, will draw you in, and you may have trouble, as did I, putting the book down. The accompanying clinical commentaries, skillfully written by S. Scott, will give you a grief counselor's perspective. This is an excellent piece of qualitative research. I highly recommend this enjoyable and enlightening book.

Janice Nadeau, PhD, LP
Licensed Marriage & Family Therapist
Fellow in Thanatology

It's been worth the wait for such a comprehensive anthology of the bereavement stories of ex-spouses. Some relationships were happy, some less so. The relationships ranged from decades to just a few years, and we can learn much from the honesty of the experiences each writer shares with us. An excellent resource for both professionals and lay readers.

Rose Cooper, BTheol, MHSc
Grief Support Services
Melbourne, Australia

These touching stories capture the complex experience of grief when an ex-spouse dies. In a world where divorce is common and we long for easy, quick answers, the authors challenge us to expand our understanding of and compassion for the growing numbers of individuals and families who will struggle to live with this conflicted loss.

Marcia Lattanzi-Licht, LHD, LPC
Psychotherapist
Author, *The Hospice Choice*